EMPIRE BUILDING

BUILDING

The Remarkable, Real-Life Story of *Star Wars*

EMPIRE BUILDING

The Remarkable, Real-Life Story of *Star Wars*

GARRY JENKINS

A CITADEL PRESS BOOK

Published by Carol Publishing Group

For Tina, Graham,
and Penny

First published in the United States in 1997 by Carol Publishing Group, 120 Enterprise Avenue, Secaucus, New Jersey 07094. Published by arrangement with Simon & Schuster Ltd., West Garden Place, Kendal Street, London, England W2 2AQ

Picture acknowledgments for inserts: pp. 1–13 © Gary Kurtz; p. 14 © Rex Features; p. 15 top left © Rex Features, top right © Fotos International/Rex Features, bottom © Rex Features/Media Press International; p. 16 © Sipa-Press/Rex Features

A Citadel Press Book
Published by Carol Publishing Group
Citadel Press is a registered trademark of Carol Communications, Inc.

Editorial, sales and distribution, rights and permissions inquiries should be addressed to Carol Publishing Group, 120 Enterprise Avenue, Secaucus, N.J. 07094

In Canada: Canadian Manda Group, One Atlantic Avenue, Suite 105, Toronto, Ontario M6K 3E7

Carol Publishing Group books may be purchased in bulk at special discounts for sales promotion, fund-raising, or educational purposes. Special editions can be created to specifications. For details, contact Special Sales Department, Carol Publishing Group, 120 Enterprise Avenue, Secaucus, N.J. 07094.

Manufactured in the United States of America

10 9 8 7 6 5 4 3 2 1

Library of Congress Cataloging-in-Publication Data

Jenkins, Garry.
    Empire building : the remarkable real-life story of Star Wars /
Garry Jenkins.
       p. cm.
    "A Citadel Press book."
    Includes bibliographical references and index.
    ISBN 0–8065–1941–X (pb.)
    1. Star Wars films—History and criticism.   2. Lucas, George.
I. Title
PN1995.9.S695J46   1997
791.43'75—dc21   97–28074
                                                     CIP

CONTENTS

I have wrought my simple plan
If I give one hour of joy
To the boy who's half a man,
Or the man who's half a boy.

Arthur Conan Doyle, Preface to *The Lost World*

PROLOGUE

On the evening of Wednesday, May 25, 1977, George Lucas arranged to take his wife Marcia for an early evening meal at one of their favorite restaurants in Los Angeles. Both were looking forward to the dinner date and their escape, the next day, to Hawaii for their first extended holiday together in six years.

Their choice of venue said much about the couple, two of the brightest young filmmakers in America. Like the Lucases, the Hamburger Hamlet on Hollywood Boulevard was down-to-earth and distinctly "un-Hollywood." Once the greats of Tinseltown had hung out at the restaurants and cocktail lounges of the area, the so-called Avenue of the Stars. Now it was the domain of the city's dropouts and dope addicts, its hookers and hustlers. In a way, the neighborhood's sad decline symbolized the fading of Hollywood's golden age itself. In the late 1970s, few stars or studio executives would be seen dead there—especially on such an eventful night.

As both he and Marcia were all too painfully aware, George Lucas's third feature as a director, a "space fantasy" called *Star Wars*, had opened at two cinemas in Los Angeles that day. After their small celebratory meal that night, the director still faced one last graveyard shift in the editing suite where he had been mixing a special sound print of the film for use the following weekend. He would probably have to head straight from the mixing room to the airport for his flight to the island of Maui the next morning. Earlier in the day he had only just made his deadline for the delivery of the final reels of the picture. In one of its two L.A. cinemas, the film had begun playing before its climactic reel had arrived in the projection room. The day had somehow summed up the four punishing years Lucas had spent fighting to bring his film to life.

Lucas had dreamed of making the movie since 1973, when he had written the story, set "long ago, in a galaxy far, far away." *Star Wars* was the tale of a young farm boy caught up in a rebellion against an evil intergalactic empire, a parable laced with influences from Arthurian legend to Greek tragedy, Flash Gordon to Captain Blood. Laden with eye-popping special effects and stirring space battles, the film was an unfashionable, uncynical, and unashamed homage to the sort of cinema Hollywood seemed to have forgotten, a throwback to the age of Errol Flynn and John Wayne, the actors Lucas himself had loved as a little boy. Yet the process of making *Star Wars* had all but broken the shy, bespectacled thirty-three-year-old from northern California. After a series of traumatic setbacks the previous year, he had been rushed to the hospital, seemingly at the point of a nervous breakdown. Lucas had already promised himself he would never put himself through the spirit-sapping ordeal of directing a movie again.

The experience had been no less draining for his wife. For months, married life had been little more than a series of snatched conversations and meetings on the staircase of their small Los Angeles home. While George worked all night, Marcia worked all day, combining work on Martin Scorsese's *New York, New York* with the cutting and polishing of her husband's movie. Their separation had become so complete, she had taken to leaving notes asking her husband whether they could meet for breakfast.

The sight of the finished film had done little to relieve the strain on either of them. If anything it had made matters worse. Days before the opening, at a screening for members of the board of Twentieth Century–Fox, the film's distributors and backers, some of the studio's all-powerful directors had dismissed *Star Wars* as an adolescent indulgence. One or two had fallen asleep in the cinema. Lucas had his allies; the studio's head of production, Alan Ladd Jr., was convinced it was a hit. Yet for every voice reassuring him his film was a success, the pessimistic Lucas heard twice as many prophesying disaster. There were those who wondered whether, at a cost of more than $10 million, *Star Wars* might even be the film that would finally bring a once-great studio to its knees after a troubled decade.

All in all then, it was understandable that George and Marcia Lucas headed for dinner that night feeling relief rather than elation, emptiness rather than excitement. They were mostly thankful their eight-year marriage had survived its most stressful period yet. It was time to forget *Star Wars* and Hollywood and look forward to the lush landscapes and perfect white beaches of Hawaii.

The Lucases parked their car on a side street near the Hamburger Hamlet then walked back towards Hollywood Boulevard. When they turned the corner they could barely believe the sight that greeted them.

Ordinarily they would have expected the sidewalk to be littered with the flotsam and jetsam of Los Angeles street life. Instead they saw a vast line of people, snaking down the neon-lit road. The line, the biggest either had ever seen, ended at the famous Mann's Chinese Theater, a stone's throw from the Hamburger Hamlet. Outside the gaudy, mock-Oriental cinema, an old Hollywood landmark with its cement hand and footprints of Chaplin and Monroe, Gable and Wayne, scores more people were jostling to see the movie, billed in giant letters under the dragon-topped marquee: *Star Wars*.

Prologue

For a moment the couple stood in disbelief. It was not long before their emotions overwhelmed them, however. "We just fell on the floor," George confessed later.

Inside the Hamburger Hamlet, the teary-eyed couple asked for a table close to the window. They spent most of their meal simply gawking at the scenes outside.

Later that night, Lucas would learn that the lines had been forming since 8 A.M. Similar scenes had been unfolding a few miles across Los Angeles, outside the Avco cinema in the chic suburb of Westwood, on the edge of the vast UCLA campus. The lines had been equally impressive outside another thirty cinemas across America, from Cincinnati to San Jose, Pittsburgh to Portland.

The first few thousand customers had sat down to see *Star Wars* at 10 A.M. The lines did not thin out until the final sold-out signs were posted at almost midnight. House records had been falling everywhere.

Over the coming months, the lines would stretch beyond the limits of Hollywood Boulevard, around America and then the world. *Star Wars* would become the greatest film phenomenon of all time.

That night he remained speechless. In time, however, George Lucas would be able to reflect on the sweet irony of his triumph. In the years leading up to that moment, he had found it hard to interest anyone in *Star Wars*. The experience confirmed what he had learned on his first two films, that working within the old establishment of Hollywood could be a bitter and disillusioning experience. Now his film was shaking that establishment to its very roots. The old empire that was Hollywood would never be the same again.

In many ways *Star Wars* would seem a metaphor for the story that lay behind its making. It too began long ago, in a galaxy far, far away...

CHAPTER 1

Junior Genius

In 1954 the young life of ten-year-old George Lucas Jr. revolved around the moment he switched on his favorite television show each evening.

The first flickering black-and-white images had arrived in the Lucas household on Ramona Avenue in Modesto, California that summer. After years of resistance, his father, George Lucas Sr. had finally bought the family a television set.

It was the age of wholesome family fare like *I Love Lucy* and *Ozzie and Harriet*. Yet for the shy, spindly George Jr. the highlight of every day came long before the prime-time shows, at six o'clock precisely. With his black cat, Dinky, draped over his slight shoulders, he would sit glued to KRON-TV, broadcasting from nearby San Francisco, impatient for the rousing theme music that introduced the *Adventure Theater* half hour. The show featured the great Hollywood movie serials of the 1930s and 1940s. Night after night, young George Jr. would watch the stirring adventures of heroes like Spy Smasher and Tailspin Tommy, Lash La Rue, and the Masked Marvel. He never missed an episode. If the program happened to clash with the family's evening meal, he would always find a way of turning the bulky television set on its revolving stand so he could keep watching from the dinner table in the kitchen.

Of all the *Adventure Theater* classics, none could compete with *Flash Gordon Conquers the Universe*, starring Buster Crabbe. For years George Jr. had followed the exploits of the all-American hero and his battle with the evil Emperor Ming in his collection of comic books. The sight of the muscle-bound Crabbe finally bringing Flash to life left a deep and indelible mark. He loved the gaudy, medieval costumes, the flame-engined rockets, the corny dialogue, and the cliff-hanging endings. At night in his bed he imagined joining Flash in his travels to the far corners of the cosmos.

Years later he would acknowledge their inspiration. "I used to love the Flash Gordon serials," he would reflect. "They were a primary influence on me. The way I see things, the way I interpret things, is influenced by television. Visual conception, fast pace, quick cuts. I can't help it. I'm a product of the television age."

By then his dreams of exploits in a far-flung corner of another galaxy had made George Lucas Jr. one of the most successful and celebrated men on earth. Back in his boyhood his fantasies fulfilled a simpler function. They were an escape from the crashing—and sometimes cruel—normality of his existence.

"There is more of me in *Star Wars* than I care to admit," Lucas would tease a fascinated world later in life. If the roots of his fantasy lay in the reality of his childhood, it is not difficult to detect the earliest and most obvious reference in the story that changed his life.

Early in the film, Lucas's young hero, Luke Skywalker

says of his home, the desert planet Tatooine: "If there is a bright center to the universe, then this is the planet farthest from it." For the first eighteen years of his life that pretty much summed up George Lucas's view of his birthplace. If there was a bright center to America, then Modesto, California was the town farthest from it. Set in the parched flatlands of northern California sixty miles south of Sacramento, the community was Modesto by name and Modesto by nature. The town's main industries were walnut farming and wine-making. The famous Gallo vineyards were a short drive away. In the late 1940s and 1950s, life conformed to the same Norman Rockwell idyll as a thousand other small American neighborhoods.

George Walton Lucas Jr. was born on May 14, 1944, the third of four children to Dorothy and George Lucas Sr. The couple were pillars of the small-town community where George Sr. ran one of Modesto's more successful businesses, the L. M. Morris stationery store. George Jr. was their only son; daughters Katy and Ann were older, Wendy three years younger. The Lucases came from wildly differing backgrounds. Dorothy had been born a member of a well-to-do Californian family, the Bombergers, with American roots leading back to the eighteenth century. George Sr. on the other hand, was the son of a poor California oil-field worker and, further back, an Arkansan family that had seen little wealth in its history. They had been driven to Modesto by the ravages of the Great Depression and had never left.

As a young boy, George Jr. was reed-thin and often sickly. So, too, was his mother, Dorothy, of whom he saw too little in his early years. The trials of childbirth seem to have done little for her health and she spent much of George's youth confined to the hospital or a bed at home. In her absence his father, George Sr. assumed a powerful, and at times overwhelming, role. He seemed to channel all his hope and anger into his only son. Their difficult, ambivalent relationship, distilled into the good and bad father figures of Obi-Wan Kenobi and Darth Vader, would lie at the very heart of his *Star Wars* story.

George Sr. was driven by a determination to be the first of his family to make something of himself. He had begun working for the L. M. Morris stationery and office equipment store as a young man. By the time George Jr. was born, he had been sold the company by its founder and built it into a thriving enterprise, selling everything from toys to typewriters.

The search for the roots of the entrepreneurial streak and pennywise philosophy George Lucas Jr. would demonstrate throughout his life need go no further than the Morris shop and the sermons his father passed on there and across the Lucas dinner table. Money did not grow on trees, life only rewarded those who worked hard. "Every generation should have to go through a Depression," George Sr. would often say. George Jr. would have to mow the lawn for pocket money and was forced to attend the local Methodist Church where he would hear a variation on the same Bible-thumping theme.

His father's words were far from empty, however. George Jr. only had to look around him to see what he meant. The comfortable family house on Ramona Avenue was a monument to thrift and hard work, built with $500 in hard-earned savings and maintained by his father's labors at L. M. Morris.

At school George Jr. was quiet and withdrawn. "A scrawny little devil," according to his father, he soon became a natural target for the bullies. They would throw his shoes into the walnut grove sprinklers on the way home. In later life he would be laden with a pessimistic nature. The phrase "I have a bad feeling about this" would be a staple in the *Star Wars* adventures. In childhood, George Jr. simply carried a fear of something menacing always lurking around the corner.

As far as his father was concerned, the bogeymen he should fear most were the big-city folk. To God-fearing George Sr. the cities were dens of iniquity, filled with hucksters and shysters, con men and liars. Worst of all were Los Angeles and Hollywood, a place he disdainfully referred to as "Sin City." Lucas later admitted that he spent much of his childhood feeling "very angry" about his father and his rabid rants against the world. Yet for all his fulmination, George Sr. could be a generous father. For a start, his son had the pick of the best toys that came into his store. A three-engined Lionel Santa Fe train set, the biggest and flashiest in town, was the pride of George Jr.'s toy box. The train set was a magnet to the town's other young boys who flowed into the house on Ramona Avenue. His toys seem the main explanation for his popularity as a child. In general he was, as he would be in later life, a quiet, withdrawn young man.

George Jr. spent much of his early childhood immersed in comic books. His passion for *Batman, Superman, Amazing Stories*, and *Unexpected Tales* stimulated an early interest in drawing, for which he had an obvious talent. On the negative side, however, it also left him lagging behind at school where his lack of literacy was a worry. According to family legend, his sister Wendy would get up at 5 A.M. to correct her brother's spelling work before he went to school.

If he was withdrawn as a young boy, he became almost invisible from the age of ten onwards when his father finally permitted a television in the house. The veto he had applied until then had little to do with any opposition to the new invention. He had been happy for George Jr. to go to a friend's house to watch television. Instead George Sr. wanted the infant technology to be properly developed before he spent money on a set. His son would apply the same good sense later in his life.

In about 1957 the family moved to the seclusion of a

walnut ranch on the edge of town, and George Jr. sank further into his shell. He would come home from school, run upstairs and spend the rest of the night playing Elvis Presley and Chuck Berry records, reading his beloved comic books and eating Hershey bars. He felt more content and safer living in his own world.

As a young boy he loved building models. He constructed his own little neighborhood, sprawling, minutely detailed streets, set in papier mâché mountain ranges with streams running through them. It was a trait his father found hard to fathom. "He was hard to understand, he was always dreaming things up," George Sr. said once.

Soon his son also developed an interest in photography. To his father's disgust he had been given his first camera by his mother rather than earning the money for it himself. "He never listened to me," he said years later. "If he wanted a camera, or this and that, he got it."

Many of George Jr.'s friends were terrified by his father. He seemed an intimidating figure. Yet slowly George Jr. summoned up the courage to defy him, usually relying on his wits to do so.

At first his rebellions were minor. Back at Ramona Avenue, frustrated by the slowness of his father's lawn mower, George Jr. had saved his allowance and persuaded his mother to advance him a repayable loan in order to buy a new one. His father had apparently admired his son's enterprise as much as he had hated his defiant cheek.

The greatest and most inevitable rebellion against the Norman Rockwell stability of his life came when comic books and television were replaced by that other great American adolescent obsession—cars. By the age of fifteen George Jr. talked of little else. Modesto and its walnut groves, with their network of long, straight back roads, was a magnet for speed merchants and dragsters. George Sr.

sensed the best thing he could do to guarantee his son's safety was to choose his first car for him. The little Fiat Bianchina he picked out had a tiny, two-cylinder "sewing machine" for an engine and would struggle to beat a motor scooter in a race.

For the remainder of his high school life, George Jr. devoted every spare dollar he had to souping the Fiat up into something quicker. A garage in Modesto, the aptly named Foreign Car Service, became his unofficial home. "My father thought I was going to be an automobile mechanic and that I wasn't going to amount to anything," Lucas laughed later.

His car gave George a sense of identity. Every night he would stretch out behind the wheel of his Fiat, by now equipped with roll bars and an open roof, and join a generation of like-minded youngsters, cruising the streets of Modesto. "For nearly four years of my life, I spent almost every weekday between three in the afternoon and one in the morning cruising up and down," he recalled.

Most nights he would park at a hamburger joint called the Round Table, where he hung out with a gang of greasy bikers he had befriended. Keen to fit in, George Jr. adopted the greasers' uniform. He slicked back his hair with Vaseline and wore grimy jeans and a blue felt coat. He became the tough guys' hundred-pound mascot. Often Lucas would be sent in to the Round Table ahead of the rest to act as the bait for fights. Gangs like the leather-jacketed Faros would surround him only to discover he had a particularly beefy collection of cavalrymen around the corner. "I was always afraid I was going to get pounded myself," Lucas confessed. It was, he admitted later, the most undisciplined period of his life. "I was a hellraiser," he said. "I hung out with the real bad element." The experience would not be wasted.

Cars soon provided an escape from the mundanity of Modesto. George Jr. had begun to follow California's racing scene. At first he had hung out in the pits, tuning up cars for other drivers. It was not long, however, before he discovered he had a knack for racing himself.

George had learned to handle his car at high speeds on a go-cart track behind the Foreign Car Service in Modesto. The flimsiness of both the Fiat and its flyweight pilot gave the car an edge over bigger, more powerful cars. Under California law people under twenty-one were forbidden to enter official races. George quickly learned that no such regulations applied at the circuit of unofficial auto-cross races held in fairgrounds all over the state. Soon he was winning trophies.

The visceral thrill of the racetracks could not have presented a starker contrast to the boredom and humiliation of the high school classroom. In many ways his gift for racing cars compensated for his lack of academic success. Lucas had not shone either at Modesto Junior High or Thomas Downey High School. His IQ hovered somewhere around the nineties, and his basic "three R" skills were dismal. "I was never that good in school. I'm not what you call a speed reader. I'm not the greatest speller, I'm horrible at math," he has admitted. "I just never considered myself intelligent in the academic sense."

His lack of interest hardly helped matters. By his senior year, George Jr. had a D average. As graduation approached, he was in serious danger of failing altogether—a prospect too painful to contemplate with a father like his. As it turned out, his high school fate—and his entire future—would be decided away from the classroom.

If there was a defining moment in the young life of George Lucas Jr. it came on the afternoon of Tuesday, June 12, 1962. Just three days before final exams at Thomas Downey High School, he had been racing his Fiat along the road that ran through the walnut groves at the back of the house. He was returning from the city library, where he had been doing a bit of last-minute "cramming."

The stretch of road was a notorious black spot—seven schoolmates had died in one single, terrible accident there when their car had hit a tree at 100 mph. As George Jr. took a left turn into the dirt road that led to the Lucas home, a Chevrolet Impala driven by another Modesto teenager smashed into his side. Partially blinded by the dazzling sun, neither Lucas nor the other driver had seen each other.

The impact sent the Fiat cartwheeling towards the trees. Miraculously, as it flipped over and over, Lucas's seat belt snapped loose and he was propelled through the hole in the car's roof and knocked unconscious. Meanwhile, his car wrapped itself around a tree "like a pretzel." The other boy was left virtually unscathed.

By the time he had been rushed to Modesto City Hospital, eighteen-year-old George was in critical condition. He had suffered massive internal hemorrhaging and was put on a respirator.

The accident marked the first time Lucas aroused the attention of the media. A report on the crash, complete with a photograph of the mangled wreckage of his Fiat, dominated the front page of the city's newspaper, the *Modesto Bee*.

It would take him four months to recover from the accident. The endless hours he spent in bed changed his attitude to life completely. As a boy, George Jr. had rebelled against the force-fed religion of the Methodist church. As he lay staring at the hospital ceiling, however, he experienced an epiphany of sorts. "When I was pulled out of the car they thought I was dead. I wasn't breathing and I had no heartbeat. I had two broken bones and crushed lungs," he recalled later. "I should have been killed. If I had stayed in the car I would have been dead." As he took a long, hard look at his young life, his racing and his endless evening drives shaped themselves into a depressing metaphor. Lucas saw he had been heading nowhere, fast. He decided things would be different when he came out of the hospital.

"Before the accident, I never used to think," he would say years later, recalling the experience. "When you go through something like that it puts a little more perspective on things, like maybe you're here for a reason..."

By 1966 George Lucas was sure he had found the reason he had been spared in his accident. Each night at the Willow Springs Raceway, north of Los Angeles, he would watch a gleaming yellow race car barrel its way around the tight circuit. As it did so, his eyes would nervously flit between the track and the marshal's stopwatch recording the speeding car's lap times.

Lucas had not lost his fascination with speed. Yet by now it had been replaced by a deeper and, as it would turn out, more lasting obsession. Standing with Lucas were the fourteen-man crew of lighting engineers, cameramen and sound recordist he now had working for him. In the darkness Lucas was completing his final feature as a student moviemaker, a film built entirely around the car and its battle with the clock.

Lucas was in his senior year as a student at the University of Southern California. It had been there that he had fallen hopelessly in love with the art of filmmaking. His decision to travel to "Sin City" had flown in the face of his father's advice. The tension that existed between them had boiled over when George Jr. had announced that he was going to study art at San Francisco State. His father, secretly hopeful that George would pick up the reins of the family business, had predicted disaster for his son. George Jr. let loose years of frustration by extravagantly declaring he would prove him wrong and that he would be a millionaire by the time he was thirty.

In the end, Lucas had spent only a term at San Francisco

State. He was persuaded to move to the more cosmopolitan USC by one of his racing friends, Haskell Wexler, for whom he had built a car. A keen cameraman, Wexler would remain a talisman for years to come.

In an attempt to make his peace with his son, George Sr. agreed to pay him a salary of $200 a month while he worked his way through university. "If I flunked out, I was on my own," Lucas recalled once.

As in high school, Lucas lacked any obvious academic brilliance. He had to take liberal arts classes to make sure he did not fail to graduate. Yet cinema soon became his passion.

As a boy in Modesto, movies had failed to make a mark. "I only went to movies to chase girls. I was totally into cars," Lucas once said. "Anyway, it took years before good movies got to my town. And foreign films—never." Thrown into a world where the heroes were Jean-Luc Godard and Federico Fellini rather than Flash Gordon and Spiderman, Lucas was reborn. He took to filmmaking like a duck to water.

Exiled to their own building away from the main campus the film majors were viewed as a collection of misfits. "We were looked at as a weird group of guys. It was mostly guys at the time. Very few women," recalled one of Lucas's classmates, Howard Kazanjian.

Lucas, slight, bespectacled, often dressed in clothes too big for him, seemed to be sizing up everyone—and everything—around him. "He was small, quiet, inquisitive, intelligent, witty—like a cat, eyes darting back and forth," recalled Kazanjian. "He was trying to figure out, was this something he wanted to do? What is this business called film? What is editing, lighting, what is all of that?" No one mistook Lucas's shyness for a lack of boldness, however. According to the course regulations, student movies were to be made in monochrome and limited to 500 feet of film. Lucas saw film as an excuse to break, not keep, rules.

"George was a rebel," recalled Kazanjian. "He said: 'I'm

gonna shoot my film in color. I'm not going to be limited to the footage I'm given or limited to the length of my completed film.'"

His talent as a filmmaker was soon separating him from others. His racing-car film—called *1:42:08*, after the yellow speedster's lap time—took everyone by storm. "It looked like [the] Grand Prix and everybody else was shooting some little movie on campus," recalled John Milius, another contemporary destined to follow in Lucas's trail. "There was a sense of there being no limits to what he would try." Lucas told Milius that he knew someone with a P51 airplane. "Think up a story so we can have a P51 in our film," he told his friend.

Lucas's films ranged from the avant-garde to the mainstream. One film consisted of artful shots of unidentifiable, gleaming surfaces. At the end the camera revealed it had been panning over the bodywork of a Volkswagen. Lucas called the film *Herbie*. Far more accessible was a documentary he made about a disc jockey called Emperor Hudson. *The Emperor* featured its titles in the middle and had a series of advertisements dotted throughout. "It was really extraordinary," Milius said later. "He was free. He said we could do anything."

Another of his enduring traits had also, by now, revealed itself. Lucas suffered fools badly. Luckily, he fell in with a group of people who felt precisely the same way. In its forty-year history, USC had never assembled as brilliant a collection of students as it had in the mid-1960s. A tight-knit group of friends formed on this basis. "If you went and saw an exciting film, you become friends with this guy," explained Walter Murch who with students John Milius, Howard Kazanjian, Hal Barwood, Matthew Robbins and others formed themselves into a mutually supportive clique, nicknaming themselves the Dirty Dozen.

The Dozen formed a camaraderie that would remain unbroken over the years. Their hero was Orson Welles; their collective dream was to conquer Hollywood, as their idol called it, "The biggest electric train set a boy ever had." The seeming impregnability of the world they wanted to take over only bound them tighter. The Hollywood of the 1960s had no place for the new cinema students. The old studio system was in its death throes, yet entry to the dream factory was still more a matter of who rather than what you knew. Even to their lecturers at USC, the film-school kids, for all their talents, were still regarded as apprentice documentary and educational filmmakers. No one believed the next John Ford or Orson Welles was in their midst.

"There were walls up in Hollywood then, and the place was very clicquish. You had to know Frank Sinatra or something," recalled Milius.

Lucas was known as the most gifted and determined of the dozen, living proof of Edison's old saw that "genius is one percent inspiration, 99 percent perspiration." "Talent is nothing without hard work," ran Lucas's variation on the theme. It was a mantra George Lucas Sr. would have been proud of himself. Lucas would spend entire nights at work at the Moviola editing machines in order to get his films right. He would neglect to feed himself or rest. At one stage he developed mononucleosis, a form of glandular fever, as a result of living off nothing but his beloved Hershey bars. He was later diagnosed as diabetic, a condition that disqualified him from the dreaded draft and service in Vietnam.

Lucas's greatest gift was as an editor. What his films lacked in content they more than made up for in pace and style. Lucas never dwelled on a scene longer than he had to. He often used montages to add to the mood of his films. If he had a personal hero as a filmmaker it was Walt Disney rather than Welles. (Welles had, after all, squandered everything he had won.) Lucas remained an enthusiastic comic-book reader, a doodler, and a drawer. He saw himself becoming an animator or director of modern-day cartoons.

Lucas graduated in 1966. By then his films were the talk of the student world. Another aspiring filmmaker, Steven Spielberg, a freshman at the rival film school at Long Beach State University, was deeply affected when he saw some of Lucas's senior work.

In time both young men would ignite the world's imagination in a manner not seen since the glory days of Disney. At the time, however, if Spielberg saw something of Lucas's hero in his boyish, student features it was for another reason. "He reminded me of Walt Disney's version of a mad scientist," he said with a smile years later.

The Dirty Dozen had a hero their own age, he was the man they would come to call the Godfather.

The bearded, piratical figure of Francis Coppola had already breached the walls of Hollywood. Of the hundreds of film-school graduates who had spilled out of the film labs and lecture halls, he was the only one to have succeeded in making a real impression inside the studio system. By the mid-1960s, a legend had already attached itself to his generous girth. For George Lucas it would become inextricably woven into his own.

The two men met in July 1967. As the star of the USC course, Lucas had won a student film scholarship awarded by Warners. His reward was six months on the Burbank lot, where he would be free to observe production in a department of his choice. He arrived on the day the studio's last founding father, Jack Warner, cleared his office and left, replaced by the 7 Arts company, a business built as far from Hollywood as could be imagined, at a Canadian tannery. As a colossus of one era walked off stage, so stepped forward one of the men who would succeed him. Choruses of "The king is dead, long live the king" were thin on the ground, however. Lucas arrived to find the studio eerily empty. For years afterwards he referred to the moment as "the day the film industry died."

Lucas had been interested in working in the animation department. The scene he found there resembled the deck of the *Marie Celeste*. As he wandered the back lot he found only one film in production, *Finian's Rainbow*, a bloated version of the popular Broadway musical about a leprechaun and his search for a pot of gold. (Rather a neat summary of Lucas's life at that precise moment.) Lucas slipped his slight and inconsequential figure on to the set, hoping to observe undetected. Soon the booming voice of Francis Coppola was demanding to know who he was.

At the age of twenty-seven, Coppola had already overcome much. He had been born in Detroit, the son of Toscanini's flautist, the composer Carmine Coppola. As a young boy his life had been overshadowed by polio and the intimidating presence of both his father and his brilliant elder brother, August. Yet, armed with a drama degree from Hofstra University, he worked his way to Los Angeles and the UCLA cinema course.

The rivalry between USC and UCLA was intense. The latter saw the former as a collection of cold technocrats, skilled in editing and photography but lacking in soul. In return the USC students regarded UCLA as a home for hopeless dreamers, incapable of translating their ideas into commercial film. Coppola had proved the exception to the rule, however. His graduation movie, *You're a Big Boy Now*, was the first student film to become a full-length theatrical release.

Coppola had cut his eyeteeth working for Roger Corman, Hollywood's prodigious purveyor of schlock horror. Under Corman's wings—along with such distinguished names as Martin Scorsese, James Cameron, Jonathan Demme, and

Ron Howard—he had worked punishing hours for little money but left with a knowledge of how to squeeze every last dime out of a budget.

His first film, *Dementia 13*, set in an Irish castle besieged by an ax murderer, was Corman to the core. Coppola wrote the script in three days and filmed it almost as quickly.

Lucas had been given his first taste of Hollywood on a scholarship with Columbia. He spent a month in Utah and Arizona filming a documentary about the making of *McKenna's Gold*, starring Gregory Peck and Omar Sharif. He had not been impressed by the wastefulness and the lack of youth he had seen there; he had been used to making movies on the run for $300 and he saw "zillions of dollars wasted."

Life seemed pretty much the same on *Finian's Rainbow* where, apart from Coppola, Lucas was the only one under fifty years of age. On a film set dominated by the old hands of Hollywood, the two students formed an instant—if unlikely—friendship. Coppola's gregarious personality threw Lucas's shyness into even starker relief. "My life has no anecdotes, Francis's life is one big anecdote," the apprentice would say of his master.

When Lucas asked Coppola for a job, Coppola hired him to be his administrative assistant. As the friendship deepened, Coppola's impresario instincts took over. An assiduous collector of people, he already saw himself as something of a guru to the young filmmakers following in his wake.

Lucas had shown Coppola a copy of what he regarded as the best of his early films, a short science-fiction film he had made after graduating from USC during a spell as a lecturer there. *THX 1138:4HB* had begun life as a page-and-a-half-long description of a man attempting to escape from his imprisonment in an underground world. By the time Lucas had spent three months filming, editing, and adding innovative optical effects, it had been hailed as the most brilliant student film in years. Coppola was highly impressed and badgered Lucas into turning it into a full blown screenplay. "If you're going to direct, you have to learn to write, and not only do you have to learn to write, but you have to get good at it," Coppola pronounced.

They may have complemented each other professionally, but Lucas and Coppola were polar opposites as men. Lucas's idea of a good evening was being wrapped up in front of the television with a tuna sandwich by 9 P.M. Coppola seemed permanently in the middle of a party: his home was a magnet for singers, dancers, poets, and philosophers.

Lucas was solitary, independent, and idealistic about the world. He could be as dogmatic as his father, particularly on the subject of Hollywood where the world was divided into black—the studios—and white—the artists. Coppola's view of the world was much more complex. For him life was an opera, and he loved the Machiavellian side of the movie business. While Coppola dreamed of taking over Hollywood, Lucas had already fallen in love with the idea of moving it somewhere quieter.

The idea of an alternative filmmaking community had taken root in 1968 when Coppola and Lucas combined on their first full-length feature together. *The Rain People*, a heavy-handed and pretentious piece by Wilmer Butler in which a depressed housewife is befriended by a mentally retarded hitchhiker as she drives across the country, was filmed on location in the remote town of Ogallala, Nebraska. While Coppola directed, Lucas doubled up as assistant cameraman, sound recordist, art director, and production manager. He even managed to use a spare camera to make a documentary about the production, *Filmmaker*. Lucas found his first experience of nonstudent filmmaking utterly exhilarating. He was also inspired by Coppola's belief in the same sort of collective "all-for-one" philosophy the Dirty Dozen had talked of at USC. On the set of *The Rain People* he had distributed share certificates promising every member of the cast and crew part of any profits the film made. As it turned out the certificates would be worthless. Yet Lucas made a deal with himself to one day do the same.

When the burghers of Ogallala donated to the ragtag crew a disused warehouse as a ministudio, he and Coppola's imaginations ran riot. Inspired by the freedom and their new facility and with little else to do but work and talk about work, the two friends excitedly agreed to form their own setup, independent of Hollywood and its interference.

Within months Coppola had browbeat Warners, then run by a former agent, Ted Ashley, into giving him the money to open a small studio in San Francisco. Their dream took shape at a warehouse in the run-down Folsom Street district where state-of-the-art production facilities, including an $80,000 sound-editing suite Coppola had bought on a whim in Copenhagen, were installed. Lucas rallied support from other members of USC's Dirty Dozen, including Milius, Matthew Robbins, Hal Barwood, Walter Murch, and the husband and wife writing team of Gloria Katz and Willard Huyck.

Coppola, appointed president of the new company, christened American Zoetrope, issued a lofty statement to the trade press outlining their principles. It declared: "The essential objective of the company is to engage in the varied fields of filmmaking, collaborating with the most gifted and youthful talent using the most contemporary techniques and equipment possible."

By now Lucas had moved to the rolling countryside of Marin County, just outside San Francisco, and was the proud owner of a new home, a new company—and a new wife.

Lucas had met Marcia Griffin while working on a documentary for the respected editor, Verna Fields, at the US Information Agency after graduating from USC. Night after night they had been locked in a room editing footage for Fields. Eventually Lucas had plucked up the courage to ask her for a date.

Marcia had found her colleague ultraserious and uptight. On their first date she told him to "lighten up." She would spend much of the rest of her life doing so. As their careers had progressed, however, they had stayed in touch. She had worked on a series of films, including *Medium Cool* with his old friend Haskell Wexler, now an up-and-coming cameraman and director. Opinionated and talented, she was a popular addition to the circle of filmmakers whom Lucas regarded as his only real friends.

After a series of painful separations, when Marcia had been hired to edit in New York, Lucas had proposed. They married near Monterey on February 22, 1969. Coppola and most of the Dirty Dozen were on hand to celebrate. The couple were homebodies at heart and struck a deal to support each other's careers and avoid more separations. Soon they had a home with their own editing room to help them stay together. It had been during their honeymoon that they had first driven through the beautiful Marin County landscape, just north of San Francisco over the Golden Gate Bridge. They found a house in Mill Valley which they turned into their first home, complete with an office and a small editing room in the attic.

In November 1969, American Zoetrope began trading on a heady cocktail of Coppola's bravado and Lucas's brilliance. The deal with Warners had been secured on the back of a deal to film Lucas's expanded *THX* script. Coppola had thrown in another of his protégé's ideas, a Vietnam war movie he had dreamed up with his USC pal Milius, for good measure.

The only catch Ted Ashley had applied to the deal with Warners was that if no finished movies resulted, Coppola would have to pay the money back. As Lucas began filming

THX 1138, however, failure was the last thing on their minds. Lucas had been given a budget of $777,000 and he began a forty-day shoot at the end of the year. The film had evolved into a bleak, Orwellian mood piece. Science fiction it may have been, *Star Wars* it was not.

Somewhere in the future humans had been confined to living in an underground environment where they were kept shaven-headed and sedated by drugs. In place of Big Brother, Lucas had created OMM, an omnipresent governing body able to monitor all its citizens with two-way TV screens and equipped with an army of robotic policemen. Anyone disobeying OMM's instructions to "work hard, increase production, prevent accidents and be happy" would be liable to receive a form of brain scrambling. At the heart of his story were two roommates, THX 1138 and LUH 3417. Discovering a sexual attraction to each other, they defied OMM by failing to take their drugs, then having sex and conceiving a child. Found guilty of perversion, THX was then imprisoned in an ethereal "White Limbo" from which no one had ever escaped. The climax of the story saw THX speeding through the maze of tunnels, evading a tribe of furry midgets and finally climbing a ladder to freedom and the blinding light of the outside world. (Lucas's final shot would become something of a trademark—a glowing, setting sun.)

Lucas filmed in the San Francisco area, using an unfinished network of new train tunnels to create his grim future and a quality cast assembled with the help of Coppola. Robert Duvall and Maggie McOmie took on the roles of THX and LUH while Donald Pleasance played the sinister SEN, who reports their misdemeanors.

Lucas found the process of directing the actors difficult, however. It was hard for him to disconnect from the technical worries of the cameras and the microphones. His shyness was also crippling. Yet he was happy with his first experience as a director. He felt his film had a message relevant to the troubled times America was suffering. In his own way, he was echoing Timothy Leary and his invitation to "tune in, turn on and drop out," reassuring everyone they were free to walk away from their problems. Soon he would be wishing that were actually possible...

CHAPTER 2

American Graffiti

Early in 1970 Gary Kurtz made the short drive out of San Francisco across the Golden Gate Bridge and the bay into the verdant valleys of northern California's wine country. He knew the area from his childhood in San Mateo County, south of the city. About fifteen minutes after crossing the bridge, Kurtz pulled up in the small, picture-postcard pretty town of Mill Valley, parked his car, and rang the doorbell of a small house off the main street.

Kurtz's first impressions of the bearded, bantamweight figure who greeted him were hardly atypical. "He was just this little guy," he recalled with a shrug. The "little guy" would cast a giant shadow over Kurtz's life, however. Together he and George Lucas would conquer the world.

The thirty-year-old producer had been in northern California planning his latest movie, *Two-Lane Blacktop,* a story of dueling drag racers in the *Easy Rider* mold, starring Warren Oates and James Taylor. The film had been financed by Universal, under a groundbreaking low budget program inspired by the success of Hopper and Fonda's drug-drenched ride into the dark side of the counterculture.

Kurtz, with director Monte Hellman, was interested in shooting the movie on the cheap, but rarely used Techniscope format and had approached Francis Coppola for advice. With characteristic pomposity, Coppola suggested Kurtz visit "one of his protégés" who had coincidentally just finished filming in Techniscope. Kurtz made the short journey from Coppola's house to Mill Valley where he found Lucas hunched over the Steenbeck editing machine he was using to complete *THX 1138*.

Kurtz thought Lucas sharp yet unpretentious—the antithesis of his melodramatic mentor. "Francis is very Italian, grandiose, great fun to be with, very outgoing," Kurtz recalled. "George is the opposite."

As it happened, Gary Kurtz was just as quiet and undemonstrative. While they talked over the technicalities of their trade, he and Lucas discovered it was not all they had in common. For a start, both had formed a passion for filmmaking at the University of Southern California.

Kurtz, born in July 1940, had grown up in the towns of San Mateo and Belmont just south of San Francisco. His family's roots lay in the Midwest where his heritage was an archetypal melting pot of influences, English, Scots-Irish, and Welsh on his mother's side, Austrian-German and Scandinavian on his father's. On his paternal grandmother's lap he would listen to tales of how she had ridden to school in North Dakota and Iowa on horseback, armed with a pistol to shoot the rattlesnakes.

Kurtz's childhood had been more Bohemian than Lucas's strict, small-town upbringing. His mother, Sarah, was a painter and sculptor. The family garage had been converted into a studio with a homemade kiln. His father, Eldo, a chemical engineer, was an amateur photographer and filmmaker. As a boy Kurtz learned to operate his 8 mm cine camera, running films from the 1930s on a makeshift screen.

Kurtz's childhood fantasies had been fired by the golden age of radio rather than television. With his parents he had spent long evenings listening to the exploits of the Lone Ranger and Sergeant Preston of the Yukon. "I loved the impact it had on my imagination," he recalled.

As he grew older, he found more inspiration in the dark of the cinemas on the fringes of San Francisco. Each Saturday he would bicycle five or six miles to the matinée show. There, like Lucas, he too had been thrilled by the spectacle of the *Flash Gordon* series.

In high school he showed his father's flair for science and mathematics. Yet his heart lay in the arts, where he was an enthusiastic drama student, acting and directing school plays and playing the clarinet. His musical ability won Kurtz a place at USC. As a freshman and sophomore, he played in the marching band and the symphony orchestra. Yet, like Lucas, he found himself drawn to the strange collection of misfits who inhabited the cinema courses. The film-school revolution, with all its repercussions for Hollywood, had yet to happen. Kurtz's photography class consisted of three students, his sound class just two. "By the time George got there in the mid-1960s, the idea of the great American filmmaker had all of a sudden exploded. Everybody wanted to go to film school," he explained. "When I was there it was a poor cousin."

Of all the words of wisdom dispensed to him, none had the impact of those Kurtz heard when he went to see one of his heroes, the great John Ford, speak at the rival UCLA shortly before he died. "He talked about working as a prop man and getting so tired he had to sleep on the floor, trading jobs with a cameraman for two weeks. I would have loved to have been part of that studio mill system," he said. As a graduate of USC, he had heeded the great man's example. "I set out to do as great a variety of work as I could."

Kurtz remained at USC working on medical information films for the United States Public Health Service. He then spent a year running the school's film laboratory. His greatest practical lessons had come at the nearest Hollywood could offer to the old studio system, as another member of the Roger Corman academy. In the course of four years, Kurtz worked on thirty or forty of Corman's films. "I don't even remember the names of some of them," he said. On one movie he would be the sound man, on the next a grip for a cameraman. One week he would be the cinematographer, another week he would be editing. On one western Kurtz was even called on to be the special-effects man. In the mid-1960s, however, his education was interrupted by the draft. Tall and sturdily built, he became a member of the Marine Corps. It was only midway through his training that he saw he had made a terrible mistake. "Basically I realized that I was a conscientious objector." When Kurtz revealed to a superior officer that he would not be able to fire a gun, he was told to keep the matter quiet. The revelation could easily have resulted in a court martial and a spell in military prison. Fortunately, his skills as a filmmaker were soon deemed more valuable than his marksmanship. Kurtz may have been the only conscientious objector in the Marines to serve in Vietnam.

Kurtz spent his time in Southeast Asia observing the war through a camera lens as he was assigned to a film unit. The traumatic events he witnessed, and the personal questions he had been forced to face, prompted a religious awakening. Kurtz would come to call himself a follower of a number of religions. At the time, however, he adopted a Captain Ahab–like beard, synonymous with the pacifist Quaker movement.

Kurtz had picked up the threads of his movie career with

another Corman graduate, Monte Hellman. It had been Coppola's Corman connection that led Kurtz to George Lucas's door. Lucas had finished filming Zoetrope's debut film, *THX 1138*, a few months earlier. Locked away in his converted attic, he, Marcia, and sound editor Walter Murch, were in the final stages of editing. As Kurtz chatted to Lucas in Mill Valley that afternoon, he recognized a kindred spirit. "We both came up in the school of doing everything ourselves," he said. "He was my kind of filmmaker."

It was a few months later, as he worked on a movie for MGM, *Chandler,* that Kurtz got a surprise phone call from Lucas. Coppola's bearded little acolyte traveled down to Los Angeles to meet him and asked whether he might be interested in producing a new project he was working on, a war movie called *Apocalypse Now*.

Coppola had typically been the matchmaker. He had been fascinated by some of Kurtz's striking 16 mm footage of American helicopters in Vietnam. He sensed Kurtz would be a perfect foil for Lucas—particularly now that his own relationship with him was in such disarray. The dream of American Zoetrope had been short-lived, wiped out by the events of what both men mordantly referred to as "Black Thursday."

Soon after Lucas had completed a cut of *THX 1138,* Coppola had, with his customary taste for drama, dispatched the first offerings from the self-styled new studio in a large black box. The box was delivered to Ted Ashley's office at Warner Bros. in Los Angeles. Its resemblance to a coffin seemed somehow more obvious when it reappeared at Zoetrope hours later.

As well as *THX,* the box had contained a selection of seven scripts, including *Apocalypse Now* and another idea Coppola was working on, *The Conversation*. The film had remained at the studio but the rest had been returned, unwanted. Ashley and his executives had taken one look at *THX 1138* and decided their investment in the brave new world of Coppola was a massive error. "They said: 'This is all junk, you have to pay back the money you owe us,'" Lucas recalled. At that stage Warner Bros. reckoned Zoetrope owed them $300,000 for the development of their scripts.

The rejection had sent the embryonic Folsom Street studio into a terminal panic. Staff walked out, legal actions were launched and Coppola temporarily relocated himself in Europe to rethink his future.

To add insult to Lucas's personal injury, Warner then went on to perform what he considered a hatchet job on *THX 1138*. "I don't feel they had the right to do it, not after I had worked on that thing for three years with no money," he protested constantly afterwards. "When a studio hires you that's different. But when a filmmaker develops a project himself, he has rights."

THX 1138 was eventually released in March 1971 to surprisingly receptive reviews. Yet its bleak message found few friends beyond the university and art house circuit. At the box office it failed to make $1 million.

The debacle had left Lucas, as he later put it, "high and dry." After three years of blood, sweat, and tears he was penniless. Only Marcia's burgeoning career as an editor was keeping the wolves from the door in Mill Valley.

In desperation, he had returned to *Apocalypse Now*, an idea that had been bubbling away for years. At USC, he and John Milius had talked of making a dark, cinema verité satire on Vietnam. Milius had mined a collection of incredible stories from veterans of the war. With Lucas he saw the film as a Vietnam version of Robert Altman's huge hit *M*A*S*H*—a surreal mix of sex, drugs, bombs, and surfing.

After some deliberation over whether he and Lucas would work as a team—he feared they might be too quiet—Kurtz agreed to Lucas's proposal and traveled to the Philippines to scout for possible locations. His mission brought bad news, however. It was soon apparent that the film would be way beyond the minimalistic budget Lucas had in mind. There were also complications in that the film technically belonged to Coppola and Zoetrope, as part of the *THX* deal with Warner Bros. Hollywood's lack of enthusiasm for making movies about a still-unfinished war settled the issue. Soon the new partnership had switched tack.

Lucas had been hurt by the criticism his San Francisco circle had heaped on him in the aftermath of *THX 1138*. "I was getting a lot of razz from Francis and a bunch of friends who said that everyone thought I was cold and weird and why didn't I do something warm and human," he said later. "I thought, 'You want warm and human, I'll give you warm and human.'"

Lucas and Kurtz discussed two ideas. One was an autobiographical piece Lucas had come up with, based on his years cruising the streets of Modesto. He saw it as a nostalgic postcard to his lost youth, drenched with the memorable music of the era. He called it his "rock 'n' roll movie." The other was less well thought out. Both Kurtz and Lucas had bemoaned the lack of films in the tradition of the old Flash Gordon adventures. They made preliminary inquiries into acquiring the rights to the old Alex Raymond series from their owners King Features. "They were way too expensive for us. They were 'hot' at the time," said Kurtz. (Ownership passed from Federico Fellini to Dino De Laurentiis in the late 1970s. By 1980—on the back of the *Star Wars* phenomenon—De Laurentiis had made a frustrating hash of his opportunity.)

Both men were admirers of the Japanese master, Akira Kurosawa. Another idea was to develop his classic 1958 *Hidden Fortress* with Toshiro Mifune and Misa Uehara. "It's about a Samurai who takes a rather obstreperous young princess across the wilds of enemy territory. It had some similarities to *Star Wars*," Kurtz said. Rights there also proved too expensive.

In May 1971, however, the "space thing" was put to one side. By then Lucas had attracted interest in his rock-'n'-roll movie at United Artists. He and Marcia had traveled to the Cannes Film Festival, where *THX 1138* was being shown as part of the Directors' Fortnight. His film proved far more to the European taste and went down well. Amid the opulence of the famous Carlton Hotel, overlooking the Côte d'Azur, Lucas had struck a deal with United Artist's David Picker. Picker, like most executives in Hollywood, preferred to cover himself with multiple picture deals. He agreed to develop *American Graffiti* in tandem with one other idea. "A Flash Gordon thing" became the second string to the deal. While the Lucases took a holiday in Europe, a friend, Richard Walters, was commissioned to write a screenplay for submission to Picker. By the time he had landed back in Los Angeles, however, Walters's first draft had left Lucas sorely disappointed. Picker read it and rejected it. If Kurtz and Lucas were willing to develop a new script for nothing, he said, he would reconsider the deal. If not they were free to take it elsewhere.

Kurtz called on his connection with Ned Tanen, the executive in charge of the low-budget program at Universal. *Two-Lane Blacktop* had not set the box office alight. Yet Kurtz's talents had been appreciated at the studio where other filmmakers—notably Dennis Hopper who had "gone missing" somewhere in Peru filming the appositely titled *The Last Movie*—had been giving them trouble. Tanen had seen *THX* as a student film and also knew of Lucas. Universal's interest spurred Lucas into rewriting the script himself. According to his friend, Walter Murch, he did so "with his old 45s playing in the background." For a month or so, Lucas tapped into the memories of his Modesto youth: his experiences as a greaser, a racer, a high school nobody. He found himself populating his story with people he had known, and most of all with people like himself. He could not see it yet, but he had a clear talent for drawing on his inner life.

Tanen liked the script and offered the duo an opportunity to make the film under the same, $1 million or less program Kurtz and Monte Hellman had made *Two-Lane Blacktop*. He had only two major conditions. The first was that the film be, once more, part of a two-picture deal. The second was that it should have a star name attached.

Once more Lucas and Kurtz were content to throw in their "Flash Gordon thing" as a second picture. Why not? It didn't even exist? Tanen's other condition caused Lucas more concern. His dislike of stars was an extension of his basic discomfort with large groups of people in general. He had found it tough working with Duvall and Pleasance on *THX* and preferred the idea of grateful unknowns who would not challenge his withdrawn manner on the set. Instead, Tanen offered him the alternative of hiring a star name as a director or producer. In the spring of 1972, one name sprang rather obviously to mind.

When Paramount had offered Francis Coppola the job of directing an adaptation of Mario Puzo's bestselling Mafia novel, *The Godfather*, he had—at first—rejected the idea of working for a studio ever again. As the repercussions of the Zoetrope catastrophe continued, Lucas had been among those who had advised him to think again. By now he was carrying around matchbooks marked "Francis Ford Coppola: The Godfather." The film had been the box office sensation of 1972, talk of Oscar glory was already in the wind.

Relations between the two friends had been strained by the Zoetrope disaster and the *THX* affair. Yet Lucas had helped Coppola out on *The Godfather*, filming montage scenes of mass Mafia slayings for the movie's climax. Coppola agreed to return the favor, consenting to produce with the tacit understanding that Gary Kurtz would do the donkey work. With Coppola onboard, Tanen gave the as yet untitled Universal Pictures Production No. 05144 the green light.

"They were already thinking of the poster— 'From the man who brought you *The Godfather*,'" smiled Kurtz.

Kurtz and Lucas set up a small office at the Mill Valley house, where extra phones were installed. At the advice of his lawyer, Tom Pollock, Lucas created a company to hire out his services for tax purposes. With Gary Kurtz and his secretary, Dorothy "Bunny" Alsup, he kicked around a number of ideas for a corporate name. "We were trying to come up with a generic name. It was going to be Mill Valley Films at one point," recalled Kurtz.

Another idea had been the English-sounding Lucasfilm Ltd. "He was a bit leery of it. He thought it was kind of an ego thing," said Kurtz. "But we thought we'd just call it that for the incorporation and worry about it later."

Lucas's story revolved around the events of one long summer's night in 1962 and a group of high school graduates' preparations for their move on into the wider world. Much of the action would center on a drive-in diner, Mel's, and the sleek, souped-up cars in which the youngsters cruised the streets. He later confessed that three of the central male parts, a nerd called Terry "the Toad," a drag racer called Milner, and a smart-alecky college-boy-to-be, Curt, were all reflections of the George Lucas Jr. who had driven the streets of Modesto.

With the help of the astute casting director Fred Roos, Lucas assembled a cast of talented unknowns. Richard Dreyfuss, Charles Martin Smith, Ron Howard, and Paul LeMat formed the central male quartet; Cindy Williams, Mackenzie Philips, and Candy Clark took the main female leads.

Shooting began in late June 1972. For twenty-eight fraught nights, Lucas and his crew would begin work at 9 P.M. and finish at 5 A.M. the following morning.

The film was beset with problems from the beginning. After three disastrous nights filming in San Rafael, where they had drawn complaints from locals, Kurtz and Lucas switched to another northern California town, Petaluma. The highly tuned cars misbehaved as did the young, inexperienced cast. LeMat, a former boxer, and Harrison Ford, Fred Roos's carpenter, hired to play the part of a drag racer, were the ringleaders. Their highjinx ranged from racing each other up a giant, revolving Holiday Inn sign to hurling Richard Dreyfuss off a second-floor balcony into a swimming pool.

Yet for everyone involved, the process of making a movie at such breakneck speed was exhilarating. "It was a giddy time," recalled Fred Roos.

To those who did not know them, Lucas and Kurtz seemed like twins conducting some silent conspiracy against the world. Both were serious and introspective. Displays of emotion were rare. Yet they complemented each other perfectly. "I felt like they were seeing through the same eyes," said Bunny Alsup.

Tanen had effectively left Kurtz and Lucas to their own devices during the month's filming. "They wrote you a check and you went away and they didn't hear from you until you'd finished filming," explained Kurtz.

Universal's trust was rewarded as Lucas and Kurtz brought the film in not only on time, but within a few stray dollars of the $750,000 budget.

By January 1973 George and Marcia Lucas's edit of the film was ready. If he had been hurt by Warners' treatment of *THX*, the sensitive director was devastated by what followed.

Universal loathed the title Lucas had chosen, *American*

Graffiti. "They thought it was an Italian film about feet," grimaced Gary Kurtz. The studio offered *Another Slow Night In Modesto* as an alternative, Coppola suggested *Rock Around The Block.* "Francis's idea wasn't so bad," said Kurtz. Both, however, were rejected by Lucas. Worse was to follow as they showed the film to Tanen at a Sunday morning screening at the Northpoint Theatre in San Francisco on January 28, 1973.

As the house lights dimmed and Bill Haley's "Rock Around the Clock" led the audience into the opening images of the inept Terry "the Toad" losing control of his scooter, there was a tangible air of excitement. George and Marcia Lucas's gift for editing had never been more beautifully displayed. Each scene, underpinned by the three-minute rhythm of a new song, was a masterpiece of timing and story-building. The rock-'n'-roll sound track, filled with classics from "Why Do Fools Fall in Love" to "The Great Pretender" and underpinned by distinctive growl of the cult, late-night disc jockey, Wolfman Jack, had large banks of the audience bobbing in their seats. Afterwards the film's makers thought the film had received "a good, solid reaction." Ned Tanen's reaction was pure rage, however. To their amazement he flew into a fury, attacking the trio of Coppola, Kurtz and Lucas for failing him.

"He said it was not fit to show an audience," recalled Kurtz, who with Lucas and Coppola, was at first stunned. "We were flabbergasted."

Tanen's outburst was the cue for what Lucas later acknowledged as "Francis's finest hour." "He just blew his top, he was so mad," Lucas said later.

Tanen refused Coppola's offer to buy the film back on the spot, and stormed out of the cinema leaving Lucas, Kurtz, and Coppola seething.

"Ned was really angry that day, he just got into his limousine and drove off," said Kurtz.

Lucas would never be as grateful to his producer as he was in the aftermath of the showdown. It was effectively Kurtz who saved his film from oblivion.

A week or so after the Northpoint screening, Tanen had cooled down enough to watch the film a second time. This time he made a list of alterations he felt would salvage the film. Lucas had locked himself away in Mill Valley, fuming at the interference. His sense of impotence was only heightened by a Writers' Guild strike which meant he could not cross the picket lines on to the Universal lot even if he had wanted to.

"George was really upset and didn't want to talk to him," Kurtz recalled. Lucas hated the idea of seeing his film changed by someone who—to his mind—knew nothing about making movies. "George was against it all. His analogy was 'It's okay to go through this nine-month period to produce a little baby, but what we want to do is cut off a little finger,'" said Kurtz. "I had to go down to Hollywood and fix this thing up."

George and Marcia had remained friendly with Verna Fields, still one of Hollywood's most respected editors. Kurtz knew she was also a close personal friend of Tanen's and cannily enlisted her help.

Fields was able to persuade Tanen to drop some of his objections. With a few, relatively minor changes—like moving a slow-paced junkyard scene featuring LeMat and Mackenzie Phillips to later in the film so as to maintain the rhythm—Tanen was satisfied.

Once the film was accepted, Kurtz then worked hard at making sure the rest of the Universal hierarchy saw *Graffiti* in the best possible environment. They knew their target audience were the young and the nostalgic. Wherever possible he packed studio screenings with as many young staff members as he could drum up. Their enthusiasm would wash over their crustier superiors.

"Normally fourteen stodgy old men sit in a room and that's it," remembered Lucas. "After about seven or eight of those screenings they knew they had a movie after all."

Eventually the film was given a theatrical release date at the beginning of August 1973. To the pragmatic producer the whole process had been little more than a tiresome piece of Hollywood power play. "I was the one who was stuck with having to make it work. All this folderal going back and forth for two months, I don't think it made any difference at all. It was a storm in a teacup," Kurtz said.

Yet it left the more sensitive Lucas nursing wounds that would never heal. Coming on top of Warner Bros. interference on *THX 1138*, the experience only deepened his disdain for Hollywood. "George is very moral and believed in doing things the right way. He also had a very Old Testament view of not forgiving," said Kurtz. "Once he was wronged he would always remember it. I suppose I didn't see it in the same light. At that point I figured it was more important to get the bloody thing finished and out there than anything else."

Even before *American Graffiti* was released, Lucas was plotting his revenge.

In the morning of April 17, 1973, armed with pads of green and blue legal notepaper and a pack of his favorite hard-leaded pencils, George Lucas left his kitchen, walked to his cramped office in the Mill Valley house and shut the door behind him. In his tiny, often illegible longhand, he began scrawling the first tentative outlines of what would eventually become *Star Wars*.

He later admitted that the first knots of anxiety he felt that day stayed with him for the next ten years. In 1983, he complained, "There hasn't been a day in my life when I haven't gotten up in the morning and said, 'Gee, I've got to worry about this movie.'"

In part he was nervous at what he was attempting. He was also still burning with anger at what Universal was doing to *American Graffiti*. He dreamed of one day turning the tables on his enemies there. If Lucas sat down to write his "Flash Gordon thing" with one overwhelming motivation, however, it was a monetary one.

While the fine details of the *Graffiti* budget were checked by the Universal accountants, the money due to him and Kurtz was being withheld. At that moment he was $15,000 in debt. "I had to start paying back some of this money," he said. To the son of penny-wise George Lucas Sr. there could have been no greater inspiration.

As ever, the process of putting pencil to paper was far from easy. Since his days at school Lucas had hated writing. The story of *American Graffiti* had been a more straightforward process. There he was, after all, recounting the formative four years he had spent cruising around Modesto in his tiny Fiat. He had also been able to enlist the help of Willard Huyck and Gloria Katz. This time he was on his own. And this time his task was the creation of an entirely new universe.

He spent much of each day soaking up a diverse collection of influences. As well as rewatching the beloved Flash Gordon adventures of his childhood he read science fiction's old and new masters, from Edgar Rice Burroughs to Frank Herbert's *Dune* and E. E. "Doc" Smith's Lensman stories.

He and Gary Kurtz had, from the outset, believed the story should have a sense of fairytale to it. "A long time ago in a galaxy far, far away was our version of once upon a time," said Kurtz. "We felt it was essentially a fairytale." Both men were interested in comparative religion and philosophy. "I have personally always been a believer in archetypal psychology and Jung's philosophies about how we take archetypal characters and use them in our lives," said Kurtz. "I think George was in that same frame of mind."

In his search for elements of fantasy, Lucas read *Grimm's Fairy Tales* and C.S. Lewis's *Narnia Chronicles,* J.R.R. Tolkien and Frazer's *The Golden Bough*. He also read Greek, Islamic and Indian mythology and the works of modern mythologists like Carlos Castenada and Joseph Campbell.

No book would be as influential as Campbell's *The Hero With a Thousand Faces*, a synthesis linking the storytelling traditions from different religions and cultures around the world. Throughout the *Star Wars* era the book—along with *Roget's Thesaurus, Webster's Dictionary, Harper's Bible Dictionary, Bartlett's Familiar Quotations* and *The Foundations of Screenwriting* by Syd Field—remained stacked on his desk at all times.

By May 20, Lucas had completed his first thirteen-page draft.

Complex, exotic, and fantastical, "the story of Mace Windu" was set in the twenty-third century, where the final two members of the "Jedi bendu," an order of knights, not dissimilar to the medieval Knights Templar, supposed guardians of the Holy Grail, were locked in a battle with an evil galactic empire. The central story bore strong similarities to that of *Hidden Fortress*. The knights, General Luke Skywalker and Anakin Starkiller escort a rebel princess, named at that stage Leia Aguilae, as she is pursued by the empire and its two villains, General Darth Vader and Valarium, the Black Knight. As insurance, two Imperial bureaucrats have been taken hostage. The duo acted as Shakespearean fools, providing comic relief to the action as did two "workmen" robots, "Threepio" and "Artoo."

The story was essentially one elongated chase, spread out over three planets—one a jungle, another a desert, and a third clouded in gas and populated by cities in the skies. In one sequence the rebels took refuge in an asteroid belt. In another they took over a space freighter piloted by a brigand called Han Solo. Midway through the complex story, the princess was captured. The rebel party, which also included a group of a dozen young boys and a "giant furry alien" called Chewbacca, a prince among the "Wookiee" race on the jungle planet, then rescued her in a spectacular attack on an Imperial convoy. The story ended with the princess honoring her saviors at a grand ceremony.

Lucas had acquired the essential attributes of a rising young director—a lawyer and an agent—before making *Graffiti*. He asked Jeff Berg at ICM and lawyer Tom Pollock to hawk the treatment around Hollywood. Both men found the thirteen pages hard to fathom.

The treatment's first ports of call would have to be the hated Universal and United Artists, where he was still obligated under the two-picture deal. On the recommendation of his old Long Beach State rival, Steven Spielberg, with whom he had become friendly since he too had broken into Hollywood, Lucas also asked Berg to see whether he could interest a relatively new executive at 20th Century–Fox, Alan Ladd Jr.

David Picker and Ned Tanen would go on to carve themselves distinguished film careers. As far as the more elephantine memories in Hollywood were concerned, however, they would always remain the men who turned down *Star Wars*.

In the mid-1970s United Artists remained one of the steadier ships in Hollywood. The studio of Chaplin and Pickford, Fairbanks and D. W. Griffith remained an oasis for cerebral cinema. No film typified their taste as well as Milos Forman's *One Flew Over the Cuckoo's Nest*, about to garner every major honor in the business. UA was not averse to the odd slice of fantasy. The studio still distributed the James Bond movies with "Cubby" Broccoli. Yet to Picker, Lucas's treatment sounded much too expensive. He was also unsure whether the special effects Lucas had described were actually possible. Three years after registering his first interest in Lucas's "Flash Gordon thing" at Cannes, Picker, with no hard feelings, formally passed on the "Mace Windu" treatment.

Tanen was not long in following. Universal still had half an eye trained on television. "Universal was a very conservative company," Kurtz said. "It was making most of its money in TV, and gearing most of its theatrical film to an eventual sale to TV." The bizarre treatment hardly seemed like prime time fare for the networks.

Tanen later admitted he had "a very tough time understanding" Lucas's fantastical outline. "I would ask most people in the world to visualize what See-Threepio means from reading a thirteen-page treatment," he sighed. Like David Picker, whose rejection had been backed by others at UA, Tanen could at least take solace in the knowledge he was not the only Universal executive underwhelmed by Lucas's idea.

The studio appears to have seen another draft, in which Lucas had distilled his story nearer its final form. To judge by the subsequent script evaluation memos the studio based its eventual decision on George Lucas rather than his story:

UNIVERSAL INTEROFFICE MEMO
Date: XXXXXX
To: XXXXXX
From: XXXXXX
Subject: The "Star Wars" screenplay by George Lucas

To my mind, we're really rolling dice with this kind of a project, but I think the concept here (at least in terms of what has been done so far with the genre) is rather exciting, and combined with the potential action inherent in the piece, it seems to me an attractive possibility in many ways.

On the other hand, a great deal of this screenplay (above the special effects and makeup problems) is going to be very difficult to translate visually. I'm thinking particularly in terms of our robot "heroes," Threepio and Artoo.

And even if all visuals and special effects work perfectly, the story could be ultimately no more than an interesting exercise if the audience doesn't completely understand the rights and wrongs involved, and just as important, have absolute empathy with young Luke. Starkiller.* And it is in these areas I believe the script still needs work. Action and adventure abounds. We still need more from the characters.

Bottom line: If the movie works, we might have a wonderful, humorous, and exciting adventure-fantasy, an artistic and very commercial venture. Most of what we need is here. The question, in the end, is how much faith we have in Mr Lucas's ability to pull it all off.

Lucas had told Jeff Berg to ask for $25,000 to develop the treatment into a screenplay. Soon he was informed the studio was formally passing. At a rough estimate, their lack of faith in "Mr. Lucas's ability to pull it all off" would cost them $3 billion.

In late May 1973, Lucas boarded a PSA shuttle from San Francisco to Los Angeles. From LAX airport he made the brief trip up the San Diego freeway towards Santa

---

* Lucas continually flitted between calling his hero Starkiller or Skywalker. It would only be on the day before filming that he finally opted for the latter.

Monica Boulevard, Century City, and the offices of the 20th Century–Fox Film Corporation.

Lucas would have spent the hour-long flight along the Pacific coast running through the three priorities he now faced.

The first and most pressing was simply to raise some money. His debts from *American Graffiti* were still piling up. Between them, Gary Kurtz reckoned he and Lucas owed some $60,000. Lucas even owed his father $2,000.

The second was to convince Alan Ladd Jr. his space fantasy was a worthwhile venture. Berg had slipped a copy of *Graffiti* to Ladd who had asked to meet its maker. Of all the Hollywood studios, Fox had the best track record with science fiction as far as Lucas was concerned. Its unexpected success with *Planet of the Apes* in 1968 had spawned a series of four likeable big-screen sequels and a television spinoff.

His third and most important goal, however, was to retain control of his next movie. If he was ever to create the kind of empire he and Coppola had dreamed of, it would be by managing his own destiny every step of the way.

Lucas arrived at Fox to experience a sense of *déjà vu*. The atmosphere must have reminded him of the day he arrived at Warner Bros. Once more he walked into a studio inhabited by little more than the ghosts of a glorious past.

Four decades after the 1935 merger between Joseph Schenck's Twentieth Century Pictures and William Fox's Fox Film Corporation, the studio built by Darryl F. Zanuck was a cadaverlike shadow of its once imperious self.

The most graphic symbol of a catastrophic decade that had almost destroyed the studio still stood on the Fox lot. Like every other visitor, Lucas would have stared in quiet disbelief at the $2 million reconstruction of a New York elevated subway built for the disastrous *Hello Dolly!* a few years earlier. The set was a rusting monument to the $16 million the studio lost on the film and the $100 million annual loss of 1969–70 which effectively brought the Zanuck dynasty to an end. After *Hello Dolly!* Fox had said goodbye to its old ways. The railroad remained as a warning to those who would forget.

The company's new chief executive was the antithesis of the old Hollywood showmen. Dennis Stanfill had moved to Los Angeles from New York and the leviathan investment banking house, Lehman Brothers. His instincts were those of blue-blood conservative Wall Street. To him, Darryl Zanuck's mantra "take a chance and spend a million dollars and hope you're right" seemed like the insane rambling of a riverboat gambler.

He was typical of the new breed of businessman now holding sway in Hollywood. A group of New York investment banks propped up Harry "King" Cohn's Columbia, Gulf and Western had gobbled up Paramount, Transamerica, a San Francisco insurance company, had acquired United Artists, while the Las Vegas hotel and airline empire of the entrepreneur Kirk Kerkorian owned the once-great MGM.

Stanfill's stewardship had been safe and steady, a series of trend-following rather than trend-setting exercises, most notably a profitable foray into the disaster movie business with Irwin Allen's *The Poseidon Adventure*. Another Allen movie, *The Towering Inferno*, being made with Warner Bros., would soon follow. In a generally unhealthy Hollywood, however, 20th Century–Fox seemed a perennially sickly child. With a number of ailing arms attached to the empire, including a struggling record company, the company's share price was ominously low. On Wall Street its stock was pinned below the $10 mark and had been as low as $5. Asset-stripping vultures circled Century City by day and by night.

Morale at the studio was at an all-time low. "As a studio it was defunct and depressing to be at," said Tim Deegan, then vice president in charge of world advertising. "Everything was gray, the people, the movies, the attitudes, the cigar smoke. It was grim, a very demoralizing place to go to every day."

"It was desperation time. Fox was almost at its lowest ebb financially," recalled another executive, Ray Gosnell, then the studio's executive production manager.

"There was just no one around, even the barber shop was closed."

Fox's plight was not unique. All Hollywood was in a seemingly terminal slump. In 1946 a staggering 78 million Americans went to the movies each week. By 1960 that figure had dropped to 23 million, and by 1969 to just 17 million. In 1971, the industry hit its nadir; a paltry 15.8 million people passed through the turnstiles each week, the lowest level it would ever reach.

Fox, like the rest of a depressed Hollywood, was in search of a savior. The studio did not quite realize it yet, but he had already arrived in the dapper form of Alan Ladd Jr.

"Laddie," as he was known to almost everyone, was the son of the late Alan Ladd, the diminutive movie tough guy of the 1940s and 1950s. At 150 lbs and 5 ft 10 in, he was a middleweight to Ladd Sr.'s featherweight. Yet he had inherited much from his famous father. He too had "the face of an aging choirboy." He too had a habit of keeping his own counsel. "His father didn't say much in *Shane*; Alan Ladd Jr. doesn't say much ever," someone once said of him. Like his father Ladd had a fastidious dress sense. Most days he wore flared trousers, gleaming Gucci loafers and a turtleneck sweater. Invariably two gold medallions, bearing the names of his wife, Patty, and daughters Kelli, Tracy, and Amanda, hung around his neck.

His devotion to his family may have been a reaction to the pain of his own Hollywood childhood. His parents' marriage had foundered long before his father became a star in

This Gun for Hire in 1942. At the age of fifteen he was handed over to his father by a mother no longer capable of coping with her drinking problems. Ladd Jr. stepped into his father's second marriage to an actress-cum-agent, Sue Carol, to find himself feeling unwanted and ignored. "It was not cool to have older kids from other marriages," said his half-sister Alana Ladd Jackson, one of Ladd's two children with Carol, often the only offspring he admitted to around Hollywood. Laddie rarely spoke of his father, who by 1964 had also drunk himself to death at age fifty-one. They were "not close" he admitted once. "He was very depressed and a heavy drinker." Yet there was an unmistakable sense of his determination to step out of his father's shadow.

Laddie had eased into Hollywood at the CMA talent agency in the early 1960s. From there he had moved to another agency, London International, and had a brief dalliance with producing his own film in England. He had been called back from Europe in 1971 by Fox's then-head of production, Jere Henshaw, and installed as a middle-ranking member of his team. "I've just hired my replacement," Henshaw was soon boasting to the board.

Laddie's credentials were impeccable. As the son of a movie star and a former agent, he had a rare insight into the temperament of creative people. As a freshman agent he once had to look after Judy Garland's weekly television show. "You never knew each week when she would appear," he admitted once. He was also, unlike most of the new breed of agents, lawyers, and accountants now moving into the executive suites of Los Angeles, utterly in love with movies. As a boy living in London with his father, Ladd would sit in cinemas from ten in the morning until eleven at night. He even took on a job picking up chewing gum off the chairs as an excuse to spend his days inside in the dark. He had watched his all-time favorite film, *For Whom the Bell Tolls*, twenty-six times. His party trick was to be able to list the credits of even the most obscure film, right down to the names of its costume makers, composers, and supporting players and its running time. To Hollywood's old order he was something of a favorite son. To the disillusioned ranks at Century City, Ladd seemed like the first production head with a clue of how to pull the studio out of its torpor.

Ladd was open to input from members of his staff and worked hard at creating a family atmosphere at the studio. Each evening at 6 P.M. or so, Ladd's door would be open for staff to join him for a drink.

"Every secretary read everything," recalled Paula Weinstein, a Ladd recruit. "They would come rushing in and say, 'You've got to read this!' People felt so connected."

His door was open to the talent of Hollywood too. The new corporate raiders were leaving disgruntled directors and writers, actors and agents in their wake. Ladd had laid out the welcome mat. Already, heavyweight directors like Fred Zinneman and Herb Ross and maverick filmmakers like Robert Altman and Paul Mazursky were joining what he liked to call his "family."

Ladd's smartest signing so far had been the renegade Mel Brooks. "Laddie was a rescuer of lost filmmakers," recalled Tim Deegan. "Mel Brooks had made *Blazing Saddles* at Warner Brothers, they had refused to release it, and Laddie scooped him up. He went on to make *Young Frankenstein, Silent Movie, High Anxiety, History of the World,* all hits."

As he arrived at Fox, George Lucas seemed like a "lost filmmaker" himself. Ladd had been an admirer of Lucas's even before he was given his sneak preview of *American Graffiti*. He was one of the few executives in Hollywood who had liked *THX 1138*. Like everyone else in the business, however, he had heard of Lucas and Coppola's problems with *Graffiti*.

Lucas was straight with Ladd about his commitments to Universal and United Artists. He had to get negative responses from them before he could press ahead with Fox. He knew, however, that his thirteen-page treatment was gobbledygook without a personal explanation from him.

The moment Lucas broke into his sales spiel, Ladd knew he had found a new adopted son. Lucas could be as silent and inscrutable as Ladd himself. (Some theorized that Ladd's habit of speaking in a barely audible whisper was affected. "Laddie discovered early in life it makes people come to you," said one colleague.) Yet Lucas's enthusiasm for his space fantasy was by now pouring out of him.

Lucas's secretary, Bunny Alsup, never failed to smile at the transformation that overcame her boss when he became wrapped up in selling his stories. "He gets very excited about his projects," she said. "Like a boy playing with his toys."

Ladd could not resist such enthusiasm. "He said he had an idea about a space picture that was a throwback to all the old movies we grew up on as kids," said Ladd.

"When he said, 'This sequence is going to be like *The Seahawk*, or this like Captain Blood and this like Flash Gordon,' I knew exactly what he was saying. That gave me confidence that he was going to pull it off," Ladd said later. Ladd saw something else in the earnest enthusiasm of Lucas. "I knew from other people and from spending time with him that he was a dead-honest person who knew what he was doing."

By the end of the meeting they had shaken on the outline for a deal memo, a standard Hollywood practice, effectively sketching out the basics for a more formal contract later. Jeff Berg and Tom Pollock helped rough the deal into a standard, "step" format. Lucas would be paid $10,000 for his first draft, more if it was accepted, $50,000 if Fox agreed to make the movie with him. He would be paid another $100,000 if he directed his film while Gary Kurtz would be paid $50,000 to produce. A preliminary budget of $3.5 million was set. Any other details would be negotiated before the film began shooting.

Ultimately, Alan Ladd Jr. had understood the treatment no better than anyone else. At that precise moment he, at least, was prepared to follow the Zanuck method of moviemaking. "It was a gamble, and I was betting on Lucas," he admitted later.

On the night of August 1, 1973, the actress Cindy Williams drove past the Avco Cinema in Westwood Village barely able to believe her eyes. As she stared at the line of people snaking out of the cinema the twenty-five-year-old let loose a squeal of delight. "I never thought I'd be in a movie with lines around the block," she screamed on the phone to her friends.

Universal's lack of faith in *American Graffiti* had continued throughout the summer. The interest both Alan Ladd Jr. and executives at Paramount had shown in buying the film had been as powerful an influence as any. Eventually the studio had agreed to open it in two "art house" cinemas, one in New York, the other in Los Angeles, at the Avco. "They said, 'Then we'll see,'" recalled Gary Kurtz.

Kurtz was in New York for the opening. Like some Broadway impresario, he sat up until midnight waiting for the first reviews to appear in the city newspapers. The wait was worth it. The reviews were among the best in years. By the time *American Graffiti* opened more widely around America, a fortnight later, people were clamoring to see the film whose striking poster asked WHERE WERE YOU IN '62? *Graffiti* touched a nerve in an America that had fallen out of love with itself. Critics loved its artfulness, audiences adored its simple sense of fun. Most of all, at a time of pessimism and paranoia—Vietnam and Watergate had dominated the headlines for, it seemed, years—it took the country back to safer, somehow happier times.

Graffiti became the classic "sleeper," opening slowly and building up momentum as it spread its way across the country. "The fifth week was better than the first, it just grew and grew," recalled Kurtz. Soon Universal's Lew Wasserman had canceled other cinema bookings, replacing the company's other releases with the "wonder film" his company had made for just $750,000.

George Lucas suddenly found himself hailed as a boy genius. Newspapers beat a path to his door to learn more about the reclusive wunderkind who had tapped so successfully into the American psyche.

His outright hostility towards Hollywood only intrigued his interviewers more. "Studios and how they're run is mind-boggling," he would say, unforgivingly. "It's amazing they're still here. How they make decisions and how they think is truly amazing."

In years gone by, Hollywood would have punished him for such ingratitude. Instead they simply mimicked the magic trick he had pulled off.

American Graffiti would go on to establish itself as the most influential film of the early 1970s. Television would reinvent it as the hit series *Happy Days*, complete with the lovable Ron Howard reprising his clean-cut turn from the film. In America—and beyond—cinema audiences would drown in a wave of rock-'n'-roll replicas, from *That'll Be the Day* with David Essex in England to *Grease* with John Travolta in America.

Within the executives' suites, its success would mark the moment Hollywood finally recognized the talent of the film school students of the 1960s. First had come Coppola, now George Lucas. Close on their tails was a new breed of filmmakers, from California Steven Spielberg and John Milius, Walter Murch, and Matthew Robbins and, from the other side of the country, the brightest products of the New York University film school, Martin Scorsese and Brian De

Palma. Nothing had contributed to the decline of Hollywood as much as the growth of television. The sweet irony was that the products of the television age were about to save the movie industry. The Movie Brats were on their way. In the immediate aftermath of *Graffiti*'s success, however, Gary Kurtz and George Lucas would be grateful for one aspect of its impact more than any other. "*American Graffiti* was the only reason we got *any* interest in *Star Wars*," said Kurtz.

CHAPTER 3

War and Peace

In August 1973, as *Graffiti* was being released, George and Marcia Lucas moved a few miles from Mill Valley to another picturesque Marin County town, San Anselmo, where they bought a modest house on Medway Street.

Shortly before Christmas, they spotted a FOR SALE sign outside an imposing Victorian mansion, high on a hill overlooking the town. It fitted perfectly George's dream of a filmmaker's retreat. A few months earlier, the idea of owning such a place would have been unthinkable. By now, however, the $150,000 asking price was looking like loose change.

Graffiti's popularity continued unabated through the winter and on into 1974. In some cinemas, it played continuously for more than a year. The film would go on to earn $117 million at the worldwide box office. Universal's share of the "rentals," the proportion of the box office repaid to the distributing company, would come to more than $55 million. "Lew Wasserman personally told me it was the highest cost-to-profit ratio film they ever had, better even than *E.T.*," said Gary Kurtz.

Lucasfilm's share of the *Graffiti* success would come to some $7 million. After taxes that would leave George and Marcia with around $4 million. It was not so long ago that he had fretted about paying his father back. Now, at the age of twenty-eight, he had fulfilled his rash prediction that he would be a millionaire before his thirtieth birthday.

Lucas kept the promise he had made to himself on the set of *The Rain People* and shared his success with those who had helped him to it. Key contributors like Bunny Alsup, Fred Roos, and Walter Murch were given cars, others were given cash. Gary Kurtz had already been given a percentage point in the film, an award that would earn him close to $1 million.

Lucas indulged himself by buying a stake in a comic-book store, called Supersnipe, in New York. Otherwise he remained the son of George Lucas Sr. and stored the windfall away in low-risk ventures like tax-exempt municipal bonds, high interest savings—and property. The house on the hill became his proudest acquisition. He and Marcia christened the place Parkhouse, and began work on turning it into a complex equipped with editing suites, offices, and a spacious screening room.

With its black shingled exterior and shadowy nooks and crannies, Parkhouse might have come straight out of a Vincent Price movie. In a room at the top, Lucas was still faced with finishing the personal horror story that was the writing of *Star Wars*.

His earnings from *Graffiti* meant he need never work again. Yet the idea of making his "Flash Gordon thing" a reality would simply not leave him, no matter how painful it might be.

"I had sort of fallen in love with it," he admitted later. "Plus I was a street filmmaker, I had never done a big studio picture, so I thought, 'This'll be the last movie I direct.'"

By now he had spent ten months on the story. It would take him another eighteen months to polish it into filmable form. Lucas later described the period as the worst of his life. Each morning he would leave his house on Medway Street and travel up the hill to his comfortable new office. His new surroundings made little difference to his writing. Every sentence still seemed like surgery. "They get dragged out kicking and screaming with a lot of pain," he said later.

He was not lacking in discipline. He would work for a solid eight hours a day, with a short break for lunch. Generally the day divided itself into "three hours writing and five hours thinking." Regardless of his progress, the routine would end each evening with Walter Cronkite and the CBS Evening News. Often Lucas would slump in front of the television back home furious that he had achieved nothing.

Lucas was plagued by nerves. He would keep a pair of scissors by his typewriter and snip away at his hair at times of frustration. The builders and decorators converting the mansion were the worst possible source of distraction for a writer in search of a little "displacement activity." Yet, word by word, page by page, *The Story of Mace Windu* evolved into an elaborate, extravagant screenplay.

Lucas made notes wherever he went. By now he had a pad crammed with idiosyncratic scribbles, some collected years back. He had come up with an idea for the name of one of his two robot characters while mixing the *American Graffiti* sound track with Walter Murch in the early hours of the morning. Lost in a sea of sound tracks and thousand-foot-long reels of film, the two men had developed their own shorthand, and given each of the reels, sound tracks and dialogue tracks a number. "Walter asked me to go over to the rack to get R2-D2, that's Reel 2, Dialogue 2," Lucas recalled. "Great name," he had thought, smiling and reaching for his notebook at the same time.

Marcia often joked that he was never off work. When she took their giant black and white malamute, Indiana, for a drive, her husband would refer to the dog as her furry copilot." The dog became Chewbacca, Han Solo's sidekick. (Indiana would remain an inspiration for years, later lending a name to Lucas's archaeologist adventurer, a certain Dr. Jones.) Chewbacca's character grew a little more during another car ride, this time with a friend, disc jockey Terry McGovern. As the car passed over an unidentified bump, McGovern apologized. "Sorry, George, must have run over a wookiee back there."

"What's a wookiee?" Lucas replied, his hand already reaching for a pen. "He'd just made it up," Lucas said later.

Lucas's characters, not unnaturally, carried hallmarks of himself—and his friends. He would never deny that his hero, Luke Skywalker, was effectively his alter ego, a conduit for all the heroic dreams he had experienced during his solitary Modesto childhood. "You can't write a main character and not have him be part of you and not be able to identify with him," he protested later.

The braggart Han Solo was modeled on the brashest of the Dirty Dozen, John Milius.

Lucas's inability to concentrate on anything else occasionally irritated Marcia, however. Often he would chatter away about his characters in bed at night. "Nothing is simply a fun moment," she later lamented.

He found unexpected inspiration in the fan mail he was by now receiving. He was genuinely moved by the letters he received from teenagers who had seen the cheap little film whose success no one seemed to have predicted. *Graffiti* had reached out to touch hundreds of them on a personal level. As the critic Charles Champlin wrote at the time: "It was a film you wanted to root for." Lucas realized that in laying bare so much of himself, he had—it seemed—helped other young Americans. "I got hundreds of cards and letters from preteenagers and young teenagers saying different versions of, 'Gosh, I didn't know that everybody has a tough time being a teenager,'" he explained later.

His mail also reflected the sheer pleasure *Graffiti* had brought into many lives. After the emptiness of *THX 1138*, he arrived at a self-realization of his own. "I discovered that making positive films is exhilarating."

It confirmed his feeling that he should aim his next film at an even wider audience. He had never forgotten the thrill *Adventure Theater* had given him each night of his life as a ten-year-old. He looked around at the heroes available to modern American youngsters, grizzly icons like Kojak and Dirty Harry, and felt sorry for them. "My main reason for making *Star Wars*," he would say later, "was to give young people an honest, wholesome fantasy life the way we had."

His idea was not, of course, entirely altruistic. It also resounded with commercial common sense. Recent statistics had confirmed something Lucas had suspected since *Graffiti* took off—the average moviegoer was not the person Hollywood had imagined he or she was.

A recently published survey by the Motion Picture Association of America had revealed nearly three-quarters of its audience was made up of people between the ages of twelve and twenty-nine. The age group that made up 40 percent of the population were the people buying 73 percent of cinema tickets. The audience was also better off and better educated than the MPAA had imagined. Students in particular were avid moviegoers. By the time he or she had finished college, the average American student had watched 600 movies.

The survey sent shock waves through Hollywood. "Given the original populist base of the movies as *the* mass medium of entertainment this observation seems to reflect not so much a shift as a revolutionary change," the film critic Charles Champlin wrote in an article accompanying the statistics in the *Journal of the Producers Guild of America* in March 1973.

Like his friend Steven Spielberg, then at work filming a version of Peter Benchley's novel about a killer shark, *Jaws*, for Universal, Lucas knew that the era of gritty realism had passed. He sensed audiences were tired of cynical issue movies. They wanted to feel more optimistic, and—more than anything—they wanted to be entertained. "You can learn from cynicism, but you can't build on it," he had told the *Los Angeles Times* at the end of 1973.

Lucas constantly added and subtracted elements from his "Mace Windu" story. He began experimenting with different variations on the central characters, using the mythological themes with which he was becoming more and more fascinated as a bedrock.

Ultimately, he admitted later, the entire *Star Wars* saga boiled down to a clutch of classical storylines that had been reproduced and reworked through the ages. Many of them had been isolated by Joseph Campbell in his seminal *Hero With a Thousand Faces*.

There was the Arthurian "Quest of the Knight," the Biblical "Renewal of Faith," and the classic science-fiction conflict of "Man versus Machine." Central to Lucas's story was the concept of "The Good Father," a constant thread in ancient and modern mythology that he was all too easily able to draw on within himself. George Lucas Sr. had, after all, been both the "Good Father" and the "Bad Father." At one point the film's paternal figure had been Kane Starkiller, father of Luke Starkiller. Lucas had by now divided him into the dark figure of Darth Vader and the more benevolent figure of a Jedi Knight, now renamed with a distinct Japanese flavoring, Obi-Wan Kenobi.

Lucas was adamant that the film should, in some way, contain a moral message. "All I was trying to say in a very simple and straightforward way is that there is a God and there is a good and bad side," he came to explain. He struggled throughout with a Jedi code of conduct within which he could enshrine his idea. At one point the film's heroes were locked in a Holy Grail–like crusade to find the "Kiber Crystal," a source of goodness. At another he had divided good and bad into two "forces" named Ashla and Bogan.

It was never difficult to spot whether his writing was going well or not. Throughout his life, Lucas's personality was one of extremes. "George was either very happy or very frustrated," said Bunny Alsup, then the first point of contact when he emerged from his writing den.

When he was happy with a section he would pass his handwritten notes to Alsup, who would correct the appalling spelling and type them into a readable form. Periodically he and Gary Kurtz would hold a war council to discuss the direction in which the story was heading. Lucas never discarded anything. He merely accepted that some of his ideas might not be achievable—yet. "At one time they went to the Wookiee planet where they met Chewbacca's family and hid out for a while. We reread that and realized it was going to be expensive enough to do one Wookiee let alone thirty-five of them," Kurtz recalled.

Kurtz was moved by the simplicity and power of the characters Lucas had assembled. "George did a really wonderful job in bringing those characters together. They could easily have been incredible clichés," he said. "But they had strength. Each one is very typical of the kind of character they need to be in this kind of story. The young boy who is cut off from his family, the mentor, just the way the characters work. If you try to reduce it to telling the story in two or three sentences you think that sounds like a hundred other stories that I've heard about."

On the days when he found the well empty, Lucas had no

shortage of friends to bounce ideas off. Parkhouse had become all that Lucas had naively dreamed American Zoetrope would be. Fellow Dirty Dozen members Hal Barwood and Matthew Robbins, and other northern California filmmakers like Carroll Ballard and Michael Ritchie took office space in the mansion.

On Fridays Lucas instigated a tradition of family-style barbecues or roasts. Marcia and Gary Kurtz's wife, Meredith, Bunny Alsup's sister, would cook and their families would sit in the northern California sun. For all the torture he was enduring, Lucas had in many ways never been happier. Parkhouse combined the Norman Rockwell atmosphere of Modesto with the pioneering spirit of USC and Zoetrope. It was little wonder his story was evolving into the ultimate feel-good film.

Yet Lucas was plagued by doubts over the riskiness of some of his ideas. At one stage the film's hero was the twelve-year-old Princess Leia. "Her brother was being held captive by the empire and she would break him out," recalled Kurtz. "The story kept changing at that time. It took a while for it to settle down." Lucas cast his net wide for feedback, even asking Coppola for his advice. (Relations had been strained once more by Coppola's decision to begin filming *Apocalypse Now* himself in the Philippines. Lucas had been furious at his friend's assumed control of a film he had always hoped to make. In reality, Coppola's Zoetrope company, rebuilt from the burning embers of the original setup, still owned the rights. "It was his to do with as he wanted," shrugged Gary Kurtz, who lost out on the producer's spot as well.) Coppola gave Lucas a flood of advice— all typically ignored by his former partner. He thought the notion of having a prepubescent young girl as the star of the film was brilliant.

By March 1975 a vast new story had metamorphosed. Now the title had changed from *The Story of Mace Windu*, via

Adventures of the Starkiller: Episode One of the Star Wars, into the simpler *Star Wars*. The only problem was that it had also evolved into *War and Peace*. Lucas had amassed five hundred pages of story. His script needed to be nearer one hundred.

Lucas divided the story into three parts, put two parts in a drawer, and distilled the remaining one into a story that would resemble the finished film. As he did so he promised himself he would somehow make the other two parts into a film one day too.

Between May and August he whittled what was the kernel of his story into a form he and Gary Kurtz felt was filmable.

Luke Starkiller was now a young boy, working on a farm on the desert planet Tatooine, owned by his uncle Owen Lars. Lars at that point remained an important figure, a disgruntled man who had stolen his nephew's savings to save his farm. Only he knew the identity of Luke's real father, Anakin Starkiller. The story's other central characters were Princess Leia, now a sixteen-year-old hostage of the evil Empire who has sent a hologram message to Tatooine hidden within a droid robot, R2-D2; "a shabby old desert rat," Obi-Wan Kenobi; Han Solo, a "tough James Dean–style starpilot"; and Chewbacca, his seven-foot tall, Wookiee sidekick. Together, Luke, Obi-Wan, Solo, and Chewbacca head off to the princess's aid. Their ultimate mission would be to destroy the "Death Star," a planet-sized space station being readied for operation by the Empire. Lying in wait was the dark presence of Lord Darth Vader, the Empire's most malignant force. The story's climax would be a spectacular air battle in which Luke led a rebel assault on the Death Star.

Lucas had by now simplified the mysticism in his script. Obi-Wan Kenobi would be a guardian of the wisdom of the Jedi Knights and the Force, a mysterious power "that binds the universe together." Lucas had found the inspiration for the idea in a story in Carlos Castenada's *Tales of Power* in which a Mexican Indian mystic, Don Juan, described a "life force." While Obi-Wan represented the positive side of this Force, Darth Vader encapsulated its negativity, or in Lucas's phrase, "the dark side." By now he had arrived at the mantra he hoped might be the message of his film, a variation on the Christian "May the Lord be with you"—"May the Force be with you."

Under the terms of the "step" agreement, and with the third draft accepted, Lucas received more money for developing his screenplay. However, until Fox finally greenlighted the film—by no means a certainty, despite the much improved new script and the success of *Graffiti*—any other development would have to come out of his and Gary Kurtz's pockets. Both men had been content to underwrite the project with their *Graffiti* windfall. As the production moved into its next phase, the producer and director set up a new company using an initial war chest of $300,000. Soon Bunny Alsup was answering the phone with the greeting "Good morning, the Star Wars Corporation."

In February 1975, Lucas was interviewed by *Esquire* magazine as part of a feature on the new Young Turks taking over Hollywood. *Graffiti* was praised as the *Easy Rider* of the 1970s, the film that had announced "something new was happening."

Asked what he was working on next, he described *Star Wars* as "the first multimillion-dollar Flash Gordon kind of movie—with *The Magnificent Seven* thrown in." He and Gary Kurtz hardly looked like a latter-day variation on Yul Brynner and Steve McQueen. As they began trawling Los Angeles for the strange assortment of professionals they needed to bring their film to life, however, the comparison was not entirely inappropriate.

Lucas's script was still dense and difficult to visualize.

Sensing the Fox board in particular would never quite grasp the concepts he was describing in his screenplay, Lucas's first priority was an artist to translate on to paper the images he saw in his mind's eye.

Of the $1 million he and Kurtz would eventually spend on the still-embryonic *Star Wars*, the few thousand dollars they gave Ralph McQuarrie, a former designer with the Boeing corporation, would prove the wisest investment of all. McQuarrie had done work for Hal Barwood and Matthew Robbins as they planned a movie called *Star Dance*. Impressed by what he saw, Lucas asked McQuarrie to illustrate four key scenes taken from the third draft of his screenplay—the robots C-3PO and R2-D2 crossing an expanse of desert on Tatooine, a "lightsaber" duel between Obi-Wan Kenobi and Darth Vader, imperial stormtroopers in action firing blaster guns and, perhaps the key to the film, the action-packed climax, a rebel assault on the Empire's moonlike Death Star.

Much of Lucas's guidance lay in the scripts. He had a few extra ideas—for instance, that the robot C-3PO should have some of the elegance of his predecessor in Fritz Lang's *Metropolis*, one of his favorite films as a USC student—and that the other robot should be "cute." He also passed on a pile of fantasy and science-fiction magazines with marked pages. Otherwise, McQuarrie was free to express himself.

McQuarrie had polished a gift for mechanical drawings animating the Apollo missions for CBS News and producing the Boeing parts catalogue. In *Star Wars* he found his metier. Soon Lucas had a set of extraordinarily evocative twenty-two inch by ten inch paintings.

Much of his early work would be modified. Chewbacca was drawn as a frightening giant, with lemur eyes and Nosferatu teeth. Han Solo was a bearded brigand, dressed Greco-Roman style in a heavy metal codpiece and breastplate. Yet some of the most familiar elements of what would become the *Star Wars* universe were in McQuarrie's original drawings.

Some were dictated from the beginning by Lucas's script. His opening sequence featured the stormtroopers burning their way through the outer skin of the rebel craft containing Princess Leia. "We realized that the air would escape," said McQuarrie. As a result the soldiers were given "breath masks," as Lucas called them. From the earliest drawings, Darth Vader was masked for the same reason. "George described him as someone in an airtight garment with a lot of wrapping and black bands and folds, kind of fluttering," recalled McQuarrie. "Darth Vader will be coming in like the wind, kind of sneaky yet big and impressive," Lucas told the artist.

Ultimately the McQuarrie paintings would be the key to unlocking the purse strings at Fox. Their immediate impact was to inspire Lucas and Kurtz to press ahead with the design work. Two other artists, Colin Cantwell, a veteran of *2001* with Stanley Kubrick, and Alex Tavoularis, brother of Coppola's favorite designer, Dean Tavoularis, were hired to produce model spaceships and outline sketches of the film's "storyboard" respectively.

Lucas had a clear idea of the look he wanted. He had been struck by how dirty the Apollo missions had been when they returned from space. In his mind's eye he saw his corner of the cosmos as a grubby, lived-in place. Its technology may be more advanced, but it would not mean it could not break down, get rusty or need a visit to the interplanetary equivalent of a car wash. In his briefings to McQuarrie, Cantwell, and his other design artists, Lucas had asked them to move away from the pristine world of the spaceships in *2001*. His catchphrase was "used space."

Lucas also wanted the *Star Wars* universe to sound "real." Through one of his mentors at USC, Ken Mura, Kurtz had been recommended a brilliant, newly graduated sound engineer, Ben Burtt. Lucas spent the first six months of the film without having met Burtt. Instead, Kurtz passed on the instruction that he was to break away from the synthesized, electronic sounds that had been the hallmark of *2001* and previous science-fiction films.

No matter how imaginative the sound and artwork they would soon have piling up at the Lucasfilm offices, however, Lucas and Kurtz knew their film would live or die by its special effects.

Since the decline in Hollywood's interest in fantasy and science-fiction movies during the 1960s, specialists had become thin on the ground. Ray Harryhausen, master of stop-motion photography in films like *Jason and the Argonauts* and *One Million Years BC* had moved to Europe. Jim Danforth and Hollywood's acknowledged SFX master, Douglas Trumbull, lionized for the elegant spaceships in *2001*, later the director of *Silent Running*, and now the boss of his own company, Future General Corporation, were the only natural choices. Yet Lucas in particular feared if he worked with either, he would not be able to exert the influence he needed. Controlling by nature, his greatest anxiety was that *Star Wars* would not be his vision. "I didn't want to be handed an effect after five months and be told, 'Here's your special effect, sir,'" said Lucas. "I want to be able to have some say about what's going on—either you do it yourself, or you don't get a say."

Lucas and Kurtz met both Danforth and Trumbull and made no secret of the difficulty of the task ahead of them— or the involvement they would demand. The effects Lucas described were far in advance of anything even Trumbull had achieved before. Yet the old masters were deterred by Lucas's hands-on philosophy rather than the challenge *Star Wars* presented. "I liked the idea of the film, sci-fi with a sense of fun, but just didn't want the problems of working with Lucas," Danforth admitted later. "He was right out front with me, told me: 'I don't know how we're going to do all this stuff, maybe we'll darken a studio and throw models at a camera, but whatever we do, I'll be right there with you.' I can't work like that so I turned it down."

Whether Lucas rejected Trumbull or vice versa remained a matter of conjecture in Hollywood. Lucas certainly claimed that the former happened. "If you hire Trumbull to do your special effects he does your special effects," he announced. "I was very nervous about that, I wanted to say, 'It should look like this, not that.'" What is in no doubt is that Trumbull soon signed up to work with Steven Spielberg and Columbia on their UFO picture, *Close Encounters of the Third Kind* and that Kurtz and Lucas reacted typically to the problem they faced. If there were no effects facilities in Hollywood willing or able to deliver the footage they wanted they would build one themselves—from scratch.

John Dykstra still recalls his first meeting with George Lucas and Gary Kurtz with a smile. It consisted of "a lot of hand flying."

In the summer of 1975, Dykstra, tall, burly, and bearded, looked precisely what he was—a rock-'n'-roll survivor. Some of his earliest experimental photography had been done for Jim Morrison and the Doors. Since then, however, he had built a reputation as a rising force in the effects business. He had been the sorcerer Trumbull's apprentice on *Silent Running* and *The Andromeda Strain* and had worked on a groundbreaking computerized camera project at the University of California at Berkeley.

Kurtz and Lucas showed him an early draft of the *Star Wars* script. It was full of phrases like, "then they attacked the Death Star." "It wasn't particularly well fleshed out," Dykstra recalled.

Lucas described the kind of look he had in his mind's eye. Much as he admired the effects in *2001* and *Silent Running*, the spacecraft in both films had been lumbering, static objects. Lucas's aim was to be able to film space battles that recreated the atmosphere of the classic aerial dogfights in World War II pictures. He wanted his craft to be able to duck and dive into the action—and he wanted his audience to feel as if they were in the cockpit.

Dykstra knew the key to achieving this would be the development of a technique—used before by Trumbull and others on a small scale —in which the camera rather than the models would be in motion. As the camera tilted, twisted and panned, the effect would be that the model was moving. Given the need to make single, composite shots featuring many elements of film, such as matte drawings of planets and other spacecraft, the movements of the camera would need to be replicated with microscopic precision each and every time. The task would require the development of a camera fitted with a "motion control" computer.

In reality, Dykstra knew the technology was years away from being perfected. "In my naïveté, of course I said we could do it," he said. "It was a huge gamble, and perhaps if I had been more aware of the impact of the gamble I would have been more fearful about it. But I wasn't."

Without Charlie Lippincott, Gary Kurtz and George Lucas might never have worked together in the first place.

Four years earlier Lippincott had been a publicist at MGM when he got a phone call from Kurtz inviting him to lunch. Lippincott had known Kurtz from his days at USC. Their paths had crossed again when Kurtz had been at MGM making *Chandler*. Kurtz had been blunt with Lippincott. "Francis called me about working with this guy you know from school," he asked him. "I really want to know if you think it's a good idea." Kurtz's major concern was that the director was no great communicator. "He's *really* quiet," Kurtz had told Lippincott.

Lippincott had long known of Lucas's talent. He recalled sharing a seat with him at the USC classes given by Jerry Lewis and later sitting on the curb outside the campus's computer laboratory while he had been filming *THX 1138*. "Short, crew-cut, and intense," he looked like his alter ego Terry "The Toad" in *American Graffiti*. Shortly afterwards it had been Lippincott, already something of a legend at marketing films, to whom Lucas had turned to to pitch *THX 1138* to the board of directors of Warner Bros. (The experience had given Lippincott his first taste of Lucas's frugality. He had given him just $100 to acquire a collection of subterranean film clips to illustrate the movie's concepts. "Anything left over you can keep," he had told Lippincott. "Needless to say I spent the $100 on films.")

Later Lucas had asked the marketing man to join him and Coppola in the Zoetrope dream. Lippincott had wisely passed up the offer, opting instead to work at MGM where he became Hollywood's first "underground publicist," specializing in publicity with the booming counterculture magazines springing up all over America.

In his time at MGM, Lippincott had gone on to work on two science-fiction films: *Westworld*, Michael Crichton's vision of a futuristic Disneyland gone wrong, and *No Blade of Grass*, Cornell Wilde's apocalyptic story of a deadly virus sweeping the world.

Lucasfilm had kept an office on the Universal lot where, despite being rejected with *Star Wars*, they had agreed to develop an idea for a sequel to *Graffiti* and another film called *The Radioland Murders*. Lippincott popped in one day after arriving to take up a new job at Universal, as unit publicist on what would turn out to be Alfred Hitchcock's final movie, *Family Plot*. Conversation soon turned to the duo's plans post *Graffiti*.

Lippincott was always going to love *Star Wars*. Like George Lucas, he had for years upheld that his young life changed the moment he first saw *Flash Gordon*. He had been a six-year-old growing up in cinemaless Oswego, Illinois when he saw the movie projected on to the wall of the town library. The *Star Wars* script stirred the same child within him.

"I read the script over the weekend and called George on the following Monday," he recalled. "I told him I'd love to work on it." Lucas had always believed Lippincott would one day run a studio. Shorn of his old hippie locks and dressed in a starchy collar and tie, he seemed the consummate company man. "You're too big for us now," Lucas and Kurtz joked. Lippincott sensed *Star Wars* might be bigger than all of them. Soon, he too was on the payroll.

One Friday afternoon in the summer of 1975, Jim Nelson was working in the cutting room at his postproduction company on Larchmont when the ramrod-straight figure of Gary Kurtz walked in unannounced. Nelson's friendship with Kurtz went back more than a decade to the time when he worked with him, Monte Hellman, and Jack Nicholson on Roger Corman's low-budget westerns. Nelson had worked with Kurtz on the postproduction work for *American Graffiti*. It had been then that Kurtz had first mentioned the possibility of he and Lucas making "a science-fiction thing." He had asked Nelson whether he would be interested in helping him produce the movie.

"Gary came in and said, 'Can you start on Monday,'" said Nelson. "I said, 'Thanks for the notice, but I'm in the middle of a picture.'" Kurtz's powers of persuasion were considerable, however. Nelson was able to persuade Kurtz to give him two weeks to finish the four films still on his company's books. Two Mondays later than originally planned, he turned up at the warehouse Kurtz had hired as the base for the early special-effects work.

The fifteen thousand square feet of warehouse space was set on a grim industrial estate near an airfield in Van Nuys,

Los Angeles. The airless brick building was surrounded by a village of faceless storage and aviation companies.

In the two weeks since he had first spoken to Kurtz, John Dykstra had begun preparing the building. The scene that greeted Nelson hardly appeared like the future of high-tech, Hollywood filmmaking. "It was just big piles of lumber and guys banging nails," said Nelson. A subsidiary of Lucasfilm Ltd. had been set up to operate the research facility. Lucas had christened it Industrial Light and Magic, ILM for short. Over the next two years the factory would earn itself myriad new names—few of them flattering.

Nelson's job was to act as a production manager-cum-associate producer. He would prepare the postproduction part of the budget with Kurtz and supervise the work at ILM and on the locations.

As he settled in to work, it was Ralph McQuarrie's drawings that made him suspect something unique was about to happen. "I never did like science fiction. But I just had a gut feeling based on looking at Ralph's stuff that if they could make the picture like what I was looking at hanging on the wall, it was going to make a fortune," said Nelson.

By November 1975, with ILM's operation under way, Kurtz and Lucas had come close to spending their first $1 million chunk of *Graffiti* profits on *Star Wars*. Suddenly they were faced with being closed down before a single frame of film had been shot.

Fox had become increasingly alarmed over the budget. Lucas had initially assured Ladd it could be made for $3.5 million, the cost of a "cheap comedy." "I think George thought it could be made like *THX*, not having a real cameraman and making it in a documentary style," said Kurtz. By now the projected cost was ballooning through the $10 million barrier.

Negotiations to finalize the figure had been going on for

months. Jeff Berg and Tom Pollock would handle many of the meetings, relaying developments back to Parkhouse and the Lucasfilm offices on the Universal lot.

Kurtz and Lucas were happy to be isolated from the haggling. They hated the hoopla of negotiating budgets. No matter how sensible, estimates were always trimmed, seemingly as a matter of principle. "They assume it is full of padding and unless they cut it it will be full of free trips to Paris or something," sighed Kurtz.

Both men saw the endless squeezing as simply another example of "sleazy, Hollywood practice." "If you are hungry enough you will do it and if you go over your budget they will take your share away regardless of whether the film was a success or not," said Kurtz. "It was not illegal but it did not seem right."

Ray Gosnell, the studio's senior "nuts and bolts" production executive, had assumed *Star Wars* was an attempt at some sort of Disney feature when he first skimmed through the script. His priorities were managing two very different, but no less high pressure, projects for the studio, *The Towering Inferno*, being made jointly with Warner Bros., and Mel Brooks's *Young Frankenstein*. Working with Brooks in particular was "always a strain," he recalled.

He did not see *Star Wars* as a major project. "Having skimmed through it very quickly, I said, 'Well that must be a cartoon, so I'll look at that later.'"

By the time he had run it over and passed it to the studio's special-effects "experts," however, the message had been clear. "They said the budget was completely unrealistic, it couldn't be done," said Kurtz. Fox estimated the special effects alone would cost between $5 million and $6 million.

Kurtz prepared his own budget, however, and figured he could pull off the effects at ILM for half the cost, just $2.5 million. "One of the things they had not figured in their costing was that they viewed each individual shot as a complete entity. We knew we couldn't do it that way. We came up with the idea of compositing a lot of shots by building up a library of images that could be used and reused," he explained.

As he searched for ways to trim the budget, Kurtz traveled to look at studio facilities in Europe. He had already scouted around Los Angeles. The prime sites, Columbia's former premises at Sunset Gower, Selznick's old studio at Culver City, and Warner Bros. Burbank were either full, winding down their film operations in favor of the booming television industry, or else too small for the scale of operation he and Lucas were now planning. By Kurtz's reckoning, *Star Wars* would require nine or ten respectably-sized sound stages as well as one huge hangar for the triumphal finale of the film.

Kurtz traveled to Rome to look at facilities there before heading to Britain and the studios that surrounded the outer ring of London, Pinewood, Shepperton, Twickenham, and Elstree. Pinewood, home of the Bond movies, seemed the most obvious base. Its massive "007" soundstage would have been ideal. Kurtz, watching every penny by now, disliked the studio's insistence that part of the staff be hired internally. Twickenham and Shepperton, despite its giant H stage, seemed too small.

Of the four studios, Elstree most vividly symbolized the parlous state of the British film industry. Located in the drab suburb of Borehamwood in northwest London, the studio had been the epicenter of a booming industry. In the 1920s and 1930s it had become an official satellite of Hollywood when MGM opened a complex of nine soundstages there. Since then, however, Elstree's decline had been seemingly irreversible.

When Kurtz arrived in London the studio was actually closed. As filming had finished on *Murder on the Orient Express* the previous year, the padlocks had been put on, permanently, it seemed. Elstree's owners, the electronics company EMI, had hoped to sell off the site as a piece of prime real estate. However, opposition from, among others, the film unions, had blocked their plans. As the wrangling wore on, the owners had decided to hire the complex out on a "wall-to-wall" basis. Staff, specialist equipment, and sets would have to be provided by its customers. Elstree would simply provide space and the most basic of filmmaking requirements. The deal suited Kurtz perfectly. *Star Wars* would require specialist props and equipment of its own. Soon he had negotiated a deal to hire the entire complex for seventeen weeks shooting from March the following year. Elstree's only drawback was its lack of one giant stage. Before heading back to Los Angeles, Kurtz also booked Shepperton's H stage for the following summer and spring.

With Elstree's savings, Kurtz was able to pare back the budget from the $13 million he feared *Star Wars* might cost in America. By October, he and Lucas had made a formal budget presentation to Alan Ladd Jr. and his heads of department.

The boardroom had been decorated with Ralph McQuarrie's drawings and each executive given a lavish, zipped black vinyl case with *Star Wars* emblazoned on its cover. The folder featured a drawing of Luke Skywalker, then a lanky cowboy waving a lightsaber. Inside, Charlie Lippincott had included dozens more of McQuarrie's beautiful drawings— from sleek "X-wing" and "TIE fighters," to a vast "sand crawler," a Death Star, and the two robots, R2-D2 and C-3PO, one short and dustbinlike, the other a less-feminine version of Lang's *Metropolis* model.

At this stage, Kurtz and Nelson had come up with a final budget of $10.5 million. When Ladd saw the figure he began shaking his head. "We were told it was just too much money," recalled Nelson.

Seemingly out of thin air an alternative figure of $8

million was produced. "I think if we'd gone in there and said the picture cost $5 million they would have said, 'No way, it's got to be done for $3.3 million.' That's the mentality of studio people," Nelson said.

Nelson would come to regret the outburst he made in response. "I said 'I don't know what the hell we're arguing over $2 million for, this movie's going to make $100 million.' And everyone laughed," he recalled.

As Nelson defended his opinion, pointing at McQuarrie's stunning drawings, a red-faced Lucas interrupted him. "I'll be happy if it makes $35 million," he told Ladd and his executives.

"I embarrassed him," recalled a rueful Nelson.

The *Star Wars* party left with the impression that if they shaved their budget by $2 million or so they would be in business. Within weeks the film was given a tentative go-ahead at a cost of exactly $7.887 million. (Hollywood budgets were often in-jokes. Francis Coppola had submitted the *THX* budget at $777,777.77 because seven was his lucky number.) Soon the gag at Fox was that the *Star Wars* budget was the same whether read forwards or backwards.

As the details were put together, however, Kurtz realized the figure was simply unrealistic. Lucas approached Ladd to explain they genuinely needed another $2 million to make *Star Wars*.

Fox's panic was understandable. What had begun, on paper at least, as a $3.5 million project was now going to cost them three times that amount. Their resistance also reflected the widespread belief that science-fiction films were simply not commercial.

Science-fiction films had, of course, predated even Hollywood itself. George Melies made his miraculous *A Trip To The Moon* in 1902. But, apart from a vogue for the genre in the 1950s, when *The Invasion of the Body Snatchers* and *It Came from Outer Space, Forbidden Planet,* and *The Day the Earth Stood*

Still tapped into America's Cold War paranoia about the Communist threat, "sci-fi" simply hadn't sold. Even the last big budget foray into outer space, Kubrick's *2001*, had taken several years to earn back its $10 million budget.

"Science fiction was *very* deadly," recalled Alan Ladd. "Market research said you just didn't do films like that."

"There was a lot of controversy about whether we should be doing a picture like this," said Ray Gosnell.

According to Lucas, there were those on the board at Fox who refused to call the film by name as a form of protest. When forced to acknowledge its existence they called it "that science movie."

As the wrangling continued, Lucas and Kurtz decided to turn the tables by indulging in a little Hollywood "hardball" of their own. They instructed Jeff Berg and Tom Pollock to tell Fox they would make the film "whether they were in or not." Ladd knew Lucas had invested the *Graffiti* profits safely and may just be able to carry out his threat. "It was a bluff—we could not possibly afford to do it," smiled Kurtz. "But it was so touch and go for a while. They were getting more and more nervous and were almost bailing out."

Ladd went to Stanfill and the board asking for an increase from the original $7.8 million to $10 million. Without it they might lose the project. By now Ladd had strengthened his position within the studio by hiring two of his oldest and most trusted aides. The English-born Gareth Wigan, a former agent, and Jay Kanter, once considered heir apparent to the formidable Lew Wasserman at Universal, were his eyes and ears around the studio. Ladd was already threatening the equality of the troika that ran the studio beneath Stanfill: himself, marketing head David Raphiel, and financial and business affairs chief Bill Immerman.

His gut feeling about *Star Wars* convinced him it would be a greater mistake to lose the film than spend $10 million on taking a chance. "He had tremendous faith in it because he had tremendous faith in George," said Wigan.

Early in December 1975, Lucas and Kurtz got the phone call they had been waiting for. The board bought the bluff. *Star Wars* was in business.

After two and a half years the final pieces in the jigsaw were falling into place. All that remained were the final contract negotiations.

To the surprise of Fox's lawyers, Lucas was happy to stick to the terms struck in the "deal memo" with Ladd back in 1973. It had been a condition of the memo that all outstanding areas, like merchandising and sequel rights, would be agreed at final contract stage. They merely wanted to negotiate those points.

"George never broke conditions of a deal memo," said Charlie Lippincott, who with Pollock, Berg, Kurtz, and others contributed suggestions as to what should be in the contract.

Despite the massively increased bargaining power *Graffiti* had given Lucas and Kurtz, they did not ask for an increase on Lucas's basic $50,000 writing fee or his $100,000 directing payment. Kurtz also agreed to accept $50,000 to produce. As agreed, 40 percent of the net profits of the film would go to the Star Wars Corporation. Far more important to Lucas and his team were the rights to retain control of *Star Wars*—and crucially its merchandising, sound track, and sequel rights. They would not inflate their fees if Fox consented to give them a majority control in the spinoff rights to the film. In effect, the Star Wars Corporation traded cash for control.

As far as Fox were concerned the sacrifice was no sacrifice at all. As the film industry stood then, music and merchandising spinoffs were virtually meaningless. Provisions for them were often referred to as the "garbage" clauses in a contract. Even those who had heard Lucas's dreams of comic books and mugs, thought them as farfetched as the story of Luke Skywalker. Fox granted them willingly but bridled at handing over the sequel rights. Their stickiness was far from unusual, as far as Jeff Berg was concerned, but Lucas was determined. In the end Lucas negotiated the rights to future *Star Wars* films personally with Alan Ladd Jr.

The final contract was full of complex formulas and future considerations. In the cold here and now of the negotiating room, however, the Fox lawyers saw their acquisition of George Lucas's services for under the $500,000 he could easily have commanded as a "hot" director as an unequivocal victory.

Their short-term triumph would be their long-term loss, however. In time, the contract would yield Lucas and his associates riches to make some at the studio sick to their stomachs. Lippincott identifies the unsung hero as Pollock's colleague at their law firm Pollock, Rigrod & Bloom, Andy Rigrod. "It is one of the most brilliantly written movie contracts I have ever read," he said. "Not from the standpoint of the studio, but of a filmmaker getting what they want."

It would be years before Fox realized the implications of the deal they had struck. Never again would they sign away sequel, merchandising, and musical sound track rights with such abandon.

"You always acquired sequel rights even then. It was a terrible oversight," said Gareth Wigan.

CHAPTER 4

An Intergalactic Gone With the Wind

At the end of 1975, the Lucasfilm office's newest addition boasted an impressive business card. It read:

Charles Lippincott,
Vice-President Advertising, Publicity,
Promotion, and Merchandising,
Star Wars Corporation,
PO Box 8669, Universal City, California.

As a seasoned media manager, Lippincott knew the first of his three disciplines inside out. After an impromptu meeting with George Lucas he was in no doubt that he would have to learn something about the fourth—and fast.

Lippincott, in common with Lucas and Kurtz, was a comic book fanatic. After reading *Star Wars* once more he had seen its potential as a colorful fantasy magazine. When he bumped into Lucas in the foyer of the Universal building one morning he had mentioned the idea. For the next three hours Lippincott listened as his new colleague outlined the infinitely more ambitious dreams he had for *Star Wars*.

Animated and boyish once more, Lucas talked about opening two stores similar to his Supersnipe shop in New York, one in Westwood Village and another in San Francisco. As well as selling *Star Wars* comics it would also stock a range of spinoff toys. He talked of R2-D2 mugs and wind-up C-3PO toys, model rocket ships and Jedi Knight lightsabers.

"The idea was to have *Star Wars* stores. We would make and sell stuff associated with the film," Lippincott recalled.

Exciting as his ideas sounded, Lippincott at first saw them as fanciful. "It was total naïveté, total off-the-wall kid stuff," he said. By the end of their conversation, however, he had realized the seriousness of Lucas's thinking. "That was the first inkling of what he had in mind. I thought, what a great idea."

Typically, Fox agreed to their bringing Lippincott into the production on the condition he worked as a unit publicist-cum-producer on two of their other films. One, a Buddy Holly biopic, became the first Fox film in a decade to be closed down, the second, a Roger Corman picture, also hit trouble after Lippincott had spent just a week on the set. By November 1975, he too was fully committed to *Star Wars*.

The toy manufacturers would have to wait until Cantwell and his colleagues had come up with approved models. Armed with Ralph McQuarrie's drawings, Lippincott's first target were the comic and book publishing markets.

Tom Pollock wanted to put the rights out to auction in the normal way. From the outset, however, Lippincott argued that the *Star Wars* market should be targeted with the precision of Luke Skywalker's raid on the Death Star. Rather than the best offer, he said, they should look for the best science-fiction publishers.

The kings of the comic jungle remained the famous Marvel imprint, publishers of *Spiderman* and *The Fantastic Four*. It needed all of Lippincott's skills to even get in through the door of its tough chief executive, Stan Lee. His "cold call" to Lee was met with a firm no. "Stan's reaction was, 'Gee, I'm not terribly interested. Why don't you come back after you've shot the movie?'" recalled Lippincott.

Drawing on Lucas's contacts at his Supersnipe shop, Lippincott engineered a second meeting via Marvel's former editor, Roy Thomas, then editing the popular *Conan the Barbarian* comics. After reading Lucas's script, Thomas agreed to get him in front of Lee if he would be allowed to edit the *Star Wars* comic. As he sat down with Lee, even Lippincott conceded he was aiming high. "No movie comic book at that time had been more than one or two issues. I wanted several issues before the film came out and several afterwards," he explained.

Lee demonstrated his toughness by offering a deal in which Lippincott and Lucas saw no royalties until the comic had sold a massive 100,000 copies. "He hardballed me," smiled Lippincott. Simultaneously desperate to get the *Star Wars* merchandising ball rolling and aware of the kudos Marvel would give the story within the key sci-fi market, Lippincott agreed. The only concession Lee granted was that further rights would have to be renegotiated.

While the comic freaks, Kurtz and Lucas, were ecstatic at having sold the *Star Wars* story to the world's leading comic publishers, the reaction back at Twentieth–Century–Fox in Los Angeles typified the year that was to follow. "They thought I was the biggest fool in the world. It was, 'Who cares about a comic book?'"

The feeling was little different when, acting under Lucas and Lippincott's instructions, Tom Pollock struck a book deal with Ballantine's Judy-Lynn Del Rey. The wife of the veteran sci-fi writer, Lester Del Rey, she was acknowledged as New York's most astute science-fiction publisher. Her reaction to the *Star Wars* script was brutally honest. "It was an interesting story, but nothing to make you jump out of your skin," she recalled later. "In the hands of a yo-yo, who needs it?'

Once more, however, Lippincott in particular was aware of the value of having the *Star Wars* name in the sci-fi marketplace in advance of the film's release. The advance Del Rey paid was so low it was "embarrassing," she admitted later. Yet Tom Pollock and Lippincott walked away with a deal for her to release a novelization, to be written by the rising writer Alan Dean Foster, a sequel, and a book on the making of *Star Wars*. Each would be published under the new Del Rey imprint she planned to launch at the end of 1976 bearing her own name.

In an office at the Goldwyn Studios in Hollywood, George Lucas was experiencing frustrations of his own. He had begun casting even before the *Star Wars* budget had been approved. His main objective had been to find the actors to play his story's central trio—Luke Skywalker, Princess Leia, and Han Solo, by now the hub of the human story at the heart of his saga.

Lucas saw them as a love triangle, *Star Wars* as an intergalactic *Gone With the Wind*. There were times when his quest could be as maddening as the legendary search for Scarlett. "I saw an actor every five to ten minutes—for six months," he said.

To spare himself the ordeal of having to make casual conversation with every actor that passed through—something he was hopeless at—he shared the expense of the office with another of the new breed of film-school graduates, Brian De Palma, casting his new horror movie *Carrie*. Some of those who auditioned left with the distinct impression that Lucas was De Palma's gofer.

Lucas was adamant that he wanted unknowns. He wanted to repeat the magic of *American Graffiti* when, with Fred Roos's help, he had unearthed a rich crop of new stars. Roos, by now at work with Coppola on *Apocalypse Now,* was once more asked for his input.

Lucas at first found little to enthuse him. For a while he considered casting a black actor, Glynn Turman, in the role of Han Solo and giving the role of Leia to a Eurasian actress. He backed down fearing the consequences if, as he intended, interracial sparks flew between Solo and Leia. "He didn't want *Guess Who's Coming to Dinner,*" said Gary Kurtz. Lucas didn't want *American Graffiti* on Mars either.

The director had remained close to a number of the *Graffiti* gang, and was bombarded with requests for roles. Cindy Williams, who had used her success as Laurie to land a role in the comedy, *Laverne and Shirley,* and was a particular friend of Roos, twisted his arm to test her for Leia. (She regretted it, hearing the most dreaded words—"We want a young Cindy Williams"—after being rejected.) Richard Dreyfuss, who had used his success as a springboard to star in what had become the biggest hit in years, Spielberg's *Jaws,* also browbeat Lucas into testing him for the role of Han Solo. As Lucas's search foundered, however, he couldn't resist choosing one of *American Graffiti's* unheralded heroes.

Each day Lucas would arrive at the Goldwyn set to discover a familiar sight. Dressed in well-worn denims, a carpenter's belt around his waist and a look of almost lethal disdain on his face, was Harrison Ford.

Ford was on his knees, constructing an elaborate door at the offices Zoetrope had taken nearby as Coppola and Roos worked on preproduction for *Apocalypse Now.* Ford, now thirty-three, had been on the fringe of Hollywood for more than a decade. After two disastrous stints within the crumbling studio system at Columbia and Universal, he had developed a knack for carpentry which he had used to supplement his sporadic forays into film. After playing the drag racer Bob Falfa in *Graffiti* he had combined another collaboration with Roos and Coppola on the Oscar-nominated *The Conversation* but then slipped back into relatively obscure television roles, including *Dynasty*, a James Michener frontier saga with Sarah Miles and episodes of *Gunsmoke* and *Kung Fu*.

Crotchety and intensely proud, Ford had been furious when his old friend Roos asked him to do work on the door while Lucas cast *Star Wars*. "I'm not working a fucking door while Lucas is there," he had told his friend. He felt it was demeaning to be on his knees outside the office while everyone else in Hollywood tested. He felt even worse when Dreyfuss, with whom he had clashed on the set of *Graffiti*, saw him slaving away in his overalls. "I felt about as big as a pea," he recalled later.

What Ford did not realize was that Roos had effectively set him up. "I would bang away every day. I kept saying, 'George, he's right under your nose.' I knew in my gut what he could do, I knew him much better than George did," said Roos, a close friend of Ford and his wife, Mary.

Eventually Lucas relented. "Harrison was there outside working all the time, banging on things. I just said at lunchtime or sometime, 'Would you like to read some of these things, because I need somebody to read against all these characters?' And he said he would do it," Lucas recalled. He instantly saw he was a natural for the part of Solo, as he described him in his script, "a tough James Dean-style starpilot, a cowboy in a starship: simple, sentimental and cocksure."

"Harrison was by far the best," said Lucas. "Within a minute or two of him being on the screen you got a whole sense of a lot of backstory with him. Part of it is just his physical ruggedness, but part of it is also the sly intelligence he keeps projecting."

Lucas yearned to find an actress with some of Ford's complexity for the part of Princess Leia, a role he saw as pivotal to the film's success. Yet, pleasant though the beauty pageant he had witnessed had been, he had been frustrated. Lucas's original vision had been of an archetypal "Hollywood blonde." None of the prom queens he saw came close to fulfilling the film's need for someone simultaneously sexy and spiky. "You would not believe some of the girls could even hold a gun, let alone shoot one," laughed Kurtz.

Less obviously glamorous young actresses like Amy Irving and Jodie Foster were considered. Marcia had recommended Foster, at thirteen already something of a veteran, as she edited her third major film, *Alice Doesn't Live Here Any More* in New York. Foster was filmed, considered, and eventually rejected because of her age.

Only the former Penthouse Pet Terri Nunn had shown the right blend of feisty beauty. She, however, lacked "regal" presence. As it turned out, the answer lay in the midst of Hollywood Royalty. Fred Roos was convinced they should recall Carrie Fisher, the precocious eighteen-year-old daughter of Eddie Fisher and Debbie Reynolds who had been tested early on. Lucas had disliked her because of her slightly surly manner and her baby-fat features.

"She was the only who was obviously young yet had a strong presence on the screen. She was someone who could be perceived as royal, was used to ordering people around," said Kurtz. She and Ford, in particular, fired sparks off each other, just as they would need to do on film. "Those two were always going to get on, they share the same jaundiced view of the world," smiled Fred Roos. The Ford-Fisher combination worked best with a boyish young actor called Mark Hamill in the role of Luke.

At the age of twenty-two, Hamill's resumé read like an A to Z of contemporary television. The son of a Navy captain, partly educated in Japan, he had already starred in 140 shows from *The Cosby Show* to *The Partridge Family, The FBI* to an ABC series called *The Texas Wheelers*. Like Ford, he looked younger than his age and had what Lucas called a naive, "gosh-golly kid" quality.

Hamill had been persuaded to put himself up for audition by an actor friend, Robert Englund. Englund, later to win a ghoulish fame as Freddie in John Carpenter's *Nightmare on Elm Street* films, had been turned down for the part of Luke but sensed Hamill may be what they were looking for. Englund's warning that Lucas would be the one who sat in the room saying nothing was unnecessary. Hamill had passed through his *American Graffiti* "cattle call" unnoticed four years earlier.

Hamill turned up at the Goldwyn studios in November. A brief, "Hi, I'm Mark Hamill, I have four sisters and two brothers," routine and he was gone, assuming once more that would be the last of it. The trip did not prove completely fruitless. Fred Roos, lurking quietly in the background, suggested Hamill might be interested in a part in *Apocalypse Now*.

To Hamill's amazement, in February 1976, an envelope flopped through his letter box containing six pages of Lucas's script, still called *The Star Wars*, and an invitation to return to the Goldwyn Studios for a full screen test. Roos, unable to convince Coppola to sign Hamill up for their movie, had been lobbying for him to be cast alongside Fisher and Ford.

Lucas boiled his choice down to two sets of three, Ford, Fisher, and Hamill and another trio consisting of Terri Nunn, the New York stage actor Christopher Walken as Han Solo, and the television star Will Selzer as Luke. One offered youth and the sardonic cynicism that Ford exuded naturally, the other a more mature mixture, with Walken's sense of menace adding an extra edge. Eventually youth triumphed.

Lucas's only worry was Carrie Fisher's weight. Eventually

her agent was told her client had to lose ten pounds before filming began. "We sent her to a health resort," said Kurtz.

Throughout the casting process, Ladd had leaned as heavily as he could on Lucas to consider at least one recognizable star name.

As March loomed ever closer, Lucas finally buckled. Of all his characters, Obi-Wan Kenobi seemed the one most likely to benefit from a sprinkling of *gravitas*. Lucas had toyed with the idea of casting the Japanese star Toshiro Mifune, an ironic nod at Obi-Wan and *Star Wars'* Samurai heritage. When he learned that Alec Guinness was in Hollywood finishing a movie, however, he saw intriguing new possibilities for the character.

Like Laurence Olivier, also passing through an uncomfortable Hollywood phase in the twilight of his career, Guinness was faced with the harsh, fiscal facts of life. For all his miraculous contributions to British cinema, perhaps the most gifted screen actor of his generation could not afford to resist the occasional fat payday in America. (To his disgust, television's endless repeats of the classics in the Guinness canon, including Ealing comedies like *The Lavender Hill Mob* and *The Ladykillers*, earned him no residuals at all. "Don't get a penny. I'm damn annoyed every time they're shown.") If *The Betsy*, in which Olivier cavorted naked with Lesley-Anne Down, represented the nadir of the colossus of the English theater's movie career, *Murder by Death*, produced by the formidable Ray Stark at Columbia, represented the lowpoint of his former understudy's screen output. "It was a silly film," said Guinness with a wince.

As he recalls, he was on the penultimate day of filming when a script arrived, unsolicited, on his dressing table accompanied by a letter from Lucas. Guinness showed little interest at first. "I thought, 'Oh crumbs, science fiction, I can't be bothered with that.'" He also disliked the idea of scripts arriving unheralded "over the transom." Holed up in his dressing room, with little better to do, however, he began reading. Guinness found Lucas's florid, breathless sci-fi babble embarrassing. Yet, he read on—and on. "I started reading it and although it was painful reading in lots of ways it made me turn the page," he said. "And that is an indicator."

Intrigued, Guinness returned to the set. "Tell me about George Lucas," he asked some of his colleagues. "Now you're talking about a real director," he was told.

On his final day in America, a curious Guinness arranged to meet the object of this reverence. His curiosity deepened when he discovered the taciturn character behind the reputation. "He was very quiet, *very* shy." Yet in his enthusiasm for his *Star Wars* script and Obi-Wan Kenobi, Lucas was once more self-assured and quietly inspiring. The Obi-Wan he described to Guinness was a slightly deranged mix of a Samurai warrior and Merlin, Dr. Dolittle and Ben Gunn from *Treasure Island*. Gifted with the ability to converse with humans, robots, and members of Lucas's intergalactic menagerie alike, Obi-Wan would be the font of most of Lucas's metaphysical wisdom. Guinness boarded his plane at LAX airport with his head spinning. "We left it that we would discuss it further, in a month or so," he recalled with an arch of an eyebrow.

The early months of the ILM operation were devoted to researching and setting up the technical capability to provide the shots Lucas wanted—no easy task. Dykstra hired only two recognized film industry veterans, Richard Edlund and Dick Alexander. The problems he faced were as theoretical as they were practical. Film set experience counted for little.

Dykstra's philosophy was to create a community of like-minded problem-solver artists. As word of the new *Star Wars* setup spread through the film schools and independent film companies of California, he was inundated with volunteers. The collection of art students and camera designers he hired bore little relation to the mainstream film community. If there was a dress code it was "long hair and Levi's."

"The first six months we were designing lenses and building cameras from scratch," Dykstra explained. Pioneering developments were also under way in the other departments—from computing to optical printing. Without a degree in engineering, computing, chemistry, and electronic design, visitors had no chance of understanding the goings-on. "From the point of view of anybody who walked through that door, it was complete gibberish."

Dykstra, still in his early twenties and headstrong, was also disinclined to explain the goings-on to strangers. His typical response, he admitted later, was to fob them off with a, "I can't be bothered explaining this to you now, just don't worry."

"Given my age and what was going on it was probably impossible for me not to have a huge ego," he admitted in hindsight.

Lucas and Kurtz had hoped to be able to go to London with a series of shots that could be used for back projection. As they prepared to leave, however, it was clear the footage was nowhere near ready. At the eleventh hour the decision was made to shoot the film using the "blue screen" method, filming against a blank background and inserting the special effect afterwards. At the time Kurtz and Lucas were deeply frustrated by the setback. "In retrospect, it was no bad thing," said Kurtz.

Jim Nelson had the unenviable job of controlling the ILM operation. "None of this had ever been done before, so it was all a giant, experimental lab," he recalled. "So it became bigger and bigger and crazier and crazier."

As new members of staff and pieces of equipment arrived,

a second story was added to the front of the building. By now it was clear that Nelson would need to remain in Los Angeles, overseeing the ILM operation. It would also be his job to buffer Dykstra and his team from the fretful attentions of Twentieth Century–Fox. Kurtz and Lucas had continued to finance the warehouse until the production had been given its green light by Fox in December 1975. Once the studio began footing the bill for the considerable expenses being run up in Van Nuys, its accountants began taking an interest in how its money was being spent.

Each Friday Nelson would have to account for his spending to Ray Gosnell's assistant John Rogers. He would also update Fox on the projected total budget—a figure that was already climbing steadily. "Of course, every week it was going up and up and up."

If Nelson was unsure of what some of the spending was in aid of, Rogers seemed equally baffled. "He would say, 'Why did you spend $200 on stationery last week?' But he wouldn't notice that I'd spent $160,000 on some obscure thing that nobody understood." At one stage, Rogers queried the vast amount of money being spent on black velvet. He did not understand the material was being used for space backgrounds. "I told him we were making dresses," laughed Nelson.

Kurtz and Lucas put the finishing touches to casting in London. The sixty-three-year-old Peter Cushing, master of the macabre as Van Helsing in the popular Hammer *Dracula* movies of the 1960s, had agreed to play the Empire's vicious overlord, Grand Moff Tarkin.

Phil Brown had been cast as Owen Lars, Shelagh Fraser had been given the only mature female role, Aunt Beru. A selection of young actors, including the young actress Koo Stark, had been cast as Luke's teenage pals. Stark, fresh from an appearance in a soft porn feature called *Emily*, would appear in a scene set in a pool hall in the town of Anchorhead on Tatooine planned for a location shoot in the north African deserts of Tunisia.

Five key roles remained uncast. While discussions with an intrigued Alec Guinness continued, Lucas looked for actors to play the two robots, Chewbacca, and Darth Vader. He was in effect looking for a burlesque troupe. Casting agents raised their eyebrows at the request for a dwarf to inhabit a four-foot robot, a seven-foot giant to play a hairy ape, a mime artist to play a gold-encrusted android, and a muscleman to play an evil, intergalactic villain. Yet with the British film industry passing through another of its almost perennial crises, there was no shortage of willing volunteers.

Dave Prowse, a 6 foot 7 inch, 280-pound gym owner, was one of the first through Lucas's door. Prowse had used his blend of athletic ability, good looks, and imposing physicality to forge a colorful career. His credits ranged from a three-year reign as British heavyweight weight-lifting champion and a spell as a professional "caber tosser," to appearances as a Frankenstein monster in *Casino Royale* and a circus strongman in the Hammer horror, *Vampire Circus*. It had been his appearance as Julian in Kubrick's *A Clockwork Orange* that had interested Lucas, however.

Prowse's first impression of Lucas, dressed in the checkered shirt, jeans, and sneakers that would remain his uniform for the next year, would be echoed by every member of the British cast and crew who met him. Compared to the rather grand directorial figures they were used to meeting on English film sets, Lucas seemed hopelessly miscast as the head of the biggest movie production in the country that year.

"George just looked like a young student," recalled Prowse.

Lucas could not have cared less. The west countryman, articulate and enthusiastic as well as physically impressive, was just what he was looking for. He offered him the choice of playing one of two characters, Darth Vader or Chewbacca. Lucas had outlined his space fantasy but had not explained the characters in detail.

"What's Chewbacca?" Prowse asked.

"He's a hairy gorilla who goes through the film on the side of the goodies," said Lucas.

"And what's Darth Vader?"

"He's the big villain of the film."

Prowse, long enough in the tooth to know the villain offered a greater opportunity and believing the Darth Vader role would not involve a mask, took no time in replying.

"I'll take the bad guy."

"Why?" Lucas asked.

"Because people will remember him."

His decision allowed Lucas to cast a 7 foot 2 inch London hospital porter, Peter Mayhew, as the gorilla. Even by the curious standards of the *Star Wars* circus, Mayhew's break into showbusiness had been bizarre. The previous year the thirty-two-year-old Londoner had featured in a newspaper article on men with oversized feet. A casting agent working on Ray Harryhausen's *Sinbad and the Eye of the Tiger* had seen the story, traced Mayhew and offered him a part in the stop-motion master's film playing a minotaur.

The following spring, members of the Sinbad crew were being hired by Kurtz for work on *Star Wars* at Elstree. Mayhew, affable and popular, was tipped off.

"They contacted me just after Easter. Word gets round and I got a phone call from one of the production secretaries," he recalled.

Mayhew met Lucas and Kurtz and was shown Ralph McQuarrie's drawings of Chewbacca. "He was described as a big hairy eight-foot monster, a bear's body with a dog's head. He was Han Solo's sidekick. He could be lovable and he could be nasty," he remembered. Mayhew signed up for what would turn out to be a six-year sentence inside a sweaty outfit made of angora wool and yak hair.

All Lucas needed now were his robots. Cabaret artist Kenny Baker, at 3 foot 8 inch reputedly the smallest man in England, had been persuaded to see production supervisor Robert Watts by the London promoter Jimmy Jacobs. If Lucas and Kurtz had agonized over other pieces of casting they had no doubt over Baker's suitability. They met him at the Harlesden offices of the Lee Lighting Company. Their primary interest was simply finding an actor to fit into their models of R2-D2.

"After about two minutes they said, 'He'll do.' I was the right size to get inside the robot," said Baker.

The matter was not quite that straightforward. With his fellow midget, 4 foot 2 inch Jack Purvis, Baker formed a double act called The Minitones. Interesting as Lucas's film sounded, its allure paled in comparison with the offer they had just received to appear on Britain's most high-profile television talent show, *Opportunity Knocks,* with Hughie Green. "Jack and I thought if we won that we'd be big names around the cabaret circuit. We were pretty well known anyway. And I thought, I don't want to be stuck in a robot really, when I could be on a cabaret tour on good money. Also if I accepted it my partner Jack would have been out of work. So I turned it down," he said.

Lucas was insistent, however. With time tight, Watts and Kurtz struck a deal with Baker. If he agreed to play R2-D2, they would employ Purvis throughout the run of the movie too. (Purvis went on to play a praying mantis-like creature in the Cantina scene and a Jawa in Tunisia.)

Lucas had imagined the other robot, C-3PO, as an acid-tongued, Bronx-accented American. Intending to dub the voice back in California, he had seen a succession of mime artists and physical performers when the slim, slightly effete Shakespearean actor, Anthony Daniels, had arrived in the Soho Square office. Another Marcel Marceau clone was completing his impersonation of a clockwork robot slowly winding down when Daniels walked in. Unsure what to do, the actor, fastidious in both appearance and behavior, sat in polite silence. Even when the other audition had left, Lucas sat meditatively making notes. "He tends to wither into catatonia, which is not a province in Eastern Europe but a state of non-talking. We sat there having a really terrific silence, not being able to think of anything to say," Daniels recalled.

Eventually, sensing it was "bad manners" to stay quiet, Daniels started asking questions. He then began to wander the room looking at Ralph McQuarrie's drawings on Lucas's walls. He was struck by the beauty of the golden robot drawing.

For the first time Lucas was suddenly animated. Daniels, classically trained and starring in a well-received production of Tom Stoppard's *Rosencrantz and Guildenstern Are Dead* in the West End, was asked to leave his résumé.

Daniels was put through the torture of a second interview. During another silence he impatiently asked Lucas if he could play the golden robot. "Sure," the monosyllabic director replied with a smile. It would take him a long time to forget the idea of the robot with the Bronx brogue. He would, however, eventually admit Daniels was about as perfect a piece of casting as he had ever performed.

"Anthony Daniels *was* C-3PO," said Gary Kurtz.

If, as he later claimed, Lucas had been choosing the actors whose personalities came closest to his imagined characters, back in Los Angeles both Harrison Ford and Carrie Fisher had quickly confirmed themselves as pretty near perfect too. Han Solo's earliest scene in *Star Wars* would involve him bantering with Luke and Obi-Wan Kenobi over his fee for outrunning an Imperial blockade. Ford proved equally mer-

cenary, haggling over his salary longer and more vo-
ciferously than anyone else.

It was a trait Lucas had been aware of on *Graffiti,* where
the actor had browbeaten him and Fred Roos into raising his
salary from a "scale" payment of $485 a week to $500 a week.
Ford had harangued Roos with phone calls along the lines of
"I've got a wife and two kids to feed."

This time his argument was that he would be left seriously out-of-pocket by traveling to England. He could
easily earn more than the $1,000 a week they were offering
running his carpentry business. Hard as he pushed Lucas
and Roos, however, they would not budge on this occasion.
"I got paid less for the role of Han Solo than I was earning as
a carpenter," he confided later, financial worries, by then, a
thing of the dim and distant past. Ford exacted revenge,
however. Unlike Hamill and Fisher, he refused to sign a deal
committing him to a possible two sequels.

While Ford had been showing the audacity of Han Solo,
Carrie Fisher had been displaying the brand of majestic
moxie Lucas wanted from his princess. The budget was so
tight that senior members of cast and crew were asked by
Jim Nelson whether they would mind traveling coach class
from Los Angeles to London for the beginning of principal
photography. As a gesture, Kurtz and Lucas had consented.
Hamill and Ford had quickly followed without any protest.

Nelson was in the Lucasfilm office on the day Carrie
Fisher was discussing her travel arrangements. Fisher's
mother, Debbie Reynolds, had somehow got wind of what
was being proposed and called through on Nelson's direct
line.

"How dare you send my daughter coach to England," she
shouted at Nelson.

"They're all going coach, the director's going coach, the
producer's going coach," Nelson replied.

"My daughter's not going coach. I'm going to put you up in front of the Screen Actor's Guild for breaking the contract."

"Carrie was sitting there in my office, hearing her mom yelling at me," remembered Nelson.

Fisher walked over to Nelson and reached for the telephone. "May I talk to my mother, please?" she asked Nelson, who gladly passed over the receiver.

The conversation was brief. "Mom, I want to go coach. Why don't you fuck off?"

She then hung up.

CHAPTER 5

"Faster, More Intense"

For centuries the Chott el-Djerid, a dry, salt-lake bed in the Saharan desert of Tunisia, had remained one of the most desolate places on earth. Barren but for its snakes and scorpions, only the silhouette of an occasional Bedouin caravan threatened the endless haze of its horizon.

On March 26, 1976, however, George Lucas and Gary Kurtz witnessed an almost miraculous sight. A day after they had set up in the stultifying hundred-degree heat, rain fell in that part of the Sahara for the first time in fifty years. As the downpour transformed the bone-dry landscape into a muddy swamp, ruining their chances of filming, the duo may have imagined they were witnessing a freak of nature. In fact they were seeing a portent of things to come.

Over the next twelve months, the making of *Star Wars* would present them with almost every imaginable test. There would be trials financial and physical, technical and temperamental. The rewards would be beyond their imagination. But the ordeal would almost break them in body and soul.

The beginning of principal photography on *Star Wars* hardly merited a mention around Hollywood. Only the official announcement of Lucas's main casting coup aroused interest at the time. On the morning of March 24, *Variety* ran a brief report: ALEC GUINNESS LANDS TOP ROLE IN "WARS."

Since their Los Angeles lunch, Guinness and Lucas had talked a lot. Guinness, disinterested in playing a crackpot but quietly impressed by the young director, had suggested making Obi-Wan Kenobi a less eccentric, nobler character. Lucas liked the idea, he thought it would deepen the divide between the goodness of Obi-Wan and the darkness of Vader. Guinness did not come cheaply. While Hamill, Ford, and Fisher had accepted $1,000 dollar a week salaries, Guinness's five-figure check was supplemented by a two and a quarter percent share in the film's profits. It would turn out—by several light years—to be the biggest payday of his long and distinguished career.

Kurtz and Lucas had allocated eleven days for the North African part of the shoot. If time pressures were not tight enough, Kurtz had booked a giant Lockheed Hercules C130 cargo plane to transport the mass of props, cameras, and lighting equipment home to Elstree. Under the terms of their contract with the charter company, the production was due to be charged $10,000 for every hour the plane was kept waiting on the tarmac.

Lucas, Kurtz, and Robert Watts had chosen Tunisia as the location for the desert planet Tatooine, Luke Skywalker's home and the setting for the opening act of the story, because of its strikingly primitive architecture and the cooperative attitude of its government. Officials, happy that the script did not contain anything to offend its predominantly Moslem population, had given clearance to film in previously unseen areas of the country.

As well as the Chott el-Djerid, setting for the exterior of

the farm on which Luke lived with his aunt and uncle Beru and Owen Lars, Robert Watts and his location managers had chosen four other main sites in Tunisia. A white-domed settlement on the island of Jerba, thought to be the legendary "Land of the Lotus Eaters" described in Homer's *Odyssey*, had been chosen as the exterior of the Mos Eisley spaceport where Luke and Obi-Wan would hire Han Solo and his *Millennium Falcon*. In the town of Matama, strange, subterranean cavelike dwellings carved by the native Berbers to protect them from the sandstorms had been picked to portray the Lars family's underground quarters. A remote canyon, beyond the Chott el-Djerid, served as the scene for Luke's meeting with Obi-Wan while another sand dune region outside the city of Tozeur had been lined up for filming of R2-D2 and C-3PO's arrival on the planet.

The rains that hit the Chott el-Djerid immediately lost the crew a day and the use of two trucks, stranded temporarily in the mud and salt. Working days were soon extended to make every use of available sunlight.

Lucas's greatest problems came when he attempted to make use of the technology flown into North Africa. A sizeable chunk of the $10 million budget had been devoted to bringing Ralph McQuarrie's art to life. The respected British production designer, John Barry, had enlisted some of Britain's brightest talents to construct the battered hardware of Tatooine, from a vast, ninety-foot "sandcrawler," in which the midget Jawas carried R2-D2 and C-3PO across the desert, an assortment of robots and Luke's "landspeeder," a sleek, hovercraft-cum-sports car.

Yet the sandcrawler was destroyed before it had been before the cameras, flattened one night by the savage Saharan winds. Kurtz asked the crew if they would take Saturday off, except for the production crew, and work on Sunday instead, which they all did. If that was not bad enough, Luke's landspeeder failed to work properly. The vehicle also proved difficult to film without its supports and wheels visible.

Lucas's greatest problems were reserved for his cherished robots, however. Kenny Baker found R2-D2 almost impossible to operate. Baker had to squeeze inside the canister, from where he had to operate switches activating the droid's lights and power. While that was manageable, achieving any fluent movement was beyond him.

"It was very hard to move because it weighed about seventy pounds," he remembered. Baker, a skilled roller skater, had suggested putting the robot on rollers. The modification hardly helped. "Every time I put the left foot forward the right foot went back, when I put the right foot forward the left foot went back. Then they thought they'd put ratchets on the rollers so that it only rolled forwards. That only worked to a certain extent because it was so slow. I could not move each leg more than about five inches at a time," he recalled.

It was only as he lost patience with the contraption that Baker stumbled on a solution. "In the end, I rocked it out of anger and frustration one day and it wobbled from side to side," he said. "While one leg was in the air I discovered I could move it if I just rocked it from foot to foot. That was the only way I could do it."

Lucas eventually gave up on using the actor in the desert and had crewmen pull the empty robot across the sand on an invisible wire. The process was almost as difficult. R2-D2 regularly fell over as the cameras rolled.

Baker's frustrations were nothing compared to the torture Anthony Daniels was enduring playing the "tin man" in the searing desert heat. Daniels's suffering had begun back in London. Costume designers had stripped him naked, covered his body in Vaseline and his private parts in plastic film before casting him head to toe in plaster. Later he had been fitted in a latex suit which left him itching his way through an entire performance of *Rosencrantz and Guildenstern*. Eventually the burnished gold costume had been constructed out of fiberglass sections. (There had been fears a plastic version would melt in the desert heat.) The befuddling process of fitting the pieces together was, Daniels complained, "like fiddling with a Rubik's cube." Most days it took a minimum of two hours. The finished effect was undeniably stunning. The Tunisian crew let out an audible gasp at their first sight of Ralph McQuarrie's original drawings brought to life.

"When I walked out of the tent it was like being a God," said Daniels. "Everybody simply froze. In the glare of the desert sunshine was this wonderful golden man."

Any sense of pride he may have felt proved short-lived. The suit was heavy, the fiberglass strands irritated his skin, the plates pinched and stabbed him, movement was restricted to jerky footsteps and arm twitches, and it was impossible to drink or relieve himself without the aid of a crew member. Even with two local helpers assigned to protect him from the sun with a parasol, Daniels sweated profusely. He lost, on average, four pounds a day in weight.

At the end of his first day inside the robot's skin the sensitive actor almost quit. "That first day in the desert, I wore it from seven in the morning until seven at night. I was hysterical by then." Daniels described the overall experience as "like living in a biscuit tin with no human contact—a kind of deprivation torture."

Predictably cast and crew fell victim to the traditional enemy of the Saharan intruder, dysentery. Anthony Waye, an experienced British assistant director, kept a diary of the first days of the *Star Wars* shoot. "Cannot abide the filthy hotel," was one of his earliest entries. Collectively the cast and crew blamed the epidemic on the breakfast boiled eggs. "Dysentery became boiled egg syndrome. At breakfast everybody ordered boiled eggs, one of the safest things to eat in a place where dysentery is par for the course. The cook had a giant cauldron of eggs and had no system for timing them. You either got one that was rock solid or totally raw— never anything in between," Waye recalled.

Bunny Alsup was stricken on the first day. The most serious casualty, however, was Stuart Freeborn. In Tunisia to supervise his designs for the desert-dwelling "sandpeople" and Jawas, the film's main makeup, costume, and creature designer went down with pneumonia brought on by the massive drop in temperatures in the desert at night. He was flown back to London where he was hospitalized for two weeks.

It was difficult to decide whether nature or technology was the production's worst enemy. The latter was almost the end of Kenny Baker one day. During filming at Luke Skywalker's home, the Lars farm, Baker had once more climbed into the belly of R2-D2. A collection of radio-controlled robots were also in the scene in which Luke and his uncle purchase two droids from the Jawas. (Baker's stage partner Jack Purvis was playing one of the Jawas, with Gary Kurtz's two daughters, Tiffany and Melissa, and five Tunisian children as the others.)

"It was the scene where we were showing off what we can do. I am wombling across the desert in my own sweet way. Suddenly Jack shouted to me, 'Look out Ken, there's a robot coming in,'" he remembered. Before he could react, a collision had sent Baker and his robot flying to the floor. "It was not exactly the M1, you don't expect something to come ploughing into you in the middle of the desert. This other robot careered into me at about twenty miles an hour and knocked me sideways. He had gone out of control."

Renegade robots became a regular threat to Baker's livelihood. "Nobody could really control them," he laughed. "The radio signals would get mixed up with whatever else was flying around and sometimes they would go a bit haywire."

There were successes in the desert, however. Mark Hamill and Alec Guinness struck up a rapport that worked well on screen. Hamill's playful sense of humor had endeared him to Sir Alec and his wife on the very first day of filming. Lady Guinness, traveling with her husband, had been relieving the boredom by sketching the Tunisian scenery and had set up near an ornate mosque. Only minutes after she settled down to capture the scene, however, an irate local ran over to her, grabbed her sketch and tore it to shreds. Guinness and his wife, surprisingly oblivious to the fact it was forbidden to photograph or draw any religious buildings in the country, turned to Hamill for an explanation.

"What did she do?" Guinness asked Hamill.

"He was probably just the local art critic," Hamill replied to Guinness's delight.

Of all the memorable sights she witnessed on *Star Wars*, none tickled Bunny Alsup as much as that when Sir Alec prepared for his first scene as Obi-Wan. Lucas, Kurtz, and the crew looked on in bemusement as the great knight of the stage lay down on the desert floor. "He laid down on the sand and rolled around to get his costume looking dusty and dirty," smiled Alsup.

Hamill had been given little instruction by Lucas before the first day's filming, but that was hardly surprising since, in essence, he had hired the leading trio to play themselves. Hamill's only clue came when, during an early take, he tried imitating his insular, soft-spoken director. "I did it just like I thought George would react in the scene," said Hamill, who had expected a rebuke. Instead Lucas muttered: "Cut. Perfect."

"I was flabbergasted. I thought, 'Oh, I see, of course, Luke is George.'" For the remainder of the film Hamill was as relieved as he was mildly unsettled. "I began to really feel like I was playing George."

Despite the early setbacks, Kurtz saw his waiting Hercules into the North African skies on time after a dozen days. For Lucas, however, there was plenty to indulge his pessimistic streak. He left Tunisia knowing many of his shots of R2-D2 and the landspeeder had been a disaster. A giant "bantha," a shaggy, mammothlike creature ridden by the sand people, had also been unusable. He knew both would have to be reshot, probably in California.

Already behind with his shooting and with serious doubts about his film's technology, Lucas left Tunisia more worried than when he had arrived. Shortly before climbing on the jet out of Africa, Lucas sent Marcia a postcard. It read: "Are you sure Orson Welles started this way?"

In the weeks before filming began, the hangarlike sound stages at Elstree had metamorphosed into a series of spectacular sets. Under John Barry, two sound stages had been transformed into two spaceports—one at the Mos Eisley spaceport on Tatooine, the other on the Death Star. Elsewhere the corridors and control rooms of the Death Star snaked around the lot.

The stage at Shepperton had been fitted out for the triumphal finale of the film, when Leia would reward Luke, Han, and Chewbacca for their heroism.

For all the vast experience it could boast, Lucas's cast had little knowledge of his revolutionary new approach to filmmaking. With the plans to use back projection abandoned, scenes were filmed against blank, blue-screen backgrounds instead. Cushing, Guinness, and their American colleagues would routinely be asked to direct their dialogue at thin air, marker boards, or specific spots in the distance. Spacecraft, planets, star-filled swathes of hyperspace, and other special effects would be added at a later date, Lucas assured them.

The process left many of them confused and some convinced they were involved in a fundamentally flawed production. "We had no idea what was going on," said Peter

Mayhew, who with Harrison Ford had to film convincing space-travel scenes aboard their ship, the *Millennium Falcon*. "When they said the spaceship is going through an asteroid field, nobody knew what that visualized like. We were told to do this, stand there. It was difficult to realize what it all meant."

"There are certain things you can bring to a movie that have substitutions in your life," Carrie Fisher complained later. "Well, you can't do that in this type of film. On the set I would have to say, 'Don't blow up my planet, please,' and all I'm doing is looking at a board with an X on it held by an assistant director who couldn't wait for the tea break!"

Often, Fisher and Ford, a philosophy student before being thrown out of college, reassured their colleagues that they needed to take what Kierkegaard called "the great leap of faith." At other times they agreed *Star Wars* simply required them to "pretend a lot."

If the cast was bemused, the crew was even more perplexed by the American and his innovative approach.

"It was a very new way of filmmaking to us. One can honestly say it was the first film to use a completely new style of moviemaking," recalled Anthony Waye. Waye, like many of his colleagues, came from the cost-conscious world of the low-budget *Carry On* and Norman Wisdom movies of the 1960s. They also inhabited an industry in which union rules and regulations were obeyed to the letter. "Those films were highly organized, you started on the dot and finished on the dot, exactly on schedule but also on budget with no wasted film."

As the mercury rose outside—1976 became Britain's hottest summer of the century—so the temperature rose inside. Relations between Lucas and his British crew had been strained almost immediately on arrival at Elstree from Tunisia—primarily because of the rigid, British union rules. In Hollywood, labor relations always came a poor second to the demands and deadlines of the studios. Work would go on, around the clock if necessary. The British film industry was shackled by a maze of regulations. And with the trade unions enjoying one of the most powerful periods in their history, few employers could afford to challenge their restrictive practices.

Lucas and Kurtz had been outraged to discover they could not work a minute past 5:30 P.M., the cast-in-stone "knocking off time" at all British studios. Union rules dictated that crews could work overtime, but only if a majority of members agreed in a ballot. When Lucas officially approached the union to request that the crew be prepared to work two hours each night after 5:30 P.M., the workforce voted to reject the proposal by an overwhelming majority.

Within days of arriving in London he was falling further behind schedule. Often Lucas's crew would finish the laborious process of setting up shots and preparing actors and extras shots only to discover there was not enough time to film anything. The whole process would have to begin all over again the next morning. Lucas would complain that half a day of shooting would be lost because his crew would not work an extra forty-five minutes.

Lucas's introverted personality only compounded the problems. "George had what he wanted in his brain, he had this fabulous picture of the end effect in his mind. The problem was that none of us knew what that was. I don't ever remember him explaining it," said Anthony Waye.

"We thought they were strange people and I suspect they thought us a bunch of idiots. But it was a new way of making movies and we were just not used to that sort of thing," recalled Ronnie Taylor, then an assistant cameraman.

Even the novices could sense a time bomb, ticking away.

"George was so uptight, super-enthusiastic, he wanted everything done exactly as he wanted it. Everybody more or less bowed down," said Peter Mayhew. "It was a meeting of the old-fashioned and the modern and the results were inevitable."

No one personified the gulf between the old school of gentlemen filmmakers and the brash new technocrats of Hollywood more pointedly than Lucas's chief cinematographer, Gilbert "Gil" Taylor. Kurtz and Lucas had originally hired the great Geoffrey Unsworth, Kubrick's cameraman on *2001*. At the last moment Unsworth had withdrawn to work with Vincente Minnelli in Rome on *A Matter of Time*. Taylor, a veteran of *Dr. Strangelove* with Kubrick and *A Hard Day's Night* with Richard Lester, seemed an ideal replacement. No sooner had filming begun, however, than it was clear the irresistible force of Lucas vision had come into collision with an immovable object. Taylor, flamboyant and used to deference, disliked Lucas's interference.

In Tunisia he disagreed with Lucas's opinions on the level of lighting needed. While others kept their opinions to themselves, Taylor made no secret of his opinion of Lucas and his newfangled filmmaking ways.

"He used to turn up on the set in his E-type Jaguar, he was a real gentleman farmer type," recalled Kenny Baker. "He was always effing and cursing, but in this frightfully Sussex farmer accent. He would say, "They don't know what the fuck they're doing this lot.'"

Relations soured further when Taylor refused to use the soft-focus lenses Lucas wanted to give the film the muted look he had in his mind. The director retaliated by moving lights, the ultimate insult to a cinematographer. Taylor blew his top.

"Gil was from the old school and he could be a little cantankerous," said Anthony Waye with a hint of understatement.

Lucas became convinced that he or Gary Kurtz would have to fire Taylor. He knew such a move would be an enormous risk, however. Not only did Taylor occupy an exalted reputation within the ranks of the British crew, his removal could easily spark industrial action. An uncomfortable standoff ensued for the rest of the shoot. Kurtz did all he could to soothe Taylor, whose complaints were sometimes valid. "I kept having to reassure him. He had not used some of the equipment before," said Kurtz. On more than one occasion, including the triumphal scene, Kurtz took over as cameraman himself.

Lucas clashed with others, however. John Barry found the director's treatment of his creative staff irritating. Too wrapped up to explain what he saw in his mind, he regularly angered the designer by issuing menial instructions. "George looked upon the people that he hired as people to facilitate what he wanted. He did not think of them interpreting things in a creative way," said Kurtz. "John and he constantly clashed about that. George would say: 'I want you to take that vent pipe and cut three inches off,' and John would say: 'You tell me what your vision is and I will do the details. I want you to tell me what you see but I don't want you to tell me how to do my job.' Eventually George realized that was the best way to do things."

The conflicts took their toll on the director. With Marcia, Lucas had rented a comfortable cottage in Hampstead. Yet he saw little of it. Most days he would be out of bed at 4:30 A.M., fretting about the day ahead. He would leave home at 6 A.M. arrive on the set at 7 A.M. ready for the start of shooting an hour later. After the final shots at 5:30 P.M., he would head to the production office at Elstree to plan the next day's filming. He would normally leave around 8 P.M., returning home to do more work until falling asleep at 10 P.M. or so. His routine continued in that vein throughout the seventy-day long shooting of *Star Wars*.

Almost inevitably, Lucas, a sickly individual since childhood, suffered from cold and flu bugs. He coughed constantly on the *Star Wars* set. "George was forever ill," said

Dave Prowse. To add to their misery, the Lucases had suffered a burglary in which all their television equipment was stolen.

As his strength failed him, Lucas retreated into his shell even more. And as transatlantic relations deteriorated, the occasional high jinks of the cast did little to restore the entente cordiale. Fisher, Ford, and Hamill would relieve the boredom by sharing jokes. A running gag between Ford and Fisher involved substituting the word *Jew* for *You* in well-known song lyrics. So they burst into renditions of "Jew Light Up My Life," "Jew Made Me Love You." Unaware that both of them were half-Jewish, a British assistant director complained that they were being antisemitic.

The trio would also laugh behind Dave Prowse's back. Prowse delivered Darth Vader's apocalyptic speeches in a rich, west-of-England accent. Fisher admitted that she had to stifle giggles almost each time she played a scene with him. "He had this Devon farmer's accent. We used to call him Darth Farmer!"

Few of the British found the Americans funny, only deepening the divide further. "The only damper on the pure fun of that set was the almost-unanimous attitude of the British crew that we were totally out of our minds," Harrison Ford complained later.

Amid the rancour, Alec Guinness became the production's beacon of light. He remained Lucas's most powerful onset supporter.

Guinness had experienced more than his share of troubled productions. He would have none of the cynicism of the British crew. "There was a certain amount of grumbling there. People were saying, 'This is absolutely down the drain isn't it?' and I said, 'Not at all,'" he recalled. "I had a great amount of confidence in George's ability to bring it together. I thought George had total dedication."

Just as he was looking for minimalism in his performance,

Guinness saw Lucas striving for the same in his direction. Rather than being worried by his director's distant, undemonstrative manner, Guinness welcomed it. "He was very quiet in all his ways of doing things, very unobtrusive. I think the English crew were a bit thrown by him. But that was something I liked very much in a way and trusted," he said.

"Like all the best directors, Lucas had very little to say during the actual filming. He simply sensed when you were uncomfortable and just walked across and dropped a brief word in your ear," he said. "Good actors don't like being told how to act and they become worried if they are made to feel part of someone else's work."

As owlish offscreen as he was in the role of Obi-Wan, Guinness also helped construct a bridge over the troubled transatlantic waters, becoming the touchstone for both the British cast and the young American actors. When Mark Hamill's humor failed him, the sagacious old hand passed on words of worldly wisdom.

"Nobody thinks I'm acting. I'm just setting up the jokes for the robots," an exasperated Hamill complained at one point.

"Be philosophical," Guinness soothed. "Nothing makes any sense in this business." The two wrote to each other for years afterwards.

No one benefited from Guinness's master class in how to behave as much as Harrison Ford, however. On the set of *American Graffiti* Lucas had found Ford undisciplined. "When he was doing *Graffiti* he was a little bit on the wild side," he recalled. At one stage Ford almost got arrested for roaring around the streets of Petaluma in a souped-up Chevrolet.

At Elstree, Lucas saw Ford paying attention to the different approach of the British actors. "I think the experience of the *Star Wars* films, especially the first one, and working with a lot of British actors, Alec Guinness in particular, mellowed him out as an actor," said Lucas. "He began to see how it was a real profession—in terms of how you act professionally on the set. American actors are quite a bit different than European actors and they approach it very differently. I think being around a lot of very professional actors that did their job and didn't cause a lot of difficulties and didn't take a lot of time and did their homework before they came on the set, all the kind of professional things you expect, caught him at the right moment. He became a very good professional actor from that point on. He disciplined his talent in a much different way."

Guinness also helped calm the fragile nerves of Anthony Daniels. He made little secret of the distress the daily transformation into C-3PO had been causing him. After the torture of Tunisia, Elstree brought new problems. Unable to get out of his outfit between takes, Daniels resorted to either standing as still as a statue or else propping his metal superstructure against makeshift leaning boards. Elstree's laborers regularly mistook him for a piece of the American visitors' bizarre sci-fi furniture. "They'd lean against me as if I were a lamppost—fortunately there were no dogs in the film," he complained. "They'd strike matches on me, and discuss their sex lives, quite unaware that I was inside the costume and could overhear every word."

Tired of the humiliation, Daniels had insisted on having C-3PO's head removed when he was not working.

Relations between him and Kenny Baker were also difficult. By now Baker was only participating in ten percent of his scenes. The rest of the time the robot was being pushed, pulled or operated by remote control—usually disastrously.

"There was still no way I could do it fast enough for the chase sequences. In the end they used a remote control one for the chases and me for the close-ups of R2-D2 reacting to the dialogue," he said.

Baker knew R2-D2's electronic "voice"—a series of beeps

and whistles—would be added afterward and saw no point in learning the script. He simply responded to what Daniels and Lucas said to him. Daniels found the task of acting against an inanimate object difficult enough as it was. As relations became strained, the two became bickering replicas of their Laurel and Hardy double act on screen.

"To put it mildly, he was a bit pissed off with me," recalled Baker. "He had to react to a dummy that was not replying. But there was nothing I could do about it. He would moan: 'You don't even learn the script.' I'd say: 'Anthony, it isn't going to work even if I do learn the script. I'm not going to whistle the bloody words and nobody will see me anyway.'"

"He was very good, but a bit hard to live with at times," Baker said of his sidekick.

(Daniels's frustration with his partner may not have been helped by the fact that each morning while he was in makeup Baker was sleeping in at his home in nearby Bushey. Transport coordinator Pat Carr could have Baker on the set at short notice. "Pat would have me at home on standby. They would call me and I'd be there in five minutes. I just jumped in the robot and I was away," Baker remembered.)

With Lucas still unconvinced about his accent, Daniels was insecure about his performance. To an unheralded English stage actor, Alec Guinness was a figure to be treated with awed respect. Despite his unhappiness, he was often too shy to even speak to the great man. When word filtered back about how impressed Guinness was with his performance in such testing circumstances, Daniels had been overjoyed. "I suspect that I wouldn't have been able to cope with *Star Wars* without Sir Alec," he said later. "I was very, very unhappy in that suit. At times I thought, 'Maybe I'm making a total prat of myself.' Then word came back to me via my agency that Alec Guinness had been saying extremely nice things about my performance. If my performance was all right with him, it must be all right."

Kenny Baker, too, saw Guinness's presence as a reassuring sign. "We all thought it was a load of rubbish at first. But I thought Alec Guinness wouldn't get involved in a load of rubbish. He must know something that we don't know." He did not, of course.

Even Alan Ladd's loyalty was tested when he saw an early assembly of footage. Ladd had flown to London to check on Lucas's progress. Kurtz and Lucas hated the old system of sending back "dailies" to be picked to pieces by sundry executives, 5000 miles from the front line. Instead they sent collections of shots back as they saw fit. "We sporadically assembled scenes and sent them back," Kurtz said.

Laddie's easy smile faded as he saw the early sequence featuring Luke leaving the farm and heading for a night out at the pool hall in Anchorhead. "He said it was just like *American Graffiti* in outer space," said Gary Kurtz. "He was really unhappy and I don't blame him. He was very concerned that he had made a serious error."

Lucas took a long, hard look at the sequence and decided to drop it, dooming Koo Stark's contribution to the *Star Wars* legend to the dreaded cutting-room floor.

Such revisions to the story were hardly unique, of course. Few films in history have been made precisely according to their original script. Alec Guinness did not take kindly when he discovered he too would be the victim of a script U-turn, however. It had been at the end of the Tunisia shoot that Lucas and Kurtz had become worried about Obi-Wan Kenobi's role in the latter stages of the film. At that stage the script described him being injured in a duel with Darth Vader, then rescued by Leia, Luke, and Han as they escaped in the *Millennium Falcon*. As ever, Lucas's fear was that it would slow the action down. "They would be dragging a cripple around for a big chunk of the movie," explained Kurtz. A script change in which Obi-Wan would die in the duel, then reappear as a disembodied "spirit guide" seemed the best solution to the problem. "It worked much better, he became the embodiment of the theological 'force' that was at the heart of the film," said Kurtz.

When the change reached Guinness's agent, Julian Belfrage of London Management, he threatened to withdraw his client from the production. Lucas and Kurtz were eventually able to explain the merits of their case. Kurtz admits it was an error. "It was something that should have been thought about earlier," he said.

In general Lucas's dealings with the actors was minimal. As on *THX* and *Graffiti*, he was too immersed within his own world to share his thoughts.

"All the actors complained to me that they were concerned they were doing all right, because George never talked to them," said Kurtz.

The producer had seen the same happen on *Graffiti*. "I remember Richard Dreyfuss asking George once, 'Am I still in this movie?'" he said. "All actors are insecure and they need the feedback. A big chunk of a director's job is to be there and help with that. That's one of the reasons why George gave up directing. He doesn't like interacting with people. He hated it."

As the production wore on, the actors grew to expect very little direction. "His biggest direction to me was 'Faster, more intense,'" said Mark Hamill.

Ford, the only actor who had worked with Lucas before, had an understanding of the man and his methods. He had learned to use the strength of his personality to overrule Lucas on the set of *American Graffiti*, where the director had wanted him to shave his long hair for the role of Falfa. Ford talked Lucas into allowing him to keep his shaggy mane hidden under a giant white stetson. At the costume-fitting stage in London, he had been horrified at Han Solo's camp, almost pantomime outfit. "I talked George out of making Han Solo wear a high pink, Peter Pan collar," he smiled later.

He also knew Lucas was open to the occasional joke.

In the run in to the first day of principal photography, Lucas had asked his friends Willard Huyck and Gloria Katz to polish up his script. His dialogue, in particular, was leaden and often humorless. "The Huycks came in at the end and added more humor. They were very good," recalled Kurtz. (If the dialogue had seemed peculiar at the casting, it looked odder still when the first scripts were handed out to the cast and crew. Bunny Alsup's favorite typewriter had been flown over to England and then Tunisia especially so she could produce daily script pages. When someone dropped it she was forced to use a French typewriter, complete with accents.)

Yet almost everyone found difficulties with the stilted, sci-fi psychobabble. Comparing lines became the subject of gallows humor on-set. Reading their script on the drive to a Tunisian set one morning, Anthony Daniels had turned to Mark Hamill laughing.

"How can you say this?" he asked.

Knowing Daniels had not seen his new lines, Hamill replied: "You think that's bad, look at your line. 'Curse my metal body, I wasn't fast enough.' How can you say that?"

"Because I've got a mask on and none of my friends know I'm in there," the Briton replied.

"It was not Noël Coward, let's face it," grimaced Hamill.

Carrie Fisher's least favorite line was: "I thought I recognized your foul stench when I was brought aboard, Governor Tarkin."

It was left to Harrison Ford to speak out on behalf of the cast. Ford would push Lucas as far as he could with his improvisational touches. Yet even he could not get the director to budge on occasions. Exasperated, Ford shouted at one point: "You can type this shit, George, but you sure can't say it."

Even Lucas's implacable features cracked.

For the youngest and most vulnerable member of the cast, however, the experience often proved too much. At times, Carrie Fisher didn't know whether to laugh or cry.

Fisher was deeply insecure about her looks, despite all she heard to the contrary. Lucas's friend Matthew Robbins had wanted to cast Fisher in a movie he was making about models on account of what was described as her "tremendous body." She, however, called herself "the Pillsbury doughgirl" and had been upset at her forced stay in a health farm. Her paranoia had been so intense as she arrived in England, she had expected another actress to be standing by to replace her if she did not pass her "weigh in."

Lucas, unwilling to make his characters overtly sexual, did all he could to deflect attention from his heroine's natural assets. Her hair was put up into a Nordic bun and she was given a full-length, high-collared white dress to wear. When he spotted some potentially distracting movement under the dress, he took further action.

"I had to wear that white dress and I couldn't wear a bra. Everything was bouncing around, so I had to wear gaffer tape for three months to keep my breasts down," Fisher said.

"We had no choice. She had ample breasts and she didn't wear a bra. She couldn't run around the set, it would have looked ludicrous," explained a faintly embarrassed Gary Kurtz.

Inexperienced and unsure of herself, she was the victim of Lucas's occasionally nitpicking manner. "Lucas always had to remind me, 'Stand up, be a princess!' And I would act like a Jewish princess and lean forward, slouching, chewing gum."

When Charlie Lippincott visited Elstree from Los Angeles

early on in the production, he shared Fisher's car on the way back into London. She began sobbing uncontrollably. "She was crying in the car. She really felt she wasn't doing a good job and she didn't belong in the film, she was very disheartened," he said.

Fisher explained she was being all but ignored by Lucas on the set. "I don't know if he really likes me," she cried to Lippincott.

After reassuring Fisher and seeing her back to her hotel, Lippincott called Lucas at home. His reaction to his colleague's description of his journey home with Fisher was monosyllabic. "He said: 'Well?'" recalled Lippincott. "I said: 'I think she really needs you to take her aside and talk to her.'"

"Oh," Lucas replied.

Lippincott explained the actress simply needed a "vote of confidence."

"Really think I ought to do that?" asked Lucas.

"Please," said Lippincott.

"Oh, all right," said Lucas.

Lippincott had seen a similar approach on his last film before joining the *Star Wars* team. Lucas seemed to share Alfred Hitchcock's infamous dictum that actors should be "treated like cattle."

"He would talk to an actor probably more than Hitch, because he didn't sit on the sidelines like Hitch did," explained Lippincott, the late director's publicist on *Family Plot*. "But he really didn't expect to have to go through a whole thing with an actor or actress. And she really needed hand-holding at that point."

Fisher's insecurities would soon lead her into the darkest period of her life. On weekends she would binge on cocaine and, occasionally, LSD. She would prepare herself for work at the beginning of the week with intakes of the depressant Percodan. It would take her years to beat her drug demons.

"Even on *Star Wars* she had drug problems," said Peter Mayhew. "It was normally after a weekend off. I can remember one Monday morning she came on and she didn't want to know anybody."

Her strongest support came in the handsome form of her fellow Americans. The trio, all living in central London, would spend nights at trendy restaurants, The Hard Rock Cafe in particular. The dynamics of Fisher, Ford, and Hamill's off-screen relationship was an almost mirror image of *Star Wars*. Hamill later admitted he had a serious crush on his costar. Fisher had been awestruck by Ford's tall good looks and laconic manner the moment she met him.

"You look at Harrison and you listen, he looks like he's carrying a gun even if he isn't. He's this incredibly attractive male animal, in every sense of the word. This carpenter stud," she said. "I've never had that same impression of anyone else in my life. I knew he was going to be a star—someone of the order of Tracy or Bogart."

The trio became inseparable—Ford and Fisher particularly so. "Whenever anyone couldn't find Harrison, you'd say, 'Have you tried Carrie Fisher's changing room?'" said Dave Prowse.

Until he had visited Berman's, the theatrical costumers, Prowse had been under the impression his face would be seen in *Star Wars*. Instead, to his disappointment, he discovered he was expected to wear an elaborate, all-black costume—part Samurai swordsman, part Horseman of the Apocalypse—complete with a flowing cape, a polished, Nazi stormtrooper-style helmet and a modified World War II gas mask.

"I didn't know it was a masked part, it wasn't until I went to Berman's that I realized my face would be covered up," he recalled.

Prowse, like the other masked actors, often found it

difficult to see exactly what was going on. During the climactic duel between Vader and Obi-Wan, he terrified Lucas by accidentally throwing Alec Guinness to the floor.

"We had been practicing the scene every spare half an hour or so," said Prowse. "It was the bit where we were sort of smashing away at each other, like the old Errol Flynn stuff." At one point the two men locked lightsabers close up before pushing each other away. "I really entered into the enthusiasm of the thing and he really went flying," admitted Prowse. As a frail-looking Guinness lay on the floor, Kurtz, Lucas, and others were panic-stricken. "Everyone raced over to pick him up."

Given the speed, scale, and surreal nature of what actors were being asked to do, accidents were inevitable. During one scene, the floor had been dusted with salt for photographic effect. No one, however, had told the actors playing the stormtroopers who had to run along the set. "They all fell flat on their backs like the first day at Harrods' sale," laughed Anthony Daniels. "They completely lost their dignity." The pyrotechnics were too much for some stormtroopers to cope with, according to Daniels. "They would wince too much at explosions and be quite un-butch!" There was much to wince at.

"They overdid the explosions a couple of times," said Kenny Baker. "They nearly blew the set apart."

Yet the frenzied pace often produced moments of unexpected humor. Filming a second unit scene in which Chewbacca is confronted with a rodent-sized robot, Lucas had the idea of reversing the old joke about the elephant and the mouse. He asked Mayhew to roar and had the mouse robot turn on its wheels in terror. The ad-libbed scene worked beautifully.

No one was better suited to the improvisational atmosphere than Harrison Ford. Unlike the comic-book obsessed Lucas, Ford had little interest in science fiction. Even as a little boy in Chicago, he had preferred Mickey Mouse and Donald Duck to Flash Gordon and Superman.

"I didn't go to those Buck Rogers matinees. I don't know anything about science fiction," he explained later. "It was simply straightforward, a clear human story. I mean I didn't have to act science fiction."

Instead he used his own arid humor to flesh out Solo's sardonic side. Ford would often turn up for a scene to announce he intended improvizing in one take.

"Stop me if I'm really bad," he would tell Lucas.

He pulled off two of Solo's best moments—first when, lost for words, he blasts a communicator to pieces and later when he cautions a sharpshooting Luke with the words, "Great kid. Don't get cocky"—by making up his performance as he went along.

Lucas remained a distant, sometimes disconsolate figure, however. "He did not like it here, he did not like the crew, he didn't like being away from Mill Valley, he didn't like the food," said Gary Kurtz, who, in contrast formed a lasting affection for London. "I don't think he had a good time here at all."

Lucas did little to hide his disillusionment. In June the *Los Angeles Times* critic, Charles Champlin, whom Lucas knew and liked, became one of the handful of journalists invited to visit the set. Ladd and Ashley Boone had felt a little early publicity—complete with a collection of high quality, appetite-whetting stills of R2-D2 and C-3PO, Chewbacca and a pair of stormtroopers, Luke and Obi-Wan—would simultaneously calm nerves inside Fox and stir interest among the public. Champlin, however, found Lucas in philosophical mood. He admitted he wondered whether he should have simply left *Star Wars* on the shelf after *Graffiti* became a hit.

"The truth is that out of what I've made from *Graffiti* I could, by living fairly modestly, get along without having to earn another dime," he confessed.

Lucas was simply not equipped for the daily warfare that came with a movie production of this scale. "When the budget goes beyond $2 million or $3 million another law takes over. You lose the personal touch, the personal contact with every aspect of the movie—unless you're a Kubrick who can take all the time that's required to oversee all the details yourself," he said.

He wished he was back in California or New York, making small, experimental films or working at the gallery. "I doubt if I'll ever do anything this big again. My personal attitudes are just not prone to this kind of enterprise," he sighed. "I like being a captain rather than a general."

As the final days of filming approached, Lucas felt like the captain of a rapidly sinking ship. With Ray Gosnell at Fox turning the financial screw even tighter, he and Kurtz knew they would have to use three units during the last week of filming. They still had the crucial opening sequence, in which Darth Vader and his stormtroopers battled their way on to Princess Leia's ship. One evening walking around John Barry's elaborate sets they realized they faced one last obstacle.

Barry had been a paragon of economy with his sets. Wherever possible hardware was used in more than one scene. The rounded computer console used to house the computerized "ticking clock" on the rebel's base in the climax, had doubled as the ceiling of a spacecraft.

"John saved us a lot of money in that sort of way," said Kurtz.

As they walked the corridors of the Death Star, however, Lucas and Kurtz realized he had been too frugal. "There weren't enough corridors," said Kurtz.

The producer had to make another begging call to Ladd in Los Angeles. "I had to ask Laddie for $50,000 more to build two more corridors."

On that occasion Ladd released the money. Soon, however, Fox's accountants were being less understanding. The call came through from Los Angeles—telling them they had seven days to finish the film.

Again Kurtz and Lucas resented the fact that it was simply Hollywood power play. Kurtz had worked out that it would have been cheaper to keep the set open for two normal working weeks than to work overtime with three camera units for a week. "That's not the point, it's psychological," Gosnell told him.

The final scenes were filmed at breakneck speed. Lucas's training as a seat-of-the-pants filmmaker at USC helped him adapt to the crisis. The sight of the sweaty, bearded figure furiously pedaling his bicycle as he raced from one sound stage to the next put a cynical smile on the faces of the older British crew members.

For Lucas the only consolation was that at least the torture was over. He had already begun promising himself he would never direct a movie again.

Gary Kurtz recognized, like his friend and colleague, Lucas was simply unsuited to the job. "He is very easygoing with a close group of friends, but in a group he is reticent," said Kurtz. He also saw the immense toll the worry took on him physically. "He was so exhausted worrying about all the details. He was afraid that if he let anything go it wouldn't be right," explained Gary Kurtz. "He almost had a breakdown because of that."

The transatlantic cousins left Elstree, deflated, divided, and doubtful their months together would amount to very much at all. For all the reassurances that the film would be transformed by the special effects, most of the cast left suspecting they had contributed to a turkey.

'Are you sure Orson Welles started this way?'
George Lucas on location in Tunisia for the filming of *Star Wars*.

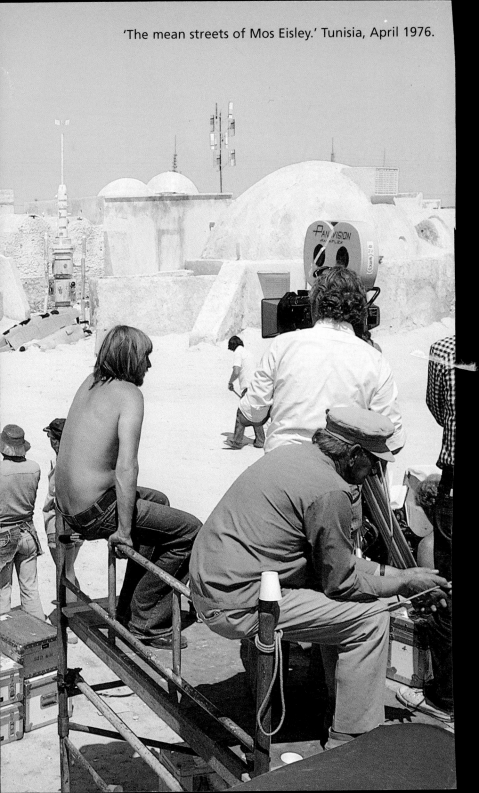

'The mean streets of Mos Eisley.' Tunisia, April 1976.

'Life in a biscuit tin.'
Anthony Daniels is shielded
from the desert sun.

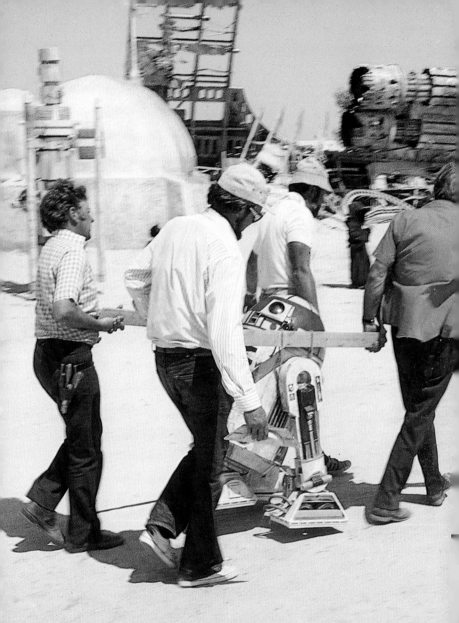

More robot trouble.
R2-D2 is dragged across the Tunisian desert.

In 'Star Wars Valley'.
Lucas, Hamill and Guinness at work in Tunisia.

Old Man of the desert:
Alec Guinness entertains Gary Kurtz's daughters Melissa and Tiffany.

Mark Hamill on set with Meredith Kurtz.

Junior Jawas. Melissa and Tiffany Kurtz at play in the Sahara.

Filming the Mos Eisley cantina. Elstree, May 1976.

'Is your landspeeder leaded or unleaded, sir?' Tunisia, April 1976.

Mark Hamill and Peter Mayhew as Chewbacca filming *Star Wars*' finale at Shepperton, summer 1976.

Above: 'Stand up, be a Princess.' Carrie Fisher forces a smile as *The Empire Strikes Back* is premiered in London.

Above right: On the awards trail. Mark Hamill collects one of *Star Wars*' myriad honours at the Sci-Fi Awards.

Right: Han Solo in full flight. Harrison Ford during a break from filming.

Left: Slaves to the Empire: (left to right) Harrison Ford, Dave Prowse, Peter Mayhew, Carrie Fisher, Kenny Baker and Mark Hamill in London prior to the premiere of *The Empire Strikes Back*.

When the war was over: Lucas with R2-D2 and C-3PO at celebrations to mark *Star Wars'* tenth anniversary in 1987.

"We all thought it was rubbish," said Anthony Daniels.

"They didn't understand, they thought we were making a really silly movie," remarked Gary Kurtz.

At the "wrap" party, a practical joke on Kurtz by the British camp summed up the uneasy, seventeen-week marriage. The Amish-bearded producer was presented with a gift, wrapped in a large box. He opened it to discover another, smaller box inside. Like a Russian doll, the package shrunk, layer after layer, until it was the size of a matchbox. When he finally saw what he had been given, his face froze.

"He opened it up and it was a little mustache," said Dave Prowse. "It went down like a lead balloon."

CHAPTER 6

Money to Burn

In the late summer of 1976 Lucas returned to San Anselmo, relieved to be back in an environment where he could at least watch his favorite television shows and get a decent hamburger. He even took Marcia for a brief break in Hawaii as a minicelebration. As he lay on the beach at their favorite hideaway, the Mauna Kea Hotel on Maui, the sound of the waves washed away the months of unpleasant memories. The idyll would be short-lived.

His first shock was the discovery that the preliminary editing work was a disaster. The assembly of shots and scenes he viewed at Parkhouse bore no resemblance to the picture he had carried in his mind in England. "We had to start from scratch," he said.

The reconstruction he was faced with amounted to an extra three-month delay. Yet he knew Fox was committed to releasing the film at Christmas. The job was beyond even the man who liked to call himself "Supereditor." He hired Marcia, already committed to working on *Carrie* for Brian De

Palma and soon to start on *New York, New York* for Martin Scorsese, and two other new editors, Richard Chew and Paul Hirsch, to help him salvage the film. Together the trio worked virtually around the clock splicing footage together, guided by notes scribbled for each of them by Lucas.

Even worse was in store at ILM, however.

During their spring and summer in England, Kurtz and Lucas had been reassured that the effects work would be ready in time for insertion in the finished film that autumn and winter. Lucas had consoled himself with the thought that *Star Wars* would come to life once he had a collection of razzle-dazzle spacecraft and pyrotechnic shootouts at his disposal. Psychologically, the sight of the finished effects would lift him and his whole, beleaguered team.

Alan Ladd Jr. had sensed there was something wrong while Lucas was in Elstree. Ray Gosnell, the technical go-between who would visit the Van Nuys warehouse almost weekly on Fox's behalf, would be "red in the face" whenever he returned. Dykstra's *laissez-faire* management style meant there were no set hours, no dress code—and seemingly no discipline of any kind at the warehouse.

One particularly hot summer's day, with temperatures inside the non-air-conditioned building way over the hundred-degree mark, an escape chute from a Boeing 747 had been inflated, greased with Mazola cooking oil, then rigged up on to the outside roof. An inflatable swimming pool had been placed at its base. Most of the staff then stripped down to their underwear and took turns riding the makeshift water slide.

No sooner had they got the hang of the ride than a limousine pulled up with two Fox executives. "Here we were, about to change the whole film industry with our work—but at that moment we no doubt confirmed their worst suspicions that we were a bunch of goof-offs," said one of the ILM team, Jon Erland.

On another occasion an ILM member insisted on talking to a party from Fox while wearing a fish-head mask. On yet another, a limousine full of film company executives arrived to see the operation's supposed mastermind, Dykstra, astride a forklift. His Kris Kristofferson–like mane flowing in the breeze, he was raising a refrigerator into the sky. "The refrigerator had died. So we had a sort of ceremony," Dykstra said, shaking his head in disbelief at the memory. The idea was to haul the appliance high in the air and then drop it to the ground, "to see what would happen."

Yet Dykstra defended his team to the hilt. Temperatures inside the brick warehouse would sometimes reach 115 degrees. "So generally we worked at night, when it was only ninety," he said. "Nobody left there before midnight, often three or four A.M. The average week was close to sixty hours."

It was only when Lucas and Kurtz arrived in the warehouse in the smog-filled San Fernando Valley that they became aware of the full extent of the problem.

Dykstra and his team had assembled a collection of formidable looking equipment, including an impressive, computer-controlled, crane-mounted camera, able to make the complex, corkscrew movements Lucas had asked for. The camera had been christened the "Dykstraflex" after its creator.

Colin Cantwell and his team had also come up with an array of stunning models. The rebel X Wing and imperial TIE fighters, Han Solo's *Millennium Falcon*, and a giant Imperial Cruiser were minor miracles of the model-making art. With Ralph McQuarrie's matte paintings and other optical developments, there was an impressive library of elements to be blended together into finished shots. When Lucas asked to see footage combining the departments' work, however, he was horrified.

In the warehouse's screening room, a crude setup with

flea-ridden sofas and the smell of aromatic cigarette smoke in the air, he watched a brief selection of shots of the models. All bar one—of the escape pod in which R2-D2 and C-3PO escape Princess Leia's ship at the film's opening—were unusable. "They had spent a year and $1 million and had only come up with one acceptable shot," Lucas fumed later.

"That's when it dawned on us we weren't going to finish the picture in time," said Kurtz.

Lucas was distraught. His express instructions to Dykstra had been to concentrate on getting shots for *Star Wars* rather than developing new technology. "John, it seemed to me, became obsessed with the research work to the exclusion of the practical matter of shooting the movie effects," he moaned.

Dykstra, however, felt Lucas had been unrealistic. Like so many directors, he argued, he had no idea of the practicalities involved in translating an idea in his mind on to film. Lucas's introverted "I know best" manner only made the situation worse as far as he was concerned. "Communication was a real hassle between myself and the director," he said later. In hindsight, Dykstra understood his employer's anger. "There were nine maniacs in this garage warehouse in Van Nuys, spending money ferociously and no film was coming out," said Dykstra. "I think if I had been George I would have wanted to kill me too."

Dykstra simply did not conform to Lucas's idea of an employee. He would often turn up for meetings in skimpy shorts, his hair, as he put it, "down to his ass." "Perhaps he was looking for someone who was more malleable," said Dykstra. "I'm sure from George's point of view, if we'd been more regimented, more organized, he would have gotten a product that was better. He might be right. But then he had the wrong guy, because that was the only way I knew how to do it."

Lucas left Los Angeles, shattered by the disappointment.

On the plane back to San Francisco he began experiencing chest pains. He stepped off the flight and headed straight to Marin General Hospital where he was diagnosed as having hypertension and exhaustion. As he lay in bed, he was not the only one wondering whether the *Star Wars* dream was over.

Lucas was discharged from the hospital under strict instructions to reduce the stress level in his complex life. In his mind he had already made a firm decision never to direct a film again. "It's like fighting a fifteen-round heavyweight bout with a new opponent every day," he said later. "I don't like to be always angry—and on this I was a lot." Yet, bitter and resentful as he was, he knew he had a few, short months to salvage *Star Wars*—and perhaps his filmmaking career. Rather than easing down, he slipped up a gear.

While Marcia, Chew, and Hirsch continued with the editing, Lucas became a regular figure on the PSA shuttle between San Francisco and Los Angeles. For a few nights each week he would book himself into a cheap hotel near the ILM factory where he set about personally supervising the special effects work. John Dykstra remained on the site overseeing the photographic work, but he was kept at a distance. Lucas was now the boss. His cool, calculating, sometimes remote manner could not have presented a starker contrast to Dykstra's freewheeling philosophy.

The transition was a difficult one to handle for the ILM team who remained fiercely loyal to the charismatic Dykstra. As ever, Lucas's perfectionism was not allied to interpersonal skills. He would often arrive at the beginning of a new week to run an eye over the weekend's work. He would walk quietly around the site, shaking his head. The tension that preceded his visits soon had Erland muttering: "I can't take too many more of these Mondays."

Lasting friendships had been forged in the heat. Lucas's

arrival dampened the spirits. "This was a big, happy family. Everybody was going camping together, fishing together," said Jim Nelson. "It was just not quite as loose when he was around."

As he stalked the offices Lucas remained silent, living deep inside his thoughts. "He'd just walk by you in the hall and never say a word. He lives in his own world, he's not a warm, friendly guy," recalled Nelson. Yet when he did not like something he wasted neither time nor words. "George is very critical, so you know, when he didn't like something, you'd know in a minute. He'd tell you 'I hate it.'"

Sometimes he would dispatch an emissary to pass on his displeasure. Peterson and Erland planned to let Dykstra shoot much of the climactic dogfight in the ILM parking lot, using a giant, sixteen hundred square foot molding of the surface of the Death Star, held together by a sea of 3M tape. Staff spent endless hours patching together the model, only to be told by Marcia Lucas—sent over to assess the model by her husband—that it had to be scaled down even further.

The tense atmosphere was not helped by an impromptu screening of some of the non–special effects scenes filmed at Elstree. The footage was unpolished and unintelligible. No music or sound effects had been added. The sight of Fisher, Ford, and Hamill in the prison-rescue sequence and the sound of Darth Vader's bizarre, muffled West Country accent left the seven or eight staff members who saw the film deflated. The artist Harrison Ellenshaw, who was working on the matte paintings, had harbored his doubts since seeing a storyboard featuring Chewbacca. "*King Kong* had just been bashed critically and here was some kind of monkey thing. I thought it was a huge mistake," he recalled.

According to Pete Kuran, another ILM staff member in the screening room that night, everyone was left dumbfounded. "The reaction was kind of like 'Uhhh?' After that nobody thought it would be a hit," he said.

. . .

Kurtz and Lucas faced the reality that *Star Wars* would not be ready for Christmas. Ladd, who had been hoping to make the film its main release for the holiday market, rescheduled it for the following summer. As the costs and the rumors surrounding the "Animal House" atmosphere at ILM grew, the troubled production inevitably began to attract unwanted attention at the studio. During the early months of filming, Fox's attitude to *Star Wars* had been "out of sight, out of mind." At the monthly board or executive committee meetings they were expected to attend, Ladd, Kanter, and Wigan were rarely asked about the film.

"It wasn't a very significant thing at all," recalled Wigan. "There were no stars in it and it was being made in England. So it was fairly off the corner of the map. And probably that was a good thing."

In the wake of its rescheduling, the mood changed, however.

"There was tremendous grumbling and real concern," said Wigan.

The fears were justified. If the most a science-fiction film had ever earned in America was $15 million and *Star Wars* was going to cost $11 million before advertising and printing costs the implications were obvious.

"In those days there was a very limited international market. You didn't consider it. The only market was domestic, theatrical and we were just beginning with sales to network television, there was no cable either," said Gareth Wigan. "It was regarded as a money loser."

Adding to the unease was the problem that no one at Fox seemed to understand the complexities of the technology *Star Wars* relied on. Gareth Wigan recalled sitting in a series of meetings with Ray Gosnell and Fox's production people.

"People would say, 'Well, this shot has sixteen elements.' And I remember saying to Ray Gosnell, "What *is* an element

Ray?" And he said: 'I don't really understand it myself, but...'"

Gosnell visited ILM weekly. He admits the new technology left him baffled—as it did most people. "Nobody understood postproduction," he said. "You would ask ILM, 'Well what did you accomplish yesterday?' They would tell you they rolled the camera twelve times but they didn't have anything finished. You can't tell somebody on the board of directors what that means."

In his meetings with Ladd, Gosnell came up with a coding system to identify shots which were completed, half completed—or even less. "One shot may have been only one fifteenth what the shot was going to be, just with the stars put in or whatever," he explained. "It was virtually impossible at that particular time. Now it seems common, everybody knows about it. At that time it was like putting your money in the middle of the street and burning it."

As the studio's unease grew, Lucas did little to calm nerves by demanding yet more money. He was still deeply unhappy with a number of the non–special effects sequences he had filmed in London and Tunisia. The Mos Eisley Cantina—conceived as a deep space version of *Dante's Inferno*—looked more like a scene from *The Tales of Beatrix Potter*. Stuart Freeborn's premature departure had left Lucas with a scene in which Luke, Obi-Wan, Chewbacca, and Han Solo mingled with a mouselike lady, a walrus-headed man and a creature that resembled a pig. He was also dissatisfied with his footage of Luke and his landspeeder and R2-D2. Kenny Baker's difficulties in making the droid move and the general unreliability of the remote-controlled models had also left him without any film in which R2-D2 was seen to move more than two or three feet at a time. He and Kurtz were forced to ask Alan Ladd Jr. for an extra $100,000 to finish the sequences.

Ladd had cushioned Lucas and Kurtz from the increasingly negative messages coming into his office. "You try to make them feel free," he explained later. "You can't go to George Lucas in the middle of making *Star Wars* and tell him, 'Some of the members of the board of directors don't like your movie.' It's not going to contribute anything to what he's trying to accomplish."

Lucas appreciated Ladd's unusual hands-off approach— even at times of crisis. "I liked the fact he left me alone," he said later. Now, however, he faced his biggest crisis. It would be the cue for Ladd's finest hour.

Ladd knew there were those on the Fox board who hated "that science movie." Yet he had much going for him. In August 1976 he had been promoted to president of Fox's film division. The move was recognition for the increasing number of big name filmmakers Ladd's "family atmosphere" was attracting to the studio.

None of his talented family would owe Ladd as much as George Lucas. Whatever his private misgivings, publicly his faith in *Star Wars* had remained unshakeable. "There never was any question in his mind, he really believed in it that much," recalled Johnny Friedkin, then a member of the Fox publicity and marketing department.

Around the Fox building, Ladd's seemingly blind belief in *Star Wars* had almost become a joke. "He kept saying, 'This is going to be the biggest-grossing picture in the history of the industry,' and we'd say, 'When did they let him out of the asylum,'" said Friedkin.

"He was the guy that went to the line on it. Certainly, had it not been successful, it would have been the end of his job," said Ray Gosnell.

Until now Ladd had never risked voicing his opinion to the board, however.

In a scene that could have come from one of his father's westerns, Ladd walked in to see the fourteen-strong body; a lone gunslinger faced with an ugly lynch mob. When they demanded to know how the *Star Wars* budget had spiraled so hopelessly out of control, he fell silent for a while then replied: "Because it's possibly the greatest picture ever made." He then got up and walked out.

Ladd was soon able to tell Lucas he had an extra $20,000 to finish his film. That, however, was the end of his money. It would have to be enough to finish *Star Wars*.

"We didn't really know what was going on, we just trusted—as it turned out with complete justification—in the genius of George Lucas to pull it off," recalled Gareth Wigan. "What else were we going to do? We had no alternative."

As winter wore on, Lucas and Kurtz began to turn the film around through the sheer force of their will. They introduced a stricter management style, with Nelson and a new appointment, George Mather, as no-nonsense overseers. Kurtz had been horrified at some of the practices. Camera crews would shoot footage of models then sit around for hours waiting to see the results from the photo-lab before moving on. "They would do this elaborate setup, shoot it, then send it off to a lab. In the meantime they sat around waiting for the footage to come back, it was insane," he said. "The fact was that ILM was not well managed." Kurtz insisted that the crew move from one setup to the next without hesitation. Rarely did they need to reshoot because of problems with the developed footage.

As he and Lucas took charge, Kurtz also realized the switch from back projection to blue screen may have been a blessing in disguise. "We were frustrated by it at the time. But it changed our concept of how to do it. We realized we could use shots over again which you couldn't the other way," he explained.

To many, Gary Kurtz was the unsung hero of *Star Wars*. As a nuts and bolts man, he was close to genius. "Gary's a walking computer. The man has got more stuff in his head than half the computers in Silicon Valley," said Jim Nelson.

He also had the ability to handle every aspect of a film's production—right down to looking after the most complex cameras. "I used to say he's the only producer you can send out on location who can fix the Nagra and Paraflex camera when it breaks. He just knows all this stuff."

When Johnny Friedkin at Fox once had a problem with still photographs from the film, Kurtz went to the laboratory to sort it out himself. "The guy was on the phone to me asking, 'Why did you send that guy? He knows more than me,'" Friedkin said.

As far as Kurtz was concerned his job was simply to allow Lucas to fulfill his vision. "If George ever really knew what Gary did behind the scenes for him, he'd be on his knees. Because he took care of everything, everything. Or hired the guy who could. Everything was kept away from George so he could be creative," said Jim Nelson.

As ILM finally fell into shape, Lucas's creative genius was allowed free rein. Lucas knew the key to the success of the film lay in the credibility of his spacecraft. Two sequences in particular—a long track along the underside of a vast Imperial cruiser at the very beginning, and the final assault on the Death Star—would define the film's success as far as he was concerned. To give his team an idea of what he wanted, Lucas assembled a montage of shots from World War I and II pictures like *The Blue Max*, *633 Squadron* and *Tora, Tora, Tora*. In time the elaborate visual storyboards would be recognized as another of *Star Wars'* innovations. At that precise moment, however, it seemed like the only way to get his message across.

If there was a turning point at ILM it came at Christmas when they were shown a finished trailer, prepared for release at cinemas by Fox. As the overture of the Mars suite from Holtz's *The Planets* rumbled into life, staff dropped what they were doing and ran to the screening room. Huge cheers greeted the end of the footage. The despair that greeted the screening of the roughcut prison sequence was replaced with elation. The knowledge that they were not working on a white elephant revived the demoralized staff. "Whenever somebody got really depressed, we'd run the trailer to cheer them up," recalled ILM staffer Lorne Peterson. ILM had finally turned the corner.

The sense that their pioneering way of filmmaking actually worked produced an adrenal atmosphere. "Another first," colleagues would shout to each other. "Some other new thing had been done that we knew hadn't been done before. This was going on every day and was very exciting," recalled Richard Edlund. Back at Parkhouse, there was, by now, more to please Lucas in the editing suite as he added the sound track to the emerging movie. Sound engineer Ben Burtt's ingenuity had produced remarkable results.

Burtt collected sounds in the way Lucas collected comic books as a child. Armed with a tape recorder he had spent days at Los Angeles Airport, the aviation company Northrup Aircraft, military bases and air shows, recording a variety of jet engine sounds suitable for the *Millennium Falcon*. He had also slowed down the sound of the Goodyear blimp as the basis for the sound of the Imperial Cruisers.

At USC he had recorded the humming sound of cinema projectors, blended it with static from the tube of his television set and produced an eerie throbbing sound suitable for the lightsabers. The sound of the lasers had been created by hitting a long cable attached to a tall radio tower. (His father had accidentally walked into one while out walking with him!) Elsewhere the inventive youngster had utilized everything from the sound of his kitchen blender and fridge to assorted animals at the Los Angeles zoo for the creatures.

Burtt had developed voices for all the main non-human

characters. Chewbacca's anguished roar was an amalgam of four different kinds of bears, a walrus, a seal, and a badger. For the Jawas he had speeded up a Zulu dialect, while for Greedo, the bounty hunting alien Han Solo would dispatch in the Cantina scene, he had hired Larry Ward, a linguistic expert at Berkeley to read in Quechua, an Andean tongue. Perhaps most innovative of all, R2-D2's electronic whittering had been achieved by scraping dry ice against scraps of metal and blowing through a length of water piping. (Lucas had rejected the idea of making the robot sound like a touch-tone telephone.)

Lucas had still to decide on voices for C-3PO and Darth Vader, however. He had disliked Anthony Daniels's Admirable Crichton voice from the moment he had heard it in Tunisia. Stubborn as ever, he had scoured L.A. for an alternative. Stan Freeberg, the comedian and impersonator, was called in to record half a dozen or so different variations. Yet the more he had watched the footage of the Englishman tottering around in his outfit, the more his voice seemed to fit.

Lucas could not stick with the accent of his film's villain, however. Dave Prowse had been primed to do post-production recording in Los Angeles. But Lucas couldn't help but lean towards Carrie Fisher's view that he was more down-to-earth Darth Farmer than Lord Vader, the most malignant force in the universe.

Lucas at one point considered using the Dirty Dozen's hero, Orson Welles, for the role. Eventually he chose the distinguished James Earl Jones, Oscar-nominated star of the 1970 hit *The Great White Hope* and one of Hollywood's few Shakespearean specialists. Jones's resonant baritone, especially when fed through an electronic filter and augmented with simulated heavy breathing, sounded truly menacing. Jones was apparently paid a mere $10,000—and given no screen credit—for an assignment he would become known for worldwide.

Dave Prowse was understandably indignant. "I was actually supposed to go into the studio and do it over," he said. "I was in Los Angeles having breakfast with Gary Kurtz and I said, 'Come on Gary why didn't you use my voice for Darth Vader?' And he said, 'Well, Dave, we just couldn't play Darth Vader with a West Country accent,'" he recalled. The man inside the mask later suspected a darker truth. "I think they had dropped a huge clanger and cast the entire film without a black person," he said. Prowse, who was subsequently grateful to Jones for never having taken credit for acting the role, was less charitable about his voiceover. "James Earl Jones did a terrible job, he sounded like a very aged old man," he complained.

The trailer may have worked inside ILM, but when it was released to a thousand cinemas across America in the run-up to Christmas the wider world were faintly bewildered. Predictably, the science-fiction community adored the montage of images of R2-D2 and C-3PO, stormtroopers and the lightsaber duel between Obi-Wan Kenobi and Darth Vader. "They were crazy to see the movie six months before it came out," Lucas said later. Others, however, were not so sure. Some people groaned when they heard the phrase: "Coming to your galaxy this summer." Others laughed out loud.

Friedkin, chief publicist Ashley Boone, and the publicity staff felt it was important to establish some form of awareness and argued they should be kept on the screen regardless. It was Alan Ladd who pulled the trailers after a phone call from Gene Wilder. The actor had been in a Westwood cinema as an audience had begun giggling at the sight of R2-D2 falling over. "Gene said, 'Laddie, they're laughing at your picture,'" recalled Johnny Friedkin. As word of the conversation trickled around Hollywood, Ladd showed his first—and only—sign of panic. "Laddie got a little bit hysterical over that," added Friedkin.

Ordinarily the brilliant young "monster maker" Rick Baker would have expected to have six weeks to make a single creature. At the end of 1976 George Lucas gave him the same period to produce two and a half dozen.

As the New Year approached, and with the last of his extra budget dwindling fast, Lucas stepped up the pace even further. The cantina scene was exercising him most.

Baker, one of the few to emerge from Dino De Laurentiis's woeful *King Kong* with any credit, worked around the clock with colleagues Jon Berg, Laine Liska, Doug Beswick, Tom St. Amand and Phil Tippett. A dozen new creatures, supplemented with a collection of castoffs from previous films, including a werewolf and a Devil's head made years earlier, were then taken to a small sound stage on La Brea where Lucas had enough money to spend two days shooting. All six of the creature makers were press-ganged into wearing the latex masks they had designed for a bug-eyed swing band. The heat in the studio was so intense it became almost impossible to breathe. "We were sweating like mad," recalled Tippett. "The masks filled up with moisture, causing us to choke on our own juices. We couldn't get any air and we couldn't see anything because the eyepieces were fogged."

It was Gary Kurtz who put them out of their misery. Tippett and the others suddenly felt a "blessed rush of air." It was only later he was able to see Kurtz using a razor blade to cut an air hole in the neck of another of the masked musicians. "I got a little freaked out when I realized that the executive producer had been working an inch away from my throat with a very sharp blade," recalled Tippett.

Lucas seemed in his element shooting the sequence,

filmed on an informal, "let's have fun with this" basis. Yet elsewhere it was still difficult to detect his sense of humor.

Another old USC pal, Dan O'Bannon, had been hired to help with the computer graphics needed in various craft cockpits and for the final Death Star sequence as the planet Yavin slowly slips into firing range. With designer John Wash, O'Bannon had struggled to overcome his aversion to the nuts and bolts of computer graphic work. O'Bannon asked Lucas at one point what would happen if the graphics failed to work out. "George looked at Dan very calmly and told him that he would have a title card made up saying that the scene was missing because Dan O'Bannon screwed up," recalled John Wash. No one was sure whether he was joking or not.

One final disaster awaited the film. Lucas had picked a location in Death Valley to film new scenes featuring Luke's landspeeder. By now near complete exhaustion, he had asked his director friend Carroll Ballard to help him with the camera work. Lucas had been pleased by the new capabilities of the landspeeder. In Tunisia its supports and wheels had been visible as had the tracks it left in its wake. At 5 A.M. on the morning of the shoot Lucas's phone rang. Gary Kurtz broke the news that Mark Hamill had been involved in a serious car accident on the Antelope Freeway the night before and was in Los Angeles County General Hospital.

Hamill woke up that morning amid a scene from an episode of *M*A*S*H*. "There's a guy moaning next to me, and some intern says 'We're gonna take him next because he's in worse shape than you are, and you're in pretty bad shape,'" Hamill recalled. "And he holds a mirror up to my face and it looks like a raspberry pie. My nose was off."

Hamill recalled nothing of his accident. "I don't even remember getting in the car." He later discovered that his new BMW had catapulted off the road and rolled thirty feet down a steep incline before hitting the ground.

Kurtz told Lucas that Hamill would be hospitalized for days. Eventually his nose would be rebuilt using cartilage from his ear. (As it turned out, the accident would release him from a commitment to the ABC television comedy *Eight Is Enough* that he had desperately been trying to escape from in case *Star Wars* was a success. ABC had threatened to cancel the series and sue Hamill in a test case if he pulled out.)

Back in Death Valley, the director frantically rescheduled his shooting plans, using a double for the shots of Luke. While he waited for the double to arrive, he went ahead with new shots of the giant "banthas." An elephant from Marine World trained to put its trunk in its mouth had been dressed up in an elaborate costume by art director Leon Erickson. Lucas's already overstretched patience ran out as the elephant repeatedly shrugged off its costume. None of the bantha closeups were usable. Only one long-range shot of the creature made it into the final version of the film.

As the sun beat down on Death Valley and the surreal scene unfolded, Lucas later recalled thinking he had reached the end of his tether. "I just wanted to get done with the damn movie."

As Charlie Lippincott hauled his bulky *Star Wars* portfolio around the floor of the annual New York toy fair in February 1977, Lucas's dreams of wind-up C-3POs and model *Millennium Falcons* looked even more fantastical than his film.

Despite the deals with Marvel comics and Del Rey books, the toy industry had proved a much tougher nut to crack.

Lippincott had been around Hollywood long enough to know toys were a difficult proposition. Most of America's major toymakers—Mattel, Fisher Price, Aurora, and Ideal—

believed it was television rather than cinema where the licensing lucre lay. Shows like the *Six Million Dollar Man* and—most of all—*Charlie's Angels* were week-in-week-out favorites. Spinoff toys featuring the series' married stars, Lee and Farrah Fawcett Majors, were the hottest properties in America's toy stores. Films, on the other hand, came and went all too quickly. The two industries had enjoyed their occasional moments of shared passion. Shirley Temple dolls, Charlie Chaplin figurines, Gene Autry guitars, Marilyn Monroe paper dolls, and Tarzan lunch boxes had done good business in years gone by. Yet of the major studios, only Disney had maintained a lasting marriage with the toy and T-shirt makers. When Ingersoll-Waterbury first launched the Mickey Mouse watch in 1933, Macy's sold eleven thousand on the first day—even in the depths of the Depression. Every generation had grown up wearing Mickey T-shirts, caps, or wristwatches. Four decades later, eight thousand Disney products were produced as part of sixteen hundred worldwide licenses generating $2 billion a year. If George Lucas had had a model in his mind as he had outlined his dream of *Star Wars* shops to Lippincott two years earlier, it had been that of Disney. Lucas had never forgotten his sense of wonder during his first visits to Disneyland as a boy. He saw R2-D2, C-3PO, Chewbacca, and Darth Vader as the heirs to Mickey, Minnie, Daffy, and Pluto.

As Lippincott was discovering, however, the toy manufacturers could not agree with him. Lippincott and Fox's Marc Pevers, traveled to the industry's main sales convention, held in New York in a glass tower on Twenty-third and Broadway in an effort to place a foot in the toymaker's door. Lippincott almost got thrown out for his trouble.

Sticking to their policy of working with the top names in each field, Lippincott had first approached Mattel, makers of such hits as the bestselling "Hot Wheels" toy cars. For

Mattel, however, the thought of joining forces with Twentieth Century–Fox only reminded them of Hollywood's greatest merchandising fiasco.

The company had worked with the studio on merchandising Richard Fleischer's 1967 spectacular, *Doctor Dolittle*, starring Rex Harrison. When the film bombed at the box office, Mattel had been left holding a multi–million dollar loss to match the studio's. Most of the three hundred Doctor Dolittle items—from clocks, watches, and hats to medicine kits and Rex Harrison dolls that would chirp "Hello, I'm Dr. Dolittle" at the pull of a string—had been returned from the shops. The value of the unsold merchandise was conservatively estimated at $200 million. The disaster had been a watershed—not just at Fox but all over Hollywood.

"*Doctor Dolittle* killed off merchandising tie-ins for the next decade," said one retired Fox promotions man. "I'll bet there are still Mattel warehouses in California bursting at the seams with it."

Lippincott would have been delighted to work with Mattel, but the company received him coolly. A representative from the company flicked through the brochure he had prepared featuring images of the key characters and models. If firms showed interest, Lippincott would provide a slide show. "They were not interested," he recalled.

The reception was even cooler elsewhere. One powerful family-run company, with interests in Hong Kong and America, even went so far as to throw Lippincott out from its stand at the toy fair. He had walked in to see one of the two sons that ran the company with their father. Marc Pevers had dealt with the company before and introduced Lippincott who offered a copy of his *Star Wars* brochure.

"He was a tall hustler in his late twenties," Lippincott remembered. "He said: 'I'm not interested in that.'" When he asked Pevers whether Lippincott was an employee of Fox, his anger built. "Marc said no. He said: 'I want him out of the office right now.'"

Lippincott and Pevers spent a frustrating week at the toy fair. By the end, only one major toy manufacturer, Kenner, a division of General Mills, was seriously interested in working on the idea of *Star Wars* toys. Even that meeting was "inconsequential," according to Lippincott.

His reception could not have presented a greater contrast to the one he was winning within the esoteric world of the science-fiction fan.

Since the late summer of 1976, when he, Kurtz, and Mark Hamill visited the World Science Fiction Convention in Kansas City, Lippincott had been drawing crowds to the striking stand hosted by the intriguing-sounding Star Wars Corporation. A gleaming C-3PO and a giant model of Darth Vader flanked the entrance. Inside Gary Kurtz and Mark Hamill happily explained the contents of the gleaming display cases, filled with X-Wing fighters, droids, and models of the *Millennium Falcon*.

Lippincott had been aware of the popularity of the sci-fi convention circuit for years. Like many others in Hollywood, he had heard tales of how the maverick Gene Rodenberry, creator of *Star Trek*, had tapped into the strange world of science-fiction fandom, particularly on the campuses of American colleges and universities. The limited success Rodenberry's original television series had enjoyed until its cancellation by NBC in 1968 had owed much to his brazen courtship of both groups. Indeed, if it had not been for a piece of Tammany Hall mischief, when Roddenberry orchestrated a massive student-led "Save *Star Trek*" demonstration at NBC's Burbank headquarters and a nationwide letter-writing campaign by the embryonic "Trekker" movement, the series would not have survived into the crucial third series which won it worldwide syndication and cult status.

Lippincott knew, however, that the movie industry had never taken the conventions seriously. The sense of mutual distrust had hardly been helped by the broken promises that led to Kubrick's *2001* failing to appear at the 1969 convention.

"They had never had a filmmaker there," he said.

When the cast and crew returned from England, however, Lippincott persuaded Kurtz and Lucas to let him take a *Star Wars* presentation around the country. Crude market research, based on the returns of other "science-fiction" films, had told them that the sci-fi fan market was worth a solid $8 million, roughly half what they needed to make Fox's money back. "I knew the movie was the star, that it had to be sold as this concept, that I had to get a primary audience for it," he said.

Many "serious" science-fiction fans viewed the Hollywood arrivals with disdain. Yet as he took *Star Wars* on tour through the winter Lippincott built a steady interest. "They were seeing something that normally never happened. Nobody went to science fiction conventions." Lippincott and Kurtz also talked to the fans and writers on their level. "We talked to them like real people." Soon their stand was one of the most popular and recognizable on the circuit. "They really got off on it," he said. By the time the tour had ended, he felt sure he had left behind a sense of anticipation to see the final film. "They felt liked, they were being accepted into something. And they loved the idea that they were the first to know."

His groundwork would prove crucial in months to come.

Lucas flew back to London, scene of so much unhappiness, still convinced he needed a minor miracle for the film to make $15 million. At least John Williams and the London Symphony orchestra provided him with one.

It had taken Williams, educated in the United States Air Force and New York's Juilliard School, more than twenty years to graduate to scoring major movies. An apprentice-ship that had taken in episodes of *Mod Squad* and *Wagon Train*, and a spell playing for the composer Jerry Goldsmith had ended when he scored Steve McQueen's *The Reivers* in 1969. Since then he had built his reputation with Oscar-winning arrangement work on *Fiddler on the Roof* and high-profile scores for Irwin Allen disaster movies like *Earthquake* and *The Poseidon Adventure*. Like everyone else in Holly-wood, Lucas had been deeply impressed by William's chill-ing, rhythmic score to Spielberg's *Jaws*. Introduced to Williams by Spielberg, Lucas explained his idea of bringing *Star Wars* to life with a stirring piece of classical-inspired music, something like Liszt or Dvořák.

Williams had suggested drawing on the influence of the great Hollywood composer, Erich Korngold, something that instantly appealed to the cinephile Lucas. Korngold had scored Errol Flynn's classic swashbucklers, *Robin Hood*, *The Sea Hawk* and *Captain Blood*.

Williams was meticulous in his working patterns. He had refused to look at any of Lucas's scripts, waiting instead for a rough cut of the film. In San Francisco he had done what he always did. "I like to sit alone in a dark projection room and watch the film from start to finish," he explained. "No distractions, just me and my response to the rhythmic impulses."

Afterwards Williams agreed with Lucas that they should avoid an electronic score of any kind. In the face of a cold, unfamiliar world on screen, Williams urged that the film needed a conventional, classical symphonic score to connect with the audience. "If you are looking at a film that is very strange but you hear music that is familiar it adds a warmth and human element to the piece," he explained.

Lucas and Gary Kurtz had only been allowed snatches of the music. In one of Williams's favorite recording rooms, at Denham Studios in Buckinghamshire, they heard the sound track in its entirety for the first time. As the orchestra struck up the main *Star Wars* overture, a rousing tumult of tympani and brass, Lucas felt the hairs on the back of his neck stand on end. By the time Williams had gone on to play the main themes he had written for the leading characters, Lucas was ecstatic. "It was the one part of the film that turned out even better than I thought," he was telling everyone afterwards.

If Lucas's greatest wish was that he be put out of his misery, by the spring he had been granted it. Soon he discovered that Fox had pulled *Stars Wars'* release date forward further. By now there were those within the studio who were convinced it had a disaster on its hands.

Expectations had been low since January, when Alan Ladd had taken a party from Fox up to see the film with Lucas at the Parkhouse screening room. Lucas held the show in his private screening room, where Ray Gosnell, Johnny Friedkin, Ashley Boone and others sank into the comfort of sofas and armchairs.

"It was a dangerous thing to do," recalled Friedkin who had feared some of the travel-weary party might fall asleep. The version they saw was still crude. The climactic Death Star battle scenes were still not ready. Where there should have been darting spaceships, the Fox team saw dogfighting Spitfires from Lucas's World War II assemblage. At the end of the show, Alan Ladd Jr. was as enthusiastic as ever. "On the bus back to the airport Laddie was going up and down saying, 'Great, huh?'" said Friedkin. Like most of his colleagues, Friedkin smiled weakly at the president of the company and replied: "Yeah, great." At least Ladd had been spared the sight of his staff asleep—the effect the unfinished *Star Wars* had on another party that traveled up to Parkhouse.

"It was the kind of place where you could really have a good nap—which most of us did," recalled Tim Deegan. "It did put me to sleep for sure and I know a lot of people around me were snoring also because I woke up a few times," he added. "It was a sleeper."

When the lights came up the bewildered team thanked Lucas for his hospitality, issued a few platitudes—"How'd you get all that on the screen for the price? You know the usual bullshit people say to filmmakers," said Deegan—and headed back to San Francisco wondering what to tell Ladd.

By the time they reached a pay phone no one had any doubt. "Everyone was in line, one after another telling Laddie what a great picture it was," Deegan laughed. Their reaction went beyond self preservation, however. By now Ladd's sense of what would and would not be a hit was proving unerring. Ladd had championed both *The Omen* and *Young Frankenstein,* despite doubts in some circles. Both films had gone on to be big hits for the studio in 1974.

"He was the straightest shooter imaginable. And he was so consistently right. There was such unquestioned faith in Ladd's judgment," said Deegan. "We figured if Laddie was behind this picture we should be too, whether we slept through it or not made no difference."

Fox's market research had no such faith, however. According to a survey conducted by a marketing executive called Alan Freeman, the title remained the main problem. Any film with the word War in it would not play well to women the research had argued. "The research said that no film with the word War in the title had ever made more than $8 million," said Gareth Wigan.

There were even fears the title could be misconstrued. Some had visions of customers paying to see a repeat of the cat fight between Bette Davis and Anne Baxter. "We thought *Star Wars* could be construed as an *All About Eve* kind of movie," smiled Johnny Friedkin.

"We invited them to think of another title—we didn't get one suggestion," laughed Gary Kurtz.

Lucas's decision to keep his office on the Universal lot rather than move to Fox helped buffer him and his team from the negativity. Inside the cramped, Lucasfilm offices, they felt an embryonic, if cautious optimism.

Charlie Lippincott had felt the film had a chance ever since he had pulled into his favorite newspaper stand on the corner of Hollywood and Cahuenga Boulevard one Monday morning in late March. He regularly bought his newspapers, magazines, and comic books at the stall where he was by now on first-name terms with its owner.

Lippincott had been sent early copies of the first edition of the new *Stars Wars* comic by Stan Lee's marketing staff over in New York. He was keen to see how the impressive looking magazine was selling on the streets. "On the ground in front of the comic section were three or four beat-up copies of the first issue," he recalled.

"Is that all you've got in, Larry?" he asked his friend.

"No, that's all I've got left. Why didn't you tell me it was going to go that fast? What are friends for?" the vendor chided him.

Back at the Lucasfilm offices Lippincott began calling all major comic stores in New York, Chicago and the Midwest. He heard the same story from each.

The surge in interest confirmed what he had first detected weeks earlier in a meeting with Judy-Lynn Del Rey. Copies of Allen Dean Foster's novelization of *Stars Wars* had been selling steadily since its publication in November. Del Rey had been unsure whether the print run of 100,000 copies, generous even within a popular book genre, had been overambitious. Without the aid of flashy displays in bookshops, however, books had continued to leave the warehouses. By February there were none left.

"They couldn't believe it," said Lippincott.

In the Lucasfilm office, Lippincott sensed a turning point.

"That was the first real indication. That's when we knew something was up!"

America's cinema owners could not have disagreed more violently with his view, however. To judge by their response, *Star Wars* was barely worth releasing at all.

Under the existing system, cinema chains made advance bids for upcoming movies. In many American states, cinema chains would be forced by the studios to put in sealed, "blind" bids. They were effectively forced to pay upfront for films sight-unseen. While it provided the studios with a way of guaranteeing a return on their investment, it made cinema chains ultra-cautious about signing up sub-standard films. *Star Wars* smelled like a sub-standard movie.

As the film's man at the commercial coal face, Charlie Lippincott had sensed the cinema owners' coolness the previous January. He had joined Fox executives at "26 for 76," an unimaginatively titled showcase for the films the studio would be releasing that year. "The general tenor was a giant yawn to complete boredom," he recalled. "Science fiction was not one of their favorite subjects. And it had no stars."

The *Star Wars* presentation was overshadowed by another Barnumesque performance by Irwin Allen, reigning monarch of the star-studded, disaster-movie market. As he outlined his latest addition to the genre, *The Towering Inferno* with Steve McQueen, the veteran, cigar-smoking owners of America's major chains had given him a standing ovation.

More than a year later, they were still unconvinced that *Star Wars* was worth showing at all. 1975 would be the summer of *Sorceror,* a remake of the classic *Wages of Fear* by William Friedkin, an adaptation of Peter "Jaws" Benchley's blockbuster, *The Deep,* the surefire sequel to the *Exorcist, Exorcist II: The Heretic* and *Smokey and the Bandit* with Burt Reynolds. If Fox had a hit on their hands it would probably be *The Other Side of Midnight*, an adaptation of a Sidney Sheldon's World War II novel with Marie-France Pisier, John Beck, and Susan Sarandon.

As advance word in the press supported the feeling that *Star Wars* was something of an also-ran, the decision was taken to bring the release forward. An opening was set for May 25, the Wednesday before the traditional opening of summer in America, Memorial Day. "We decided that we'd better open early if we wanted to have a chance," Ashley Boone later confessed.

The effect was minimal. To judge by their bids for *Star Wars*, cinema owners were clearly wary of being left holding a dud. Fox received advances of around $1.5 million, a fraction of the normal $10 million a major movie could expect.

"Embarrassing," Boone later called it.

"People ask why *Star Wars* only opened in forty theaters. *Star Wars* only opened in forty theaters because we could only get forty theaters to book it. That's the astonishing thing," said Gareth Wigan.

In fact it may only have been a combination of luck and Hollywood hucksterdom that allowed *Star Wars* to open at that many venues.

Lippincott, Ladd, Boone, and the marketing men at Fox were convinced that—particularly with evidence of some grassroots support within the sci-fi fraternity—*Star Wars* needed a "tentpole" opening at high-profile cinemas. The Avco cinema in Westwood, on the edge of the massive UCLA campus, was booked but attempts to get a cinema on Hollywood Boulevard, the heart of the city's cinema district had failed. "They could *not* get a Hollywood theater," said Charlie Lippincott. In a piece of good fortune, with only weeks to go before the opening, Ted Mann, new owner of what was once the Graumann's Chinese Theater, learned Universal's *Sorcerer* had been delayed. He agreed to run *Star*

Wars before the Friedkin film opened. "The deal was we were only supposed to be there for a month," recalled Lippincott.

Elsewhere, however, Fox was forced to bend rules. While interest in *Star Wars* was almost non-existent, advance word on *The Other Side of Midnight* was strong. In a flagrant breach of the law, for which the studio was later fined $25,000, a small number of cinema owners were given a simple choice. "Fox said, 'If you don't book *Star Wars*, we won't let you have *The Other Side of Midnight*,'" said Wigan. "That was the relative relationship between the two films."

By the time it came to ordering final prints of the film, Fox could do little but err on the side of extreme caution. Only ten prints of *Star Wars* in the full 70-mm format were ordered. They would be earmarked for screening at select cinemas in Los Angeles, New York, and San Francisco. With each copy of the wider-screen format costing $7,000, Fox saw no reason to spend more. Every other cinema would have to make do with the standard 35 mm prints, which cost just $1,000 each.

With time now against it as well, the advertising campaign was pared back to the bone. Since the withdrawal of the trailer there had been little in the way of promotion apart from within the college and sci-fi communities. Normally a film would be launched with a campaign of magazine and newspaper advertising, one-sheet billboards and advance screenings. But with the film unfinished and no one sure about posters, after-market research had advised against using the film's high-tech hardware for fear of alienating non-science-fiction filmgoers. *Star Wars* would be launched with a whisper.

"All the things you do on a normal film—we didn't do them," admitted Johnny Friedkin.

Lucas retired to the cocoonlike comfort of the editing room for the run-in to the May 25 release date. The final "answer" print still had to be turned in and approved by Fox, who—technically at least—had the right to the final cut. By now, Lucas had reduced the 400,000 feet of footage into 123 minutes of film. Yet it was still too long. To maximize its turnover at the cinemas, *Star Wars* had to be under two hours. Lucas looked long and hard and eventually decided to cut all the scenes featuring Luke's boyhood friend and fellow rebel pilot, Biggs Darklighter. Garrick Hagon's one chance of lasting fame was lost. Out too went the confrontation between Han Solo and the galactic Godfather who had put a price on his head, Jabba the Hutt. Lucas had been desperately disappointed with his monster makers' efforts on the slimy creature. He thought it looked "disgusting."

Lucas spent his confinement back at the Warner Goldwyn Hollywood Studios in Los Angeles, the only place available at the time with the editing facilities he needed. Marcia was already installed there editing *New York, New York* for Martin Scorsese. Over the next few weeks Lucas and his wife barely saw each other, however. Scorsese had the editing suites from 8 A.M. until 8 P.M. Lucas took over for the graveyard shift from 8 P.M. until 8 A.M. Both were holed up at the small Los Angeles apartment they had bought with the *Graffiti* money. Occasionally Marcia would scribble her husband a note, "Can we meet for breakfast?"

Lucas was by now too close to his film to make serious sense of the conflicting opinions he was hearing. Within ILM and Lucasfilm there had been growing optimism that the film had evolved into something extraordinary. If in doubt, however, its creator always feared the worst. Unfortunately, there was no shortage of opinion to support his natural pessimism.

Lucas had invited members of his inner circle to see the film at Parkhouse. Bill Huyck and Gloria Katz, John Milius, Hal Barwood, Matthew Robbins, Steven Spielberg, Brian De

Palma, and the *Time* magazine writer Jay Cocks, watched the film, then had dinner with Lucas and Marcia.

Spielberg was already familiar with his friend's pessimistic streak. "Oh, he complains. George ran down *Graffiti* too. Before I'd seen it he said, 'Forgive me.' I went in expecting a turkey," he recalled.

In this case, however, there was strong support for the view that *Star Wars* was a turkey. Silence greeted the end of the movie. His friends left the screening offering condolences rather than congratulations.

De Palma was the most openly critical. Throughout dinner he made cruel jokes about the "almighty Force." Spielberg and Cocks were more supportive, offering advice on improvements and additions that might salvage the film. Lucas sat quietly eating his meal, nodding politely at each contribution. He accepted an offer from Jay Cocks and De Palma to rewrite the opening crawl he had inserted to explain the background to this story.

As he said goodbye to his guests, Lucas went to bed convinced he had made a potentially career-wrecking move. "It's just a silly movie," he said to himself.

Perhaps predictably, the board of directors at Fox thought even less of it.

A lavish evening had been organized around the screening for the fourteen directors and their wives at the Warner Goldwyn Hollywood screen. Once more the film was preceded by a cautionary announcement that some of the special effects still had to be added to the movie.

If even the experienced movie men of Fox had found the patchwork print unusual, the directors, captains of industry and commerce drawn from boardrooms across America, thought it was simply a catastrophe.

"Some of the directors fell asleep—so did one of the secretaries," recalled Johnny Friedkin, who sat in the screening room that night.

Friedkin, Gareth Wigan, and other Fox executives canvassed all fourteen directors. "Three thought it was brilliant, absolutely brilliant, three were on the fence about it, and the rest were convinced it was a disaster, an absolute disaster," said Wigan.

According to Lucas himself, one director grudgingly came up to him afterwards and offered his opinion that the film might do okay. He soon issued a caveat, however. "But I know nothing about movies," he said.

Within days Wall Street detected a sudden rush of interest in Twentieth Century–Fox stock. The flurry nudged the share price, then hovering around the $11 mark, up slightly.

In time there would be claims that the movement was prompted by Hollywood whispers of a new "wonder film" on the books at Century City. Executives at other studios, Universal in particular, were later revealed to have been among the prospectors.

The reality, according to those within Fox's hierarchy at the time, was the polar opposite of what became the prevailing wisdom. After the directors' screening, the word had spread through the corridors of corporate America. Twentieth Century–Fox was about to take an $11 million bath.

"The truth, I believe, is that there was somebody who thought that the film was going to be a catastrophe and that Fox would be on the block," said Gareth Wigan. "They wanted to accumulate shares in order to take it over because the studio was going to be involved in a disaster."

CHAPTER 7

Heading for Hyperspace

On Thursday, May 26, 1977, Twentieth Century–Fox's Tim Deegan was relishing a rare break from the madness of Hollywood. With his girlfriend, he had fled to the Hawaiian island of Maui for a vacation.

As Deegan recalls, his girlfriend was at the wheel midway through the three-hour drive up the slopes of the famous Mount Haleakala volcano when he began reading her snippets from a newspaper for fun. His relaxed smile gave way to a look of mild bemusement when he got to the financial pages. Deegan, the owner of a sizable chunk of Fox stock, could not help but notice an unusual rise in his company's share price on Wall Street the previous day.

Visions of takeovers and boardroom coups flashed through his mind all the way up the spectacular mountainside. By the time he saw a phone booth at the visitor's center at the top of the seven thousand foot crater Deegan's curiosity had got the better of him. "I didn't want to call the studio. I was on vacation. So I called Art Murphy at *Variety*," he remembered.

Murphy, one of Hollywood's most seasoned reporters, was as amused as he was baffled by his old friend's inquiry. "Where are you, on the moon?" he asked. "Sort of," the advertising executive replied, casting an eye around the surreal, steaming granite landscape.

"*Star Wars* opened yesterday," said Murphy, putting his friend out of his misery. "The biggest opening in history, the projections are that it will be the biggest movie ever."

Gary Kurtz had sensed that something remarkable was happening the previous evening, Wednesday, May 25, as he had guested on a radio phone-in show in Washington. Accompanied by Charlie Lippincott, the producer had spent the morning in New York, appearing on NBC television's *Today* program. The next day he would be in Massachusetts, a guest on another breakfast television show, *Good Morning Boston*.

Questions and answers had been routine until he took a call from a college student. The caller said he was not a science-fiction fan but had seen and liked *Star Wars*. He then started reeling off highly detailed questions about the characters and story.

"You seem to know quite a bit about it," Kurtz told the caller.

"Yeah, I saw it four times," he replied.

Thrown for a moment, Kurtz asked how that had been possible given that the film had only been released that morning.

"I sat through the whole day," the student replied.

Soon cinema managers across America would be forced to change their admission policies. "The normal procedure until that time was that you could go in when you wanted and leave when you wanted," explained Kurtz. "*Star Wars* forced the cinema owners to initiate a program of clearing the cinemas so as to get people in."

It may have been the first, but it was certainly not the last time *Star Wars* would reinvent the rules of cinema.

Lines had begun forming since the doors had opened at 8 A.M. for the first 10 A.M. shows that morning. They had remained there until people were turned away from the final screenings that night.

By Thursday morning, the early figures had set the Twentieth Century–Fox offices alight.

"It was unbelievable," recalled Gareth Wigan. "The mathematics were astonishing."

Cinemas in Orange County, Minneapolis, Denver, and Sacramento had reported all-time house records for a single day. Other cinemas in Detroit and Phoenix recorded the biggest receipts ever for a Fox film. By the time the accountants had finished it emerged that *Star Wars*'s opening day totaled $254,309 from just thirty-two cinemas. The company's previous opening day records, set by *The Towering Inferno* and *The Sound of Music*, had been hopelessly shattered. And all this on a Wednesday!

It was the Hollywood screenwriter William Goldman who most memorably summed up the reality of the movie industry. "Nobody knows anything," he wrote in his seminal *Adventures in the Screen Trade*. No film summed up that truism as completely as *Star Wars*.

If there had been a turning point as far as Alan Ladd and Lucasfilm had been concerned, it had been at the scene of Lucas and Coppola's famous showdown with Ned Tanen. The first major public screening had been arranged at the Northpoint in San Francisco at the beginning of May.

By now Lucas's film was complete, the last ILM effects delivered and inserted late in April. As John Williams's stirring brass theme filled the theater, the opening crawl outlined the plot of "Episode IV: A New Hope" and the camera panned to the surface of Ralph McQuarrie's exquisitely executed Tatooine, the house fell silent. By the time the vast Imperial Cruiser had completed its seemingly endless rumble overhead, the entire audience had broken into spontaneous applause. The reaction would be repeated time and time again over the coming years. Hisses greeted each appearance of Darth Vader, cheers accompanied the moment when Obi-Wan Kenobi dealt a lethal lightsaber blow to a bug-eyed bully in the cantina sequence, applause rang out as Luke dispatched his climactic payload into the heart of the Death Star. Thunder greeted the moment the house lights came up once more at the end.

"It was pretty rare in those days for audiences ever to applaud a movie in any circumstances," said Gareth Wigan, who had traveled up for the screening with his son. "I think there were twelve times when the audience applauded that morning."

Afterwards the audience milled around slightly unsure what to do. "The manager came in at the back of the theater, he couldn't get people out. They wouldn't leave," said Wigan.

The emotion of the moment proved too much for Alan Ladd Jr. "Laddie walked out of the screening crying," recalled Charlie Lippincott.

"As the first spaceship went across the screen they started applauding," Ladd admitted later. "I didn't expect that, it brought tears to my eyes."

Word of the screening, inevitably, filtered into the Hollywood gossip mill. Lippincott later learned that two executives from Columbia had been sneaked in by a connection at the cinema. Impressed by what they had seen, they sent word flying around that Star Wars was far from the disaster the rumors had claimed it to be. "It started an underground current, the word-of-mouth was great," said Lippincott.

The screening proved useful in other ways too. Lippincott had seen a five-year-old girl crying at scenes featuring Darth Vader, particularly when he choked a rebel officer at the opening. Afterwards he, Lucas, and Kurtz decided to ask Ladd to lean on the American certification board, the MPAA to give the film a stiffer PG rating rather than the innocuous G rating. The move was far from altruistic. It helped dispel the idea that *Star Wars* was a kid's movie, box-office death to the crucial preteen market.

As a minor buzz percolated around Hollywood, Lucas once more found himself the subject of press interest. *Time* magazine, encouraged by Jay Cocks, said they were planning a possible cover, an incalculable boost for any movie. (No one had forgotten the benefits *Love Story* enjoyed after Ali McGraw's all-American smile had beamed from the cover of *Time* seven years earlier.) After Lucas had spent a few brief hours on the record about *Star Wars*, however, there were those who wondered whether he had actually done more harm than good. While everyone else had stuck resolutely to the party line, avoiding any references to science fiction or children's movies, Lucas simply sold his film the way he saw it. "All he would talk about was 'I think this is a film that will appeal to the child in all of us,'" recalled Gareth Wigan.

"We thought the moment you sell it as a children's film, no adults would go. It sounds just like an old Saturday matinee. Which of course George thought it was. Everybody was tearing their hair out. Everybody was saying, 'Oh, my God it would have been better if we hadn't let him speak to anybody,'" he added.

With little advertising planned, it became clear that the critics would be more important than usual if the film was to find a wide audience. Their verdict alone would not sink the movie—there were still those on the lot who remembered that *The Sound of Music* had broken all records despite often derisive reviews—yet if *Star Wars* was to build all-important word-of-mouth, it needed the power of praise on its side.

Johnny Friedkin's main concern had been that the major critics, Charles Champlin of the *Los Angeles Times*, Jack Kroll at *Newsweek*, and Vincent Canby at the *New York Times*, might be away at the Cannes Film Festival in late May. "We didn't want it reviewed by a bunch of second stringers," he recalled. A series of press screenings had been arranged in New York and Los Angeles. Where necessary, Friedkin had flown key critics in to Los Angeles specially to see *Star Wars* before they left for France.

It was at the main press screening at the Astor Plaza in New York on the Monday before *Star Wars* opened, May 23, that Friedkin sensed what might be about to happen.

"It was insanity, absolute, the audience went berserk," recalled Friedkin. Instructions had been issued to fill the audience with youngsters. Friedkin had invited his eighteen-year-old son who in turn had brought five friends with him. "They just sat there at the end of the picture and said 'Dad, you're a vice-president, can't you get them to screen it again?'"

Friedkin returned to Los Angeles, convinced that the critics would be kind.

Every Hollywood publicist carried around a list of the key opinion-forming newspapers and magazines: *Time* and *Newsweek*, the New York and Los Angeles *Times* at the top, *Variety* and the *Hollywood Reporter* lower down, America's city newspapers somewhere alongside them. By Tuesday, advance copies of the reviews had begun to dribble in to the publicity office. Friedkin and Boone wasted little time in placing pristine, blown-up copies on Alan Ladd and Dennis Stanfill's desks. They were among the best any of them had ever seen.

On May 20 *Variety* set the tone. "*Star Wars* is a magnificent film. George Lucas set out to make the biggest possible adventure-fantasy out of his memories of serials and older action epics, and he has succeeded brilliantly," the review began. "Like a breath of fresh air, *Star Wars* sweeps away the cynicism that has in recent years obscured the concepts of valor, dedication and honor. Make no mistake—this is by no means a children's film—with all the derogatory overtones that go with that description. This is instead a superior example of what only the screen can achieve, and closer to home, it is another affirmation of what only Hollywood can put on a screen." As the review ended a new phrase crept in, soon to become common currency. "This is the kind of film in which an audience, first entertained, can later walk out feeling good all over." Soon everyone would be invoking the feel-good factor.

Charles Champlin certainly did nothing to deflate it. "George Lucas has been conducting a lifelong double love affair, embracing the comic strips on the one hand (or with one arm) and the movies on and with the other. Now he has united his loves in *Star Wars*, the year's most razzle-dazzling family movie, an exuberant and technically astonishing space adventure...*Star Wars* is *Buck Rogers* with a doctoral degree but not a trace of neuroticism or cynicism, a slam-bang, rip-roaring gallop through a distantly future world."

Even the patrician Jack Kroll in *Newsweek* became a breath-less child. "I loved *Star Wars* and so will you, unless you're...oh well, I hope you're not," he opened his review. "It's the last chance for kids to have fun before they grow up to be Oedipus. And we hollow-eyed Oedipuses can, if we try, go back and enjoy the fun of our pre-guilt stage."

Early proofs of America's other great weekly news maga-zine, *Time*, were, if anything, more positive. It devoted six pages to an article simply titled "*Star Wars*: The Year's Best Movie." *Time* had intended putting the film on its cover. Lucas cared little that he had been blown off by the election of Menachim Begin in Israel. None of the new breed of

EMPIRE BUILDING

director, not even Coppola, Spielberg, or Scorsese, had been anointed in this way.

"*Star Wars* is a combination of *Flash Gordon*, *The Wizard of Oz*, the Errol Flynn swashbucklers of the '30s and '40s and almost every western ever screened—not to mention *The Hardy Boys*, *Sir Gawain and the Green Knight* and *The Faerie Queene*," *Time*'s critic went on. "The result is a remarkable confection: a subliminal history of the movies, wrapped in a riveting tale of suspense and adventure, ornamented with some of the most ingenious special effects ever contrived for film."

By the time Vincent Canby in the *New York Times* chimed in, hailing it as "the most elaborate, most expensive, most beautiful movie serial ever made," *Star Wars* had achieved a remarkable clean sweep of the most influential reviewers. Where they led, almost every critic in America soon followed.

By Friday news of the opening Wednesday was dominating the trades. The *Variety* headline screamed:

FOX'S *STAR WARS* HEADS FOR HYPER SPACE:
FIRST DAY B.O. 255G, HOUSE RECORDS TUMBLE.

"There was only one topic of conversation in the film industry yesterday—the smash opening of George Lucas's *Star Wars*," the report began.

That morning, nine more cinemas opened with the film. No matter where the location, the lines were there waiting.

At Fox the euphoria was a blend of relief and unadulterated shock. Much of the earlier negativity had been taken with a pinch of salt within Alan Ladd's circle, the most somnolent screening dismissed as proof of another old Hollywood saw: "Boards of directors know nothing about making movies." Yet for all the optimism generated by the

158

Northpoint screening, no one had dared predict the tsunami unleashed that Wednesday morning.

"We knew we had something amazing, but we didn't know that everybody was going to react," said Gareth Wigan. Typically there were plenty ready to claim the glory. "What's the expression, success has a thousand fathers and failure is an orphan," smiled Wigan. Those who had predicted disaster were even quicker in covering their tracks. The thousands of women lining up to see *Star Wars*—fully aware it was set in space rather than the Bel Air mansion of some fallen screen diva—left Alan Freeman's damning market research report looking rather ludicrous. All trace of it was obliterated from the Fox files. "As I recall, every copy of it was called in and shredded," said Tim Deegan. "It became a huge embarrassment."

To the less opportunistic members of staff, however, there was no doubt Lucas and the footsoldiers from his *Star Wars* Corporation deserved the lion's share of the praise. "We didn't do the things you do on normal films, we didn't have time," admitted Johnny Friedkin. "The lines were there because Gary and Charlie went to a sci-fi convention every goddamn weekend. Somehow Gary and Charlie translated the heart and the essence of the film. People asked, 'Well, how did the lines get there?' That's the only answer."

"It was completely below anybody's radar," said Gareth Wigan. "In those days there was no research, no polling. But there was an underground awareness."

The office was alive with stories about the lengths to which people had gone to see the movie. "There was one we all heard and loved of a kid from Boston who had hitchhiked to New York," said Wigan. "The film was being screened in Boston, but he wanted to see it in six track and there were only two six track prints, one in New York and one in Los Angeles. And he hitchhiked from Boston, all day and night so as to stand in line for the first performance in Times

Square of the six track print the next night. It was unbeliev-able, and it just grew and grew."

There was no doubting where the credit was due within the Fox organization either. The after-six drinks flowed a little more freely in Alan Ladd Jr.'s office. He was even persuaded to break the terms of his contract (he had stipu-lated that he would never have to talk in public) and give his first interviews to the press. Ladd laughed at the battle he had fought to get the film past Dennis Stanfill and his directors. "How do you do a synopsis of this movie for a board of directors? Imagine: 'Well you see, there's a golden-haired, gorilla-shaped Wookiee named Chewbacca copilot-ing this pirate spaceship...'"

The fraught final months had taken their toll, he admit-ted. He had successfully quit smoking until the morning of the Northpoint screening. "When it was over I walked out to the lobby and lit up; I've been smoking ever since."

No one on the staff at Fox begrudged him his moment of public glory. "If it hadn't been for Laddie, Fox would never have made it," said Ray Gosnell. "Laddie just fought and fought and fought and his persistence got it made. He put his job on the line—and from day one," said Johnny Friedkin. "Anyone else who takes credit for it is full of it!"

Mark Hamill was the first of the cast to get the news of the amazing scenes. "Hi kid, you famous yet?" Lucas had asked him as he called him at 10 P.M. on Wednesday night, back in his editing suite after finishing dinner with Marcia. Typ-ically his director had gone on to ask him whether he could come over for one final piece of voiceover looping! During his limousine drive across Los Angeles, Hamill's chauffeur took him past the Avco in Westwood. He resisted the driver's suggestion that he lean out of the window and shout, "Hi, it's meee!" as they slid by the massive lines.

The morning afterwards Harrison Ford sat in his manager

Patricia McQueeney's office with his head in his carpentry-calloused hands. After years of heading nowhere, he had finally made his breakthrough. While most of the critics had hailed Lucas and his designers as the heroes of the hour, a few had taken the time to spot the sly craftsmanship in his performance.

"Outstanding," *Variety* called him. "Ford has all the gusto, macho, and humor of Jeff Bridges, but he's better looking as well as a fine actor," wrote Ruth Batchelor in the *Free Press*. "For me he is the discovery of *Star Wars*."

"Patricia, this is a miracle," Ford told McQueeney.

George Lucas headed off for his prearranged holiday with Marcia in Hawaii, relieved, at least, that he had avoided complete embarrassment. Alan Ladd Jr. knew where he was if he needed him—a creature of habit, Lucas had once more withdrawn to the Mauna Kea Hotel.

The question at Fox was whether *Star Wars* could continue doing business through the Memorial Day weekend. The extravagant projections made during its first day were based on the phenomenal, dawn-till-dusk sellouts at a relatively small number of cinemas. Nine more venues were opening with the film over the weekend. Only after the final screenings on Monday night would they know whether Wednesday had been a freakish flash in the pan.

By the time Alan Ladd Jr. called George Lucas on the following Tuesday morning, they had their answer. This time the news was even more spectacular. On a desk in Ladd's office a copy of *Variety* read: MAMMOTH 6 DAY DOMESTIC TAKE THE BEST SINCE *JAWS*. "Domestic box office for George Lucas's *Star Wars* totaled a sensational $2,556,418 at the end of the holiday weekend," its report went on.

It took only the most cursory analysis of the latest figures to see that *Star Wars* was already becoming a phenomenon more powerful than Spielberg's shark, however. *Jaws* had opened "wide," on more than 100 screens. *Star Wars* was only showing at the forty theaters brave—or weak—enough to take a chance. On the holiday Sunday alone, *Star Wars* had taken in $595,000—an average of $13,000 per cinema, a respectable figure for a week at many cinemas. Its average over the week was $10,000 per cinema per day. Even at the height of its success two years earlier, *Jaws* had only managed half that figure. The statistics were almost unbelievable.

If *Star Wars* owed its flying start to the core sci-fi community, the film's jump to light-speed at the box office was now down to something else.

As the lines grew and grew throughout the week, Fox dispatched teams to clean up the mess they left behind. The sidewalks outside cinemas playing *Star Wars* had become a sea of empty drink cans, newspapers, hamburger wrappers, and cigarette packs. At the same time editors everywhere dispatched teams to find out: why? Soon *Star Wars* made the quantum leap from trade paper headline to national news story.

At the Avco in Westwood, *Star Wars* had rewritten the house records at the thousand seater cinema. Every day since May 25 lines had formed at 8 A.M. in readiness for the first 10 A.M. show. For the next sixteen and three quarter hours, until the last of the Avco's seven shows, they remained. The crowds, students and businessmen, mothers holding their babies and kids in baseball uniforms, clutched brown paper bags with snacks, exchanged opinions on the film and behaved impeccably. Inside they did what audiences everywhere were doing, whistling and hissing, shouting and screaming as the action unfolded. "They go in there and have a ball, cheering and applauding," the shell-shocked manager, Albert Szabo kept saying. Szabo was a movie theater manager of the old school—right down to his ever-spotless tuxedo and bow tie. After thirty years in the business he thought he had seen it all.

"I remember crowds," he told the *Los Angeles Times*. "Crowds at my theaters for *The Godfather, That's Entertainment, Dr. Zhivago, 2001: A Space Odyssey*. But I have never seen anything like this."

Szabo had hired sixty extra staff to handle the crush. By the first week of June the crowds were, if anything, bigger. "Last weekend we turned away five thousand people," he told the *Times*. The scenes were being repeated all across America. "This isn't a snowball, this is an avalanche," said Szabo.

Nowhere was *Star Wars* better loved than on Wall Street. On May 23, Fox shares had been suspended amid rumors of a takeover by the Nashville tycoon Claude Cockrell Jr. Their price then had been $11.50. During the next three weeks brokers bought and sold almost six million shares—just under half the company's total stock. By then the share price had reached $22.50, its highest level in years.

"No one doubts that the success of *Star Wars* is behind the stock's climb," said the *Wall Street Journal*. The financial world had already begun number crunching on Fox's behalf. Analysts estimated *Star Wars'* rentals could be as high as $150 million worldwide (half the $300 million worldwide box office already being projected). After Fox deducted its $40 million distributor's fee and the costs of making, marketing, and printing the movie, that would leave around $80 million to be split 60–40 with Lucasfilm. If it was already obvious that George Lucas would soon be an enormously wealthy man, it was equally plain to see that Fox's fortunes had been transformed in an instant. "If the movie lives up to box office expectations, some analysts believe it could provide the financial ingredients for the possible transformation of Fox into an entertainment conglomerate like MCA Inc. or Warner Communications," said the *Wall Street Journal*.

In the corridors of corporate America, Dennis Stanfill was suddenly lauded as a financial Lazarus, the man who had saved Twentieth Century–Fox. "When has a movie ever caught the public's imagination this way?" he said during a rare interview in June. "When they see it they love it, they want to own a piece of it."

Suddenly the old studio seemed alive again, saved at the eleventh hour by the kind of classic speculation for which its old master Darryl Zanuck was famous. "It was a great moment," recalled Ray Gosnell. "It brought Fox back from near bankruptcy into contention as being a major studio."

As in all the best Hollywood stories, the transformation had been an even greater cliffhanger than anyone could have imagined. Ironically few inside the studio knew just how close Fox had come to selling off a large chunk of the profits about to rain down thanks to *Star Wars*.

Such was the lack of belief in Lucas's film, the company had all but finalized negotiations to sell a share of the film and its profits to a German tax shelter. The routine practice of offsetting potential losses by selling stakes to wealthy businessmen—who would in turn use their investment to set against their tax bills—had been outlawed by the IRS in December 1976. West Germany still provided a loophole, however, and Fox lawyer Donald Loze had been working to ease the pain if "that science movie" flopped. On May 2, at a price of $12 million, he had struck a verbal agreement to sell *Star Wars* as part of a $24.2 million package that also included *The Other Side of Midnight* and *Fire Sale*. The deal would have given Fox's German partners, who would have been credited only for their "production services" with a sizable slice of any profits on offer if the film succeeded. A day later, on May 3, however, Loze called the Los Angeles investment company handling the deal, Bel Aire Associates, breaking the news that *Star Wars* was no longer part of the package. The lawyer explained that given the involvement of Lucas and his company the paperwork involved would be "too complicated" to complete before the film's release on May 25. Stakes in the other films were, however, still for sale. The U-turn saved Fox from forking out millions in profits. Predictably Bel Aire Associates later attempted to sue the studio. They too, it seems, saw it as something more than a coincidence that the deal fell apart so soon after news of the Northpoint screening bubbled back to Hollywood. It seems their $25 million suit was unsuccessful. (Such was the seeming lack of faith in all things science fiction that Columbia—to its regret—went ahead with the sale of a sizable share of its upcoming *Close Encounters* to a German shelter.)

Lucas had touched a nerve with *Graffiti*. But this time he had hit the bull's eye on almost every level.

His film might have been custom-made for the mass of young, educated, middle-class moviegoers Hollywood had identified as its lifeblood back in 1972.

For the young there was the simple, escapist exhilaration of a movie beyond anything they had seen before. "There hadn't been any exciting science fiction for at least twenty years, since *Forbidden Planet* in 1955. That meant there were two generations of kids who didn't know what that was all about," said Gary Kurtz.

For the film-school generation there was a technical *tour de force,* full of gorgeous tableaux, innovative editing, and unashamed homages to genres from westerns to the *Wizard of Oz*, Errol Flynn swashbucklers to even Leni Riefenstahl's *Triumph of the Will* if you searched hard enough. In this sense it was post-modernist before the term popped into common usage.

Yet *Star Wars* worked perhaps most powerfully of all on a

deeper level still. The pain of Vietnam had finally come home, the shame of Watergate had left America hanging its head. The most optimistic nation on earth had never felt more pessimistic. In *Graffiti* Lucas prescribed nostalgia. Now, as the film's title promised, here was an offer of a new hope.

It marked the dawning of a new era. "Today, movies say that the system is corrupt, that the whole thing stinks. When movie after movie tells audience that they should be against themselves it's hardly surprising that people go out of the theaters drained, numbly convinced that with so much savagery and cruelty everywhere, nothing can be done," wrote the distinguished critic Roger Simon, defining the mood of the moment in the *Chicago Sun-Times* that summer. "That has been the theme not only of movies, but of pop culture in the seventies. Helplessness, dread, cynicism, and random cruelty. Victory is beyond us, we are taught. Survival is the most we can expect. Well, not in *Star Wars*. There the bad guys get zapped with death rays and the good guys get a kiss on the cheek and a medal. There is a tremendous amount of action but no blood. No sex. Not even a little flash of thigh. It's hard to believe people want to go see it. But they do. So maybe the seventies are over and the first movie of the 1980s has begun. Not a moment too soon."

Of course the irony was that in pointing the way to the future, Lucas had simply invoked the memories of his own—and America's—past. *Star Wars's* roots lay in the "Adventure Theater" of Lucas's childhood and the sheer sensory thrill of a Saturday morning matinee. Previous generations had cheered Charlie Chaplin and John Wayne, rooted for the values of Frank Capra's *Mr. Smith Goes to Washington* and *It's a Wonderful Life*. Now their heirs hissed Darth Vader, raised the roof as they roared on Luke Skywalker then left the cinemas smiling, muttering "May the Force be with you" all the way home. *Star Wars* celebrated a golden, bygone age, an era of good guys and bad guys, heroism and hope. Lucas had written a story for a generation growing up without fairytales. As the historian Les Keyser wrote, seeing the movie became "a celebration, a social affair, a collective dream, and people came again and again, dragging their friends and families with them."

Or as Alan Ladd Jr. put it: "He showed people it was all right to become totally involved in a movie again, to yell and scream and applaud and really roll with it."

Amid the endless stream of statistics that attached themselves to the *Star Wars* phenomenon one was telling. A startling 5 percent of those who saw the film watched it at least twice.

Jaws had brought people back to the cinema. *Star Wars* brought them back to stay. In 1977, a year utterly dominated by Lucas's film, weekly audiences in America exceeded 20 million people for the first time since 1963. It would mark the beginning of a lasting renaissance in filmgoing. In the two decades that followed, only twice—and then marginally—would the figure slip below the 20 million mark again. The sense that a new era was at hand was obvious all over Hollywood.

Gareth Wigan was walking by the Mann's Chinese one evening in early June when he saw the familiar figure of Irwin Allen stumbling out into the night. As the two men greeted each other, the sixty-one-year-old producer looked dazed. "I don't understand it. I don't understand it," he told Wigan, shaking his head. "There's no stars, there's no love story, what are they clapping at?"

"He was completely bewildered," recalled Wigan. No one had done more to draw Twentieth Century–Fox from the brink of oblivion. Yet, for Allen's generation of showmen, the writing was on the wall. "It was like a change of generations right in front of your eyes," said Wigan. "It was poignant, like a world had passed him by."

The feeling was much the same at a screening to the elders of the industry at the Academy of Motion Pictures Arts and Sciences soon after the opening night. The great and the good of Hollywood had come to cast a critical eye over the film rewriting its history almost daily. They too left with eyes open wide in wonder. "The people in the audience were just stunned," recalled Jonathan Dana, then chairman of Atlantic Films. "It you could ever say that jaws dropped at a movie, that was it."

Dana sensed a change in the entertainment world he had not felt in more than a decade. Afterward he compared the moment to another that had shaken show business to its core. "It was like when the Beatles appeared on the *Ed Sullivan Show*," he said. "Business was never the same after that."

CHAPTER 8

Wookiee Cookie

When Alan Ladd Jr. and his team had first suggested Twentieth Century–Fox's record division release John Williams's *Star Wars* score as an album, the company's chief, Alan Livingston, had dismissed the idea out of hand. "He said we couldn't, orchestral scores wouldn't sell," recalled Gareth Wigan.

Ladd and his colleagues had not given in easily, however. Eventually a deal was struck whereby they would underwrite any losses the sickly Twentieth Century Records incurred if the record flopped.

"With tremendous arm twisting, tremendous interference and with the deepest reluctance on his part, they put out 20,000 albums," recalled Wigan.

By the beginning of June sales of the album stood at 200,000 copies and Williams's score had become the first orchestral work to enter the national music charts. Another 150,000 LPs were being printed to match the demand. Eventually sales of the record would exceed one million in America alone.

As the box office bonanza grew with each day, so too did Charlie Lippincott's conviction that Lucas had not been dreaming when he talked of stores stuffed full of *Star Wars* products. Soon the press were asking him for clues as to what to expect. "The merchandising income may net $1 million by itself," he told them. "And that's conservative." Highly conservative to judge by the scenes all over America as the *Star Wars* phenomenon spilled from the cinemas to the shopping malls.

Within weeks of the record-breaking opening, the hulking figure of Darth Vader had become as familiar as Ronald McDonald in the major department stores of Los Angeles. One enterprising chain had hired him—minus Dave Prowse to the English actor's anger—to celebrate a special "*Star Wars* Week" with a series of personal appearances. Thousands turned up to eat "May the Force Be With You Meals"— alfalfa sprouts, vegetable drinks, and R2-D2–shaped cookies! As they did so, the stores set about the real business of the day—capitalizing on the biggest merchandising boom a Hollywood film had ever spawned.

There were products to suit every pocket—from $1.50 souvenir programs to $30 masks of Chewbacca, Darth Vader and C-3PO. A "Super 8" home movie, featuring segments of the movie for projection at home, was selling as soon as it arrived in the stores. Soon, George Lucas had come in on the act. He claimed he thought of the concept of the "Wookiee cookie."

Like every other licensed item, however, the cookies— sugarless to protect young teeth—weren't allowed near the streets until Lucasfilm approved them. Having tapped into one of the richest marketing veins in American history, he was in no mood to lose a grip by churning out inferior products. "We are trying to keep as clean as possible, trying to stay away from cheap junk items," Charlie Lippincott told the *Hollywood Reporter*.

Lippincott and Lucas's strained persnicketyness relations with Fox. The studio had verbally accepted a jewelry manufacturer's offer of $500,000 for the license to make *Star Wars* brooches, rings, and various other trinkets. When Lucas got wind of the deal he vetoed it, much to the studio's fury. "I don't want to have junk with the *Star Wars* name on it in every five-and-dime store in America," had been Lucas's final word.

Lucas could, of course, afford to be choosy. Only now was Twentieth Century–Fox beginning to realize the implications of its *Star Wars* contract. Lucas was entitled to an unheard of 50 percent of every single merchandising deal. As if to rub salt into the wounds, the director confirmed he had always suspected he would make more money from *Star Wars* spinoffs than the movie itself.

"In a way this film was designed around toys," he told the *Los Angeles Times* as the fever spread. "I'm not making much for directing this movie. If I make money it will be from the toys."

If Lucas's smile was broad, the smiles on the faces of the businessmen who had backed a hunch that his movie would work were even broader. In the town of Bear, Delaware, the grin on the face of Harry Geissler was as immovable as the Darth Vader drawings printed on his company's high-quality T-shirts. Geissler had made a fortune on the rights to print show business tie-in merchandise from T-shirts and posters to badges and belt buckles. The popularity of shirts featuring the Osmonds and Wonder Woman, tennis stars Bjorn Borg and Vitas Gerulaitis and—most of all—Charlie's Angels, had made him the pioneer in a booming new business. Geissler paid $100,000 for the exclusive rights to the *Star Wars* characters. By the end of July he had already recouped his investment twice over. Within a year it had earned him $1 million. Soon Geissler was negotiating to acquire the rights for the two next most lucrative markets, the Far East and western Europe. "Sometimes, the gravy can exceed the actual meat," he smiled.

Stan Lee at Marvel Comics was looking equally smart. To the acute embarrassment of those at Fox who called Lippincott's deal "dumb," Marvel was at full capacity as it struggled to keep pace with the phenomenal demand. Original copies of the first two editions of the *Star Wars* series were already selling for three to six times their original 30-cent cover price. By August 1977 the company was into their third reprint of the opening three editions of its *Star Wars* comic alone. The only dampener was that sales had long since passed the one hundred thousand mark after which royalties were due to Lucasfilm. Under the terms of his deal with Lippincott, Lee also faced having to renegotiate for further editions. It was soon Lippincott's turn to play hardball.

Del Rey, too, were the envy of their market. Within weeks of launching a new imprint, Judy-Lynn Del Rey's name was all over the bestseller list. Soon booksellers who complained they had no space to stock the *Star Wars Blueprints*—a collection of drawings of spacecraft—were reordering. Del Rey praised Lippincott and Lucasfilm as the pioneers of a new era. "Should I insult the rest of Hollywood? Better not. Let's just say others could learn from Lucasfilm how to do a tie-in," she told the trade magazine *Publishers Weekly*. She, too, had her chance to rib those who had doubted her. The moment she saw the film stills Lippincott had sent back from Tunisia, she had yelled, "We're going to make zillions." Her then-publisher had given her a look which she translated as, "Go play in traffic, the adults are working."

Lucas knew through Spielberg that *Jaws* had breathed a little new life into movie merchandising. A *Jaws* chewing gum had proved a lasting hit and by the time the film had finished its year long run more than three hundred thousand board games had left the shelves. This, however, was something else.

The thousands of phone calls that poured into Fox and the Lucasfilm offices were soon too much to handle. The *Star Wars* office moved across the road from Universal to a small office on Riverside Drive in North Hollywood. An extra five members of staff, primarily secretaries, were hired to help deal with the deluge. A system was devised whereby messages were filed according to their importance. One pile was marked, "Call back immediately," another "Call when convenient," a third, "Why bother." As the calls continued, Charlie Lippincott enjoyed bothering with one more than any other.

The "hustler" who had thrown him off his stand at the New York toy fair a few months earlier literally begged him to allow his company a slice of the *Star Wars* pie. Lippincott claims he was "polite" in his reply. He learned soon afterwards that the firm had gone bankrupt.

Like the hapless toy company executive, Wall Street had not failed to notice one gaping hole in the booming merchandising marketplace. Shares in both Mattel and Ideal had hit highs for the year early in June as Fox and Lucasfilm made noises about an imminent announcement about a *Star Wars* toy contract. As it turned out, neither of them would win out. At the New York toy fair in February only Kenner had shown interest in making a range of *Star Wars* toys. Afterwards a copy of Lucas's script and McQuarrie's drawings had been circulated at the company's Cincinnati HQ.

The company's senior designer, Dave Okada, had been as skeptical as most other senior designers about the viability of movie-inspired toys. He had seen the Dr. Doolittle debacle unfold at Mattel, where he had also worked on the unsuccessful launch of a multi-million-dollar astronaut toy, Matt Mason. In the wake of Vietnam, the accident-prone NASA moon shot program and the ill-fated Apollo 13 mission in particular, a question mark loomed over the entire market for military and space toys.

"The feeling was that the mothers of America were afraid of having their children grow up to be spacemen," he said. "There was also still a backlash from Vietnam. For mothers, who are the ultimate gatekeepers, it was not a very pacifist-oriented toy line."

Yet, as he and the company's chief executive, Bernie Loomis, had looked at Cantwell's drawings and McQuarrie's designs—each copy slashed with a razor blade for security reasons—they sensed a worthwhile gamble. Okada was impressed with the "oddness of the visuals." He also liked the names. "The X-Wings not only had a cool name, but had cool features and for a toy person like myself that was an instantaneous fun thing."

By April, Okada and Loomis were sitting down with Lucas at the Century Plaza Hotel in Century City signing a deal to make a complete range of *Star Wars* toys. Kenner would sell $1 billion worth of toys every year for the next seven years.

By the end of the summer Hollywood's business barometers were all pointing in the same direction. "Although there are no projected figures on how much money merchandising will bring in from *Star Wars*, the amount will be astronomical, and possibly the largest ever for any motion picture," said *Variety*.

As the summer holidays wore on, *Star Wars* had spread its wings wider across the country. By the end of June there were 460 cinemas showing the film, by the end of August some 900. Back in May, 70 mm prints of the film had been kept to a minimum. Now the laboratories were turning them out at the rate of two a day. As the *Star Wars* phenomenon spread into every major town and city in America, so, too, the media's feeding frenzy intensified. At the end of June, Ted Mann had been forced to remove *Star Wars* from the Chinese Theater to honor his commitment to screen Friedkin's *Sorcerer*. Within a month, he had renegotiated with Fox to have *Star Wars* return to the cinema where its phenomenal success had been born—the first time in the cinema's fifty-year history a film had returned there.

Mann marked the moment by bestowing the ultimate Hollywood accolade. As the lines returned to the Avenue of the Stars on the morning of August 3, Darth Vader, C-3PO and R2-D2 entertained them by immortalizing their tire-tracks and footprints in the Hall of Fame cement. The story ran in almost every newspaper in the country.

By now it was apparent that *Star Wars* would have no major rival at the box office. One after another its rivals had come and gone. *The Deep, Sorceror*, and *Exorcist: The Heretic* all faded in the face of the growing phenomenon. Only *Smokey and the Bandit* registered as a genuine success that summer.

"We were incredibly lucky that there was very little that was entertaining," admitted Gary Kurtz. "There was so little competition that summer—of any kind."

As the opposition disappeared so the records continued to tumble. By the end of August *Star Wars* had reached the $100 million mark at the box office faster than any movie in history. It had also eased its way past *Jaws* as the biggest box office hit in American cinema history. By the end of the year it would pass *Jaws*'s rentals record as well. In among all the remarkable statistics that summer, however, one fact left America shaking its head in wonder more than any other. Nowhere had *Star Wars* been as popular as in San Francisco, a home to both the film's producer and director over the years. By the end of the year the number of people who had seen *Star Wars* exceeded the 750,000 population of the city!

• • •

Asked an all-too-familiar question during an interview at the opulent Beverly Wilshire Hotel in June 1977, Mark Hamill had leaned back into his sofa and smiled at the bottle of Dom Perignon on ice before him. "How has this changed my life? I'm ordering forty-three dollar bottles of champagne I can't even pronounce," he had replied. It would not take long for the champagne to fall flat, however. As the most famous faces connected with *Star Wars* were to discover, success came at a questionable price.

For Hamill, Carrie Fisher, and Harrison Ford May 25 had been a watershed. That morning their lives had been transformed beyond all recognition. Now, their features were emblazoned on T-shirts, belt buckles, lunch boxes, and tote bags from Seattle to Saratoga. George Lucas had also set each of them on their way to becoming millionaires in their own rights.

As he had done on *Graffiti*, Lucas awarded bonuses to those he felt had helped him the most. Alec Guinness had negotiated a two and a quarter percent share of the profits in advance, the most astute financial move of his entire career. It would earn him around $6 million. Lucas felt his leading trio should benefit too. Hamill, Ford, and Fisher were given a quarter percentage point of the profits. In time the gift would earn them some $650,000 each. In time, each would wonder whether it was worth it.

As *Star Wars* fever broke, the trio had been sent on a three-week long, rock-'n'-roll style tour. Crowds turned up for each public appearance, television cameras jostled for the best positions at their press conferences. The trio did their best to shine light on the phenomenon. "*Star Wars* is a silly movie, but wonderfully made," was the best a nonplussed and often bored Ford could come up with. Their elevation to iconhood seemed barely credible to friends who met them on the road. Earl McGrath, a Los Angeles art collector and former rock-'n'-roll manager, had arranged to meet his old friend Ford as the tour took in New York. When he arrived at the posh Sherry Netherland Hotel on Fifth Avenue he had paid little attention to the crowd of mainly women fans loitering outside. McGrath, whose money had helped Ford set up his carpentry workshop when he was almost broke years earlier, was as amused as he was baffled by his friend's behavior as they walked out through the lobby on their way to dinner.

"I have a car outside," Ford reassured him.

"We don't need a car," McGrath replied, puzzled.

"Yes, we do," his friend said as he grabbed his arm and ran him through the throng. The Han Solo Fan Club chased them all the way to the waiting limousine.

All three found the job of impersonating latter-day Beatles "unnatural and embarrassing,"according to Fisher. Amid the madness they let off steam like Animal House students. "We had a huge food fight in my suite at the Sherry Netherland," she recalled. "It was terrific: spinach in my hair, beer down shirts. We tried to clean up before George and Marcia Lucas came in—like mom and dad—but there was still a piece of spinach on the mantel."

The surreal circus was somehow less shocking to Fisher. She had, after all, grown up in the glare of publicity. "I don't mind the attention, I grew up on a movie-star map," she laughed. Yet even she realized *Star Wars*'s peculiar brand of stardom differed from that of her parents. Soon after *Star Wars* took off she began to find adolescent male fans hanging around outside her house. One evening she discovered one sitting in her kitchen. She had to call a neighbor, the brother of her then-boyfriend, Dan Aykroyd, to throw the intruder into the street. "I felt helpless," she said later. The insecurity only deepened her dependency on drugs, by now an every-day part of the life she led with friends like John Belushi and other members of the anarchic *Saturday Night Live* television show.

Fisher's unhappiness was not helped by the paucity of work that came her way in the wake of *Star Wars*. Apart from a television production of *Come Back, Little Sheba* with Sir Laurence Olivier and Joanne Woodward, Fisher found herself reduced to guest appearances on shows like *Saturday Night Live*.

Years later, in drug rehabilitation, a roommate would attempt to intimidate her by announcing: "I was in San Quentin."

"So what? I was in *Star Wars*," would be Fisher's acidic reply.

In the afterglow it was Ford who benefited most professionally. He was, after "a bloody long night," an overnight star. *Star Wars* had put the first stamp on his passport. In the months that followed he flew to the Philippines to appear in *Apocalypse Now* (where he wore a name badge emblazoned with the name Col. G. Lucas!), Yugoslavia for *Force Ten From Navarone*, and then back to England for the World War II movie *Hanover Street*. The films were part of a concerted effort to establish himself away from the deck of the *Millennium Falcon*. Yet, he too was soon harboring regrets. By the time he returned to Los Angeles, Ford's thirteen-year-old marriage was in ruins. He found it hard to excuse *Star Wars* from blame.

His wife, Mary, whom he had met at college in Wisconsin, had seemed ill at ease in her few public appearances on the arm of Han Solo. Friends wondered whether she had found marriage to a struggling carpenter-cum-actor preferable.

"You could never picture Mary in the Hollywood scheme of things," said one old friend, Walter Beakel. "She was very supportive, but the struggling was somehow easier to comprehend than the success."

Within a year of *Star Wars'* success Ford had moved to a rented flat in west Hollywood, within a short drive of his two sons, Ben and Willard. "Success separated us more and more—and I will never forgive it for that," he would say of his marital break up.

Hamill was, perhaps, the least equipped of the three to cope with the success. His traumatic car accident had left his face and his confidence badly scarred. "All life had to offer was Peter Lorre's old parts," he joked later. The only role he had been offered after *Star Wars* had been in Hal Barwood and Matthew Robbins' limp adolescent road movie, *Corvette Summer*. In general, the only scripts that came his agent's way were "garbage," he admitted. "Many studios seem afraid to take the chance and hire me because of my *Star Wars* association," he complained at the time.

Hamill's long-running relationship with a dental hygienist, Marilou York, foundered almost as soon as Luke Skywalker turned him into the most famous pinup in America. Hamill had used his windfall to buy a beachside home in Malibu. As he looked out of his window each morning he would see the small group of devoted female fans he called "Charlie's Angels" standing outside in the hope of seeing him. "They became my protection squad," he confessed. At the age of twenty-five, he was simply unable to resist the temptations. Soon he was spending his money in the clip joints and casinos of Las Vegas. "I had to taste groupies and fame," he confessed. "I went to Las Vegas to date thirty-eight-year-old showgirls. I wanted to scale all these women."

For much of the year that followed the release of *Star Wars*, Hamill "wallowed in self-pity." It was only the intervention of an old friend, actress Diana Hyland, that had pulled him back from the brink of self-destruction, he admitted later. Hyland, with whom he had worked on television, had seen him depressed and drinking and told him he was "letting himself down." A few days later Hamill heard she had died. "I was so self-involved I didn't know she was ill, let alone [that] her illness was terminal."

It had been Francis Coppola who had first warned Lucas of the dangers of success. Coppola had been lauded like some cinematic demigod when *The Godfather* was released in 1972. It was, he said: "no different than the shock of death— you're in a transition period and when you come out of it, you're a different person." If there was one thing George and Marcia were determined to do post-*Star Wars*, it was to defy Coppola's predictions and remain themselves. As the box office headed beyond the $200 million mark, Lucas's share of the "rentals" was growing exponentially. Ultimately he would bank around $20 million after taxes.

Yet his only extravagance was a Ferrari, and typically a used one at that. Instead, he remained hidden away in San Anselmo. "I'm an introvert, I don't want to be famous," he told *People* magazine as they came to profile him and Marcia. "I get nervous when people recognize me and say, 'I loved your movie.'"

Asked what their plans were, he and Marcia held hands and talked of starting a family. "Getting our private life together and having a baby. That is the project for the rest of this year," Marcia smiled.

If Lucas needed any reminding of the dangers of fame, he had only to visit his office in Los Angeles. "Some guy came into our Los Angeles office claiming to be a Jedi Knight and pulled a knife on a secretary," Lucas recalled. "Another real lunatic insisted he wrote *Star Wars* and came to pick up his $100 million check."

Even Alec Guinness saw his share of the insanity. "People became fairly lunatic about it," he said. "I had a letter from a couple somewhere in California, who were having marital trouble, inviting me to visit them. It was along the lines of: 'Would you as Ben Kenobi come and spend a week with us and sort out our marriage?'"

Guinness was later persuaded to attend a science-fiction convention in San Francisco. "I had a question and answer business, that was kind of all right," he explained. "But then there was a boy of about twelve or thirteen who suddenly stood up and said: 'I've seen *Star Wars* 110 times.' I said: 'please come round and see me afterwards, which he did with his mother.'"

Guinness warned the boy he was becoming obsessed. "I said, 'I beg you never to see it again because this is going to be an ill effect on your life,' whereupon he burst into tears."

For some the fantasy was infinitely preferable to the reality of their own day-to-day existence. "People were seeking something which didn't exist for them," said Guinness.

"It is bizarre, people do lose track of what's real and what's not," said Gary Kurtz. "They are living a fantasy life because they can't deal with their own lives."

For Lucas, however, the path was clear. He stepped up his plans for a permanent withdrawal from Hollywood and its multi-layered madness.

In France they smiled "*Que La Force Soit Avec Toi*," in Holland "*Moge De Kracht Met U Zijn*," in Mexico "*Que La Fuerza Te Acompane*" and in Denmark "*Ma Kraften Vaere Med Dig*."

If 1977 had been the year America discovered *Star Wars* mania, 1978 began as the year the world felt the Force.

Since May 1977, Fox had been laying the groundwork for the film's worldwide release. Lucas had personally overseen foreign language dubs of the film to ensure his dialogue did not sound too silly in other tongues.

Nowhere was the mania greater than in *Star Wars*'s home itself. In 1978, London became a mirror of every American city the previous summer. The lines stood in the wind and rain outside the Dominion, Leicester Square, standing in line to see the 10:50 A.M. showing—the only one not booked solidly until March. The advance box office of £170,000 was the biggest London had ever seen. Sphere's paperback of the

Lucas/Foster novel had sold 700,000, 95-pence copies before Christmas.

As the records fell, so the merchandising madness descended with them. Household names from ICI to Letraset, Waddingtons to Walls foods staked their claims for a corner of the market, unleashing *Star Wars* wallpapers, Princess Leia notepads and jigsaw puzzles, and—least credible of all—*Star Wars* sausages on an unsuspecting British public! Even the trendy London hairdresser Michaeljohn found it hard to resist the gold-rush offering clients a twenty-first century sphinx-style "*Star Wars*-inspired" perm for the hair-raising price of £12.

The scenes were repeated across the Channel when *La Guerre des Etoiles* opened there a month later. By now Fox was using troops of stormtroopers and Darth Vader lookalikes to drum up publicity at major city openings. Like an invading army they were soon sweeping through Spain, Italy, and Germany.

The Philippines had become the first foreign country to be shown *Star Wars* in the early autumn of 1977. Reaction there encouraged Fox to tackle areas of Asia where American movies had fared poorly in the past. In India, notoriously indifferent to imports, *Star Wars* racked up new records when it was released in January. The Sterling picture house in Bombay and the Safire in Madras sold out every single seat of their twenty-eight and twenty-four week runs.

There were territories that proved immune to the fuss. In some cases, the hype proved hard to live up to. In May 1978, Chile gave the film the cold shoulder at the box office. Returns were respectable, yet less than the dire remake of *King Kong* and the film version of *Jesus Christ Superstar* when they visited Santiago. After a year of waiting to see what the fuss was all about, Chileans were disappointed with what their critics called "a minor comic strip." The film was withdrawn after six weeks, as it was in Scandinavia, where *Star Wars* also left audiences cold.

Predictably, the crumbling Communist regime in the Soviet Union saw the film as a piece of blatantly subversive propaganda. It was not just the grim empire imagery that upset the party newspaper, although *Izvestia* did claim the film was an attempt to make the rest of the world "anti-Soviet." The Kremlin's main grievance was that Hollywood was obviously plotting to sabotage the SALT nuclear arms treaty!

Star Wars's triumphant march was not hindered by its success at the Academy Awards in April 1978. The most remarkable year in Twentieth Century–Fox's recent history was crowned when the studio picked up a record-breaking thirty-three nominations that year. While *Julia* and *The Turning Point* picked up twenty-three of them, the remaining ten were for *Star Wars*. Lucas was nominated for best director and best screenplay, *Star Wars* for best film. Other nominees included the four Johns, John Mollo for costume design, Dykstra and his team of Richard Edlund, Grant McCune, John Stears, and Robert Blalack for special effects, Barry for his design, and Williams for his score.

Lucas regarded the highlight of the American awards season as an offensive and meaningless piece of Hollywood pageantry—nothing to do with filmmaking, everything to do with cold-eyed commerce. Yet he reluctantly slipped into a tuxedo and a limousine and braved the spotlights at the Dorothy Chandler Pavilion on Oscar night. He was there as much for Marcia, nominated with Chew and Hirsch for the best editing prize, as for himself.

The trusty barometers of the Writer's Guild and Director's Guild had given Lucas and Gary Kurtz a clue as to what to expect. As anticipated, it was another Hollywood-hater, Woody Allen, who won best screenplay, best picture, and best director for *Annie Hall*. Allen didn't even turn up.

Star Wars left far from empty-handed, however. The four Johns all won, as did Ben Burtt, awarded a special Oscar for his sound achievements. Even Lucas felt a spark of pride when Marcia took the tally to five statuettes. Her smile seemed one of the brightest on a subdued night for the awards.

Buoyed by the success, Fox decided to rerelease the film in America that summer. In five weeks *Star Wars* sold another $46 million in tickets. (It took in another $23 million when it was rereleased an unprecedented third year running in 1979.)

Fox had left potentially the biggest overseas market, Japan, until last, delaying opening there until August in the hope of benefiting from a traditional twenty percent rise in summer audiences.

In August, in the face of advice from his team, Alan Ladd Jr. flew over to Tokyo for the premiere. At first he was convinced he had witnessed a disaster. The audience at the giant domelike cinema, decked out to look like a vast R2-D2 for the occasion, sat in silence. When the final strains of John Williams's score drifted off into the night, they simply rose and filtered out of the cinema. Over dinner afterwards it took a while for Ladd to believe his hosts' assurances that silence was the greatest compliment an audience could pay a film. Soon the figures provided all the reassurances he could want.

Within two months Fox's rentals from Japanese cinema chains stood at $18.3 million. By the end of its run it had earned almost $21 million. Until then the most the studio had ever made from a single film in any foreign market had been $6 million when *The Poseidon Adventure* opened in Japan.

By the time *Star Wars* was finally withdrawn from American cinemas in November 1978, it had earned an all-time record of $273 million gross and $164 in rentals at the US and

Canadian box office. With overseas rentals already at $68 million, *Star Wars* had earned its owners $232 million. By the end of the following year the worldwide box office would go on to gross a total of $430 million.

For decades, the studios had seen the foreign market as an interesting sideline business. From now on they would view it rather differently.

At 8 P.M. on the evening of Sunday, September 17, 1978, the ABC television network premiered its most expensive television series ever. *Battlestar Galactica*, a space saga, set in a distant galaxy in the seventh millennium A.D., had been made by Universal in Hollywood, at a reported $1 million an episode. As lasers flashed, imperious spacecraft lumbered overhead and a dashingly handsome young hero called Starbuck led the battle against a half-human, half-machine enemy, the Cyclons, it looked worth every cent. Viewers and critics who found something strangely familiar about the series were not alone, however.

Weeks before transmission, on June 23, Twentieth Century–Fox had issued a lawsuit, suing Universal for what it saw as a blatant theft of *Star Wars*. If science fiction had been "deadly" before May 25, 1977, it had been resurrected in the most spectacular fashion. Seemingly every studio and television company in Hollywood had become involved in a frenzied race to the stars.

Warner Bros. had committed $20 million to bringing the *Superman* comics to life. Marlon Brando had been paid a bewildering $2 million for a cranky cameo as the Man of Steel's father in a spectacular version of the story being produced in England by the Salkind brothers. Disney was preparing to put its inimitable imprimatur on the genre with *The Cat From Outer Space*. It was also spending more serious money on developing a Jules Verne–like, spectacular about a deep space mission, *The Black Hole*.

Paramount, whose then-parent company, Gulf & Western had ditched plans to launch a fourth national television network with a new series of *Star Trek* as its centerpiece, hurriedly dusted down a relic of the genre. One of the abortive scripts was hurriedly translated into *Star Trek: The Movie*. Thanks to *Star Wars*, Kirk, Spock, and company were allowed to boldly go where everyone in Hollywood was now headed. In the meantime, the studio reissued George Pal's 1950s classics, *When Worlds Collide* and *War of the Worlds* to tap into the vogue.

Even the then-president of Paramount Pictures, Michael Eisner, admitted that without Fox's success, his company would, in all likelihood, have left *Star Trek* on the shelf. He shrugged: "I doubt whether there would have been the impetus to change *Star Trek* from a television series to a movie without *Star Wars*." (Gene Roddenberry remained jealous of *Star Wars*'s success until his death in October 1991. In his autobiography he confined his thoughts on the most influential science fiction movie of all time to one sentence.)

Of all the studios, Universal seemed the most halfhearted in their search for movies in the mold of the one they had passed up. A remake of *When Worlds Collide*, to be cofunded with Paramount, was attempted but perished in the face of terrifying special-effects costs. With rare candor, Ned Tanen admitted he saw little point in trying to bolt the stable door. "I'm not interested in chasing *Star Wars*," he announced. "You can't do it. *Star Wars* is an incredible bullseye—a unique phenomenon." Instead, the studio concentrated on bringing the thrills of *Star Wars* to the small screen. It had also snapped up the rights to the old Buck Rogers series with an eye on another television series.

If imitation was flattering, outright lifting of ideas—to Lucas's mind, at least—was not. (Lucas would never get the chance to dismiss the most hurtful and faintly preposterous plagiarism charge he received. In a foreword to a collection of short stories, published after his death in 1986, Frank Herbert, author of the benchmark sci-fi novel *Dune*, moaned that *Star Wars* used "so much" of his novel, he counted "sixteen points of identity.")

In many ways it was hardly surprising that the stirring aerial dogfights in *Battlestar Galactica* bore some similarity to the rebel assault on the Death Star. Universal's special-effects wizard was none other than John Dykstra. After *Star Wars* had shut down in the spring of 1977, Dykstra had remained at the Van Nuys warehouse where he had begun almost immediately on preliminary work for Universal.

The influence of *Star Wars* did not end there, however. Jim Nelson and many of the original ILM artists also contributed to the series. It seems a curious coincidence that some of them had lost out when Lucas had handed out his bonuses that summer.

Nelson had fallen out with Lucas just before the release. The ILM overseer had been expecting to be acknowledged as an associate producer on the final credits.

Lucas told him he did not agree and suggested he was credited further down the titles with the technicians. He did not feel Nelson had contributed anything "artistic" to the film. After a blazing row in which he told Lucas he had "no idea" of the role he had played in the production, Nelson took his name off the credits completely. Despite Lucas's pleas that he reconsider, *Star Wars* was released without any mention of his contribution at all.

Nelson's anger was understandable. The strain of working within ILM had turned his brown hair gray. "Lucas gray, I call it." He had stopped running his own thriving company and taken a considerable salary cut on the strength of the promise of a share in the film. "I gave up a $100,000-a-year job to go to work for $25,000 a year. I had to pay my own health [insurance], pension, and everything else. I took home around $224 a week," he said.

He wondered whether his outspoken attitude had damaged him in the eyes of the director. It was no coincidence that neither he nor John Dykstra had been invited to stay with the company in the wake of *Star Wars*. Rebellious natures had no place in Lucas's new empire, it seemed.

"I liked George. But George is very difficult to work with; you must agree with George and if you don't agree with George then George doesn't like you," Nelson said. "Dykstra would argue with George all the time and so would I. It didn't pay off!"

"The reason George likes to work with young people is because they don't have much experience or power," said Ben Burtt. "With me, he could still be in charge."

Dykstra had been most hurt by comments Lucas supposedly made that "on a scale of one to ten, the effects in the movie were a five." "Although George was cordial to me whenever he saw me, and he did congratulate me on the Academy Award, we weren't particularly close friends to begin with and we weren't particularly close friends at the end of the movie," he said.

When Dykstra had been approached to continue the work he had pioneered at ILM on a Universal television series, he had had no hesitation in accepting. Such was his bargaining power in the post-*Star Wars* world, he was even able to negotiate a producer's credit.

Lucas had got wind of the series early on and demanded to be shown it. *Battlestar*'s producer, Glen Larson, had handed Lucas an early episode in an attempt to placate him. When Fox filed its lawsuit against him, Larson had initially made much of the fact that the creator of *Star Wars* did not have his name attached to the legal papers. To Lucas's fury, he even claimed he was "satisfied with it."

"I did see the first episode of this proposed series and I feel strongly that Glen Larson and Universal Pictures have attempted to copy what I created for *Star Wars* and are continuing to attempt to pass their series off as some sort of *Star Wars* for television," he said, pulling no punches in a public letter to *Variety*.

"I feel this will ultimately be very harmful to what I have created and I strongly hope that Fox will be successful in attempts to protect us," he added.

Fox failed to halt the series being aired, however. As *Battlestar Galactica* went on to become one of the winter's biggest TV hits, the off-screen drama rolled into a series of court hearings that would last years.

CHAPTER 9

Double or Nothing...

George Lucas liked to claim he was not a gambler. "I'm a bad poker player," he would say. "I don't have the ability to bluff."

If there had been few in Hollywood who believed him, there had been fewer still on the morning of February 24, 1978.

The *Variety* headline ran: IT'S DEFINITE NOW: 20TH FOX GETS THE "STAR WARS" SEQUEL.

To many in the industry it had been news that Fox did not have the rights to the sequel in the first place. As they read on, however, their belated admiration for the negotiating skills Lucas had displayed in 1975 had paled before their amazement at the *chutzpah* he was now showing.

Lucas announced that while Fox would distribute his follow up, to be called *The Empire Strikes Back,* he would finance the film completely himself. Behind the headlines, the move was even more audacious than it appeared. The reality was that he had mortgaged his entire *Star Wars* fortune.

According to the reports the sequel would cost Lucasfilm around $10 million. In fact, he already knew the budget would be almost twice that. Lucas had loaned almost every dime of the $20 million he had earned personally from *Star Wars* back to Lucasfilm as collateral against a loan for the $18 million he and Gary Kurtz had calculated *Empire* would cost.

If the film worked, the company would pay him back his money. If it did not, the banks would come to him for compensation.

On one level Lucas was simply practicing what he had preached. He had nothing but disdain for the conglomerates who made money in movies then siphoned it off elsewhere. Dennis Stanfill and the Fox board had used its $150 million bonanza to diversify its interests, making investments in a midwestern bottling company, a golf course in Pebble Beach, and a ski resort in Colorado. He was putting his money back into the industry. Yet on another level, his gamble was the ultimate game of double or nothing.

Ever since the first flush of success with *American Graffiti*, Lucas had dreamed of building a genuine alternative to Hollywood amid the peace of Marin County. He likened the idea to that of a rock musician constructing his own recording studio in his backyard.

He had discreetly begun buying land in a secluded valley near San Rafael. A 1,882 acre site known as Bulltail Ranch had been his major acquisition so far. He had paid $2.7 million for the property after his first wave of *Star Wars* profits arrived in 1978. Negotiations were already under way for a further thirteen pieces of adjoining land. In moments of relaxation, he would doodle the blueprints of the ranch-style home and production outbuildings he one day hoped to place there. Yet Lucas knew that to fulfill the plans he had for his own personal studio, he would need "serious money." He had projected a cost of more than $20 million over the course of the next six years. With the Lucasfilm operation in Los Angeles still drawing on his resources, the $20 million or so he had earned from *Star Wars* was not enough.

He had gambled before and won. This time he had everything to gain—and everything to lose.

Halfhearted talk of a sequel had begun even before *Star Wars* had been completed. In the final weeks of filming at Elstree, Alan Ladd Jr. had suggested to Gary Kurtz that he film a little extra footage. "Right at the end of shooting Laddie said, 'What about shooting material for another film?'" said Kurtz. "Based on the principal if we could do it cheaply, then we'd have something else." The notion was soon forgotten in the face of the hideous pressure he and Lucas were under to simply finish *Star Wars*.

By the time he had flown to Hawaii in the middle of June 1977, however, Ladd was deadly serious. He knew from his conversations with Lucas that *Star Wars* was merely the tip of an extraordinary iceberg. For Lucas, however, it was a question of how he could survive the process once more. He had already decided to give up directing and he knew he could not face the torture of writing another *Star Wars*. In his mind he made the decision to delegate control, even though he must have known how impossible that would be in reality.

Lucas had struck the deal for the sequel only using Tom Pollock for the legal side of matters. Lucas made no secret of the debt he owed Berg for brokering the deal with Fox. On the other hand, he felt the company had been more than adequately rewarded with its ten percent of his gross earning, by now a colossal $4.5 million fee. To no one's surprise, ICM failed to see it quite that way. It insisted that as it had negotiated *Star Wars* it should also negotiate its sequel. Once more flying in the face of Hollywood convention, Lucas told the most powerful agency in the business to "buzz off." He could hardly have been surprised when it too launched a legal offensive against him.

By late 1978, the production was already beginning to take shape. Lucas was determined that the lessons of *Star Wars* would be taken on board. Gil Taylor, John Dykstra, and the recalcitrant elements who had made life so difficult for him on *Star Wars* were the first victims. Meanwhile, many of the original ILM team had already been relocated to a site he had bought fourteen miles or so from his ranch, in San Rafael. The backbone of the team that had completed *Star Wars*, more manageable talents like Dennis Muren and Joe Johnston, moved to northern California to head up the operation. The undisciplined madness of the Van Nuys warehouse would be a thing of the past.

Gary Kurtz had been the natural choice to produce. With Lucas he had asked Leigh Brackett, the highly regarded writer of *The Big Sleep* and *Rio Bravo,* to develop the outline of the second story Lucas had mapped out in his Luke Star-killer epic.

The ring binder full of notes Lucas had given Brackett amounted to a scene-by-scene synopsis of what would be her finished story. Luke, Leia, and Han began the story hiding at a rebel base on the ice planet Hoth. Discovered by a probe droid dispatched by Darth Vader, they would fight a spectacular air and ground battle with the imperial forces before abandoning the planet. While Han and Leia were pursued by Vader, Obi-Wan would send Luke to the swamp planet Dagobah, where he would be instructed in the ways of the force by the Jedi master, Yoda.

The third act would climax with Luke rushing to rescue Leia and Han from the clutches of Vader on a cloud city above the planet Bespin.

After Brackett turned in an excellent first draft, Lucas had expected she would then go on to provide a customary rewrite or two. What he did not know was that Brackett was suffering from terminal cancer. She died within days of delivering her script.

Lucas was then forced to redraft the script himself. After scrabbling around he hired a promising Chicago copywriter, Lawrence Kasdan, to apply the final brush strokes. Kasdan quickly added depth to the characters, especially the central love triangle of Luke, Leia, and Han Solo.

When the deal with Fox had been announced the return of the three American stars had been taken for granted. Yet it was far from cut and dried. Lucas had ensured that Carrie Fisher and Mark Hamill had been signed up for three films from the beginning. His foresight was admirable. Both were still finding the experience of being pop cultural icons a faintly unpleasant one. Since making *Corvette Summer* with Barwood and Robbins, Hamill's only other appearance had been in the *Big Red One*, a war drama with Lee Marvin that had failed to even find a release date. His misery had not been helped by his slow recovery from his facial injuries and persistent rumors in Hollywood that he had been scarred for life. At least he had turned a corner personally and, reunited with Marilou York, had married in December 1978. The couple were expecting their first child in the summer of 1979.

As his career had been becalmed, Hamill admitted he had felt let down by Lucas. All he had been able to do was suggest, semijokingly, that Hamill retire while he was at the top. "There's no pressure to put out a product, and if you do get a part you can say: 'The role was so good it lured me out of retirement,'" he had told the young star.

Hamill found it hard to mask the resentment he felt at his fate. "Thirty years ago the studios would have built our careers."

Fisher, still unconvinced she had anything major to contribute to acting, had concentrated on developing her gift for comedy on *Saturday Night Live*. "I'm famous in this weird way because I'm this children's cartoon character," she had opined. "It hasn't translated into jobs."

However, the major job was persuading the recalcitrant Harrison Ford back into the fold.

Ford had continued to capitalize on his success as Han Solo and found it easy to win roles. Yet *Heroes, Force Ten From Navarone* and his most recent movie, *The Frisco Kid*, a comic western with Gene Wilder directed by Robert Aldrich, had been disappointments. *Hanover Street*, with Lesley-Anne Down, had been an unmitigated disaster. The reviews were so bad Ford had refused to even look at the film.

His major worry remained that he might be pigeonholed as Solo. As he discussed the script with Lucas and Kurtz, he made it clear he wanted to broaden the role.

"He wanted to be more Clark Gable–like and roguish. Like most actors he was also really worried about being stereotyped," said Kurtz.

Fortunately, Ford saw that Kasdan's screenplay bristled with more energy and humanity than any of Lucas's *Star Wars* drafts had done. Soon he had committed himself to another outing in the *Millennium Falcon*.

Only one major piece of American casting was needed. Billy Dee Williams was cast as Lando Calrissian, an old gambling friend of Solo's who would appear in the third act in the Bespin cloud city. Much as he and Lucas may have denied it at the time, Kurtz now admits that the appearance of the first black actor in *Star Wars* was an attempt to quell the criticism the film had taken in a racially sensitive America. Lucas had been accused of "rampant racism" for failing to use a single black performer in his film. "It was an oversight," Kurtz conceded.

Of the British cast, the most stubborn proved to be Anthony Daniels. Like Dave Prowse, he had been angered by the lack of credit he had been given and the widespread use of his screen image in America. Prowse reacted with the virility of Vader. The muscleman, who hired an agent in the U.S., answered his own fan mail and quickly became something of a cult figure on television. "I was determined to get the credit for it," he said.

Daniels, however, simply fretted much like C-3PO. He had found the insinuations that C-3PO wasn't even played by an actor the most hurtful. According to Daniels, publicists for *Star Wars* had at one stage claimed, "C-3PO is entirely mechanical." "They denied I existed," he complained. Daniels even let rip at Lucas publicly, accusing him of "opening one door only to slam another in his face." While Lucas took his point, it only deepened the director's dislike of dealing with temperamental actors.

Eventually, Daniels was offered a higher billing and a guaranteed profit participation in the film. The temptation proved too much.

Kurtz's toughest assignment was finding a director willing to pick up what many regarded as the ultimate poisoned chalice. "Half a dozen key names in Hollywood did not want to have anything to do with *Empire*. You could see why," said Kurtz. "It was a sequel to the biggest selling film of all time. So number one, if they screw up it's all their fault. Two, if it's another big hit all the credit was going to go to George. So why bother, unless you're getting tons of money; why take on a totally thankless task like that."

Eventually Kurtz interviewed an old friend, Irvin Kershner, whom he had met way back in his post-USC documentary days. Back then Kershner had been making an antidrug documentary, *Stakeout on Dope Street*. Since then an eclectic career had taken him from the United States Information Service in Africa and the Middle East to directing *The Eyes of Laura Mars* with Faye Dunaway. Kershner had, as a musically gifted child in Philadelphia, wanted to grow up to be

Stravinsky or Prokofiev. Tall, goateed, and intellectual, Hollywood saw him as an unlikely choice to conduct the latest symphony of the space opera that had captured the imagination of the world. Yet Kurtz and Lucas had been impressed by the distinctly un-Hollywood director. Anyone who quoted a 1950 prediction by Aldous Huxley's that fantasy was the future of film, was always going to appeal! Like many middle-aged fans of the film, Kershner had watched *Star Wars* with his son. He had enjoyed the film's mythical undercurrents and saw them deepening with the arrival of the new character, Yoda.

"Kersh was into Zen, as I was. We were both excited about the Yoda character," said Kurtz. "He had lines like, 'There is no try, only do.' That's a very Zen concept. We both thought it was great to be able to use things like that in an entertaining way."

Lucas and Kurtz agreed to once more base the production at Elstree. What it lacked in sophistication, Borehamwood more than made up for in economy and privacy. The two men's first major difference of opinion came when Kurtz drew up a budget of $18 million—almost double the cost of *Star Wars*. He saw no way of making the film for significantly less. In the three years since *Star Wars*, inflation had bumped up the cost of all film material by a factor of three or four. And no agent in the entertainment world would now allow his client to work for George Lucas for nothing. "The problem with being a hit was that no one was going to work for a minimum, they all wanted top dollar," said Kurtz. Eventually Kurtz was given the $18 million he needed. Lucas would not allow him to forget whose money it was, however.

The villagers of the remote Norwegian outpost of Finse were used to rather lonely winters. Each year, between October and March, eighty or so of them remained snowed in there, mostly railway workers assigned to keep the vital Oslo to Bergen line open during the relentless blizzards.

In the first week of March 1979, however, the population almost doubled. More than seventy American, British, and Norwegian visitors crammed themselves, two to a room, into the town's main accommodation, the Finse Ski Lodge. Soon their Swedish snowcats and powerful helicopters helped them establish two base camps high on the blue ice glacier, 6,000 feet above the village. Each was equipped with emergency heating, lighting, and food supplies to last days.

The technology at their disposal would have been the envy of any invading army. Captain Robert Scott would certainly have appreciated it when he left Finse, the training camp for his ill-fated expedition to the South Pole, almost seventy years earlier, in 1910. Yet it did not take long for mother nature to reassert her authority. Three years after the rainstorm in Tunisia, the weather once more wreaked havoc with the *Star Wars* team's first days of filming.

Kurtz and Kershner had led the team to Finse at the end of February, hoping the worst of the winter would be over. No sooner had they unloaded the tons of equipment shipped over via London and Oslo and welcomed Carrie Fisher and Mark Hamill to the ski lodge, than a series of furious snowstorms broke. Then a succession of avalanches had left them completely cut off.

If there had been any doubts over the movie's status, the media's reaction to the news removed them. The first days of filming on the first film had been a nonevent. The beginning of principal photography on its sequel was instantly broadcast from Bergen to Bogota. Soon the film's unit publicist, Alan Arnold, was issuing a statement from the Finse Ski Lodge assuring children everywhere that Luke and Princess Leia were safe.

Gary Kurtz found it hard to see the delay as a publicity opportunity, however. It only compounded the mounting problems his production was facing before a single frame of film had been shot.

Kurtz and associate producer, Robert Watts, had chosen Finse the previous year. Its barren wastes seemed perfect for the surface of the ice planet Hoth, where the first act of *The Empire Strikes Back* would be played out. Even when the weather did clear, however, shooting conditions were hideous. Kershner's priority was to film key opening scenes featuring Luke riding across the tundra astride a giant llamalike Tauntaun and his attack by a Wampa snow monster. (The monster's slash to his face would provide an explanation for the lingering hint of scar tissue after Mark Hamill's accident.)

Forced to reschedule while snowed in at the ski lodge, Kershner decided to change his plans and film a scene in which Han rescues a frost-bitten Luke, wrapping him in the carcass of his Tauntaun. The change forced Harrison Ford to undergo a grueling trip from London, the final stage of which was conducted on board a snow plow he had hitched a ride aboard. He arrived bleary-eyed at midnight on the night before his 6 A.M. start the next day. Like Hamill, he headed out into the sub-zero cold wearing two pairs of thermal long johns, four pairs of socks and a walkie-talkie strapped underneath his costume in case of problems.

The constant threat of new blizzards and the biting 40 mph winds made even the simplest piece of filming near impossible for Kershner. Often the weather would change in an instant, forcing him to abandon set up scenes and head for the safety of the base camps—named Camp Kurtz and Camp Sharman (after production supervisor Bruce Sharman)—or Finse itself. When the ferocity of the storms produced dreaded zero visibility white outs, the half-hour march back to the lodge could take as long as an hour and a half.

For all their experience, Kershner and Kurtz had never

faced a challenge like it. "The camera equipment had to be winterized with special lightweight oil in the gears to stop them from freezing up," recalled the director. "And you had to handle the film carefully in case it became very brittle and cracked."

"There was so much wind blowing, with snow and ice, that it would cover the lens. You could do a take for twenty to thirty seconds then it would just cloud over," he added. "And if you touched a camera without gloves on, your skin immediately glued to the metal. You had to take a razor blade and slice away the skin a little bit to get it off. It was kind of an adventure."

Despite the difficulties they had encountered three years earlier, Kurtz and Lucas had stuck with Elstree as the base for the rest of the shoot. Fueled by the profits of *Star Wars*, a new sound stage had been built at the studio, its cost shared between EMI and Lucasfilm.

Lucas, Brackett, and Kasdan's story had divided itself into three distinct acts—the first on the ice planet Hoth, the second divided between the swamp planet Dagobah and the *Millennium Falcon*'s attempts to elude Darth Vader, and the third in Bespin City, a community in the clouds where Solo would be frozen in carbon after being betrayed by his friend Lando Calrissian.

At first Kurtz had toyed with the idea of filming the Dagobah scenes back in Tunisia. Instead, with art director Norman Reynolds, he had opted to create the dank "swamp" planet at Elstree's Stage 3. As the Arctic storms kept him penned inside the Arctic Circle, that decision was looking inspired. Time was already against him.

Kurtz's problems had begun long before the Norwegian part of the shoot.

No one had been able to ascertain whether it was a discarded cigarette or an electrical short that started the small fire on Stage 3 at Elstree on the night of January 24, five weeks before principal photography was due to start. The carnage it had caused was beyond doubt, however.

The alarm had been raised quickly but the driveways of the studio complex were so congested by equipment that the local fire brigade found it impossible to reach the fire. They could only stand helplessly by as the flames spread through the building. By the following morning all that remained of the stage was a smouldering ruin.

With *Empire* due to take over the stage weeks later, Kurtz was instantly forced to look for two more sound stages. He was also hindered by the fact that the fire had further delayed Stanley Kubrick who was completing *The Shining* at Elstree. "Kubrick was driving me crazy. He stayed on two stages that we needed desperately to build on," said Kurtz. "I kept saying, 'Stanley, I've got to have that stage.'" At least Kurtz offered Kubrick an easy scapegoat for the failure of the more hurried scenes in his flawed masterpiece.

After an initial appearance to bolster his troops in London, Lucas headed back to Marin where he was to oversee the special effects side of the film at ILM. (He was also committed to finishing a misguided sequel to the film that made his name, *More American Graffiti*, for Universal.) Having succeeded in creating a believable new world in *Star Wars*, Lucas was determined the illusion would be maintained. Each effect was "a little time bomb" he would fret. There were thousands, "and if you don't catch one, it could do you in."

Yet in many ways the challenges were less demanding this time. John Dykstra's pioneering camerawork on *Star Wars* had shown the way ahead for the photographic work. Ralph McQuarrie's genius was once more on line and Joe Johnston, who had joined the ILM operation towards the end of *Star Wars*, had emerged as a brilliantly innovative model-maker. Even the perfectionist Lucas had been delighted at the first sight of the *Empire*'s newest weapon, elephantine walking tanks, christened AT-ATs, that would feature in the opening act's climactic battle on the planet Hoth.

With Lucas in America, *The Empire Strikes Back* was very much Gary Kurtz's film. Kershner had primarily been his choice as director. He had also been largely responsible for key crew appointments, including Peter Schuzitsky, photographer of Ken Russell's lavish piece of lunacy *Lisztomania*, as a replacement for Gil Taylor.

From the outset, however, Lucas left neither man in any doubt whose money was financing their operation. Kershner had been offended by his brusqueness.

"The very first day of shooting, he came up to us and said, 'You know this is my own money and we have to be careful with it, so be sure you do a good job,'" recalled Kurtz. "Kersh felt really incensed by that, he felt it was unnecessary pressure. Kersh did this all the time, it didn't matter if it was his money or Fox's money. Kersh felt it was uncalled for, especially on the first day."

Luckily Lucas had not accompanied them to Norway. "In a way it was fortunate he was not around because Kersh was bothered by him," said Kurtz.

Having picked up the poisoned chalice, Kershner was determined to make the film he wanted. As a director his instincts were more performance-minded than Lucas's. "In the first movie the situations were so powerful you didn't have the time to watch the characters,'" he said, setting out his agenda to the film's publicist, Alan Arnold, at the film's outset. "They were totally in the service of the story. In the new film the characters will still be in the service of the story because the narrative must flow, but they will be more defined. They have rivalries, jealousies, sexual tensions."

The cast found Kershner the polar opposite of the monosyllabic Lucas. Lucas did much of his work at the storyboard stage. He arrived on set with a clear picture in his mind. The occasional input of actors was acceptable but hardly encouraged. Kershner on the other hand picked his way meticulously through every scene. He welcomed debate and discussion and was far more improvisational than Lucas. No one responded to his style more willingly than Harrison Ford.

Ford had learned much from his experiences away from the *Star Wars* universe. He had suffered at the hands of the boorish Robert Aldrich on *The Frisco Kid*, and been left looking foolish with the lame lines given to him in Peter Hyams's *Hanover Street*.

"Harrison did a lot of [those films] to consolidate his position, to get the billing," his manager Pat McQueeney said. "You go in with high hopes, but he ran into some trouble. One thing he learned is that an actor is really at the mercy of the director."

If Ford had learned one great lesson away from *Star Wars* it was to never let up in looking after oneself on a film set.

"The special effects take so much attention that you tend to let the action slip by. I didn't want that to happen, and Harrison was constantly calling me on it," Kershner recalled. "If we did just two takes and I'd say, 'That's great,' he would say, 'Wait a minute, wait a minute. What's great? Was it great for the special effects or for me?'"

"And I'd say, 'Harrison, I wouldn't say 'great' unless it was for you.' And he would give me that wonderful look of his, you know that wry look, and we would move on."

The sight of director and leading man walking off towards Kershner's trailer, arms waving around in deep debate became a familiar one.

"He probably more than anybody would get into an intellectual debate with Kersh about why certain things were happening," said Kurtz. "He loved that kind of stuff. In the end I had to lean on him a bit."

The mutual, Three-Musketeer support system Fisher, Ford, and Hamill had struck up on *Star Wars* seemed strained. Three years on, Fisher and Ford seemed particularly ill at ease.

The *Empire* storyline raised the sexual stakes between Solo and Leia. Gone was the asexual dialogue of *Star Wars*. In its place, Kasdan had inserted a more playful, if still rather cartoonish, relationship. The first exchanges came during filming of the evacuation of the rebel base on the ice planet Hoth. Amid the chaos, Solo would challenge Leia to reveal her true feelings for him. Whatever the cause, the residual tensions between Fisher and Ford were worked out in front of a full crew.

"It got a lot hotter than it should have between Harrison and Carrie. I think it was, "Let's get rid of it through performances in front of the cameras rather than keeping it bottled up," said Peter Mayhew.

Fisher, in particular, was prone to walking off the set, Mayhew recalled. "It would build up, build up, build up. Then one or the other of them would storm off."

Fisher had, by now, begun what would prove to be a tempestuous relationship with singer Paul Simon. She would often arrive at work at 7 A.M. having had only a few, brief hours of sleep. "He was in New York and would call her up in the middle of the night," said Kurtz. At times the producer understood Lucas's frustrations at working with actors. "That part was uncomfortable," he admitted. "It was like holding together a sinking ship."

Lucas's insistence on keeping his cast in the dark about the story did little to calm nerves. *Empire*'s most dramatic twist was to be the revelation that Darth Vader was in fact, Anakin Skywalker, Luke's long-lost father. (To Dave Prowse's anger, he acted out an alternative dialogue at Elstree only to discover the truth at a premiere in America.)

The tensions boiled over during filming of the most technically complex of the non-special effects scenes, Han

Solo's lowering into a carbon-freezing chamber, filmed on Stage Five in the third week of June.

The vast, elevated soundstage—a precarious network of metallic walkways and platforms—had taken weeks to erect. Much of the filming took place twenty feet above the studio floor, often a risky business given the subdued lighting and steam clouds Kershner had insisted on for the scene.

An earlier scene had already frayed Kershner and Hamill's nerves. As Hamill and Prowse had filmed a lightsaber duel between Vader and Luke, the director had criticized his star's facial expression. Hamill, suffering in the oppressive heat and increasingly worried about his now heavily pregnant wife, had taken exception.

When Kershner shrugged and told Hamill he would see what he meant when he saw the finished movie, the argument degenerated into childishness.

"I don't even want to see the movie," Hamill snapped.

"Really," the ordinarily calm Kershner replied before shouting, "Cut the lights, cut the camera, cut everything." If Hamill was not interested, why make the movie, he asked?

Within moments, both men's faces were wreathed in embarrassment.

The shakiness of relations between Fisher and Ford only added to the uneasiness. The freezing scene would finally offer a resolution to Han and Leia's prolonged will they-won't they flirtation. Han's freezing, insurance in case Ford proved unpersuadable for a third outing as Solo, was their moment of truth.

As originally scripted, Leia would seize the moment to tell Solo: "I love you. I was afraid to tell you before, but it's true."

"I'll be back," Solo would reply.

Ford's instincts told him the exchange could be improved. He had set to work on Kershner, locking himself away alone with the director suggesting new lines for both him and Fisher.

Kershner was concerned that Ford wanted to drop the line, "I'll be back." "It's almost contractual," he said.

He eventually came up with a line in which Leia says, "I love you," and Han replied simply, "I know." "Beautiful and acceptable and funny," he told Kershner who, once more bowed to the actor's undoubted gift for improvisation.

Fisher, as insecure about her ability to extemporize as Ford was secure in his, flew into a rage when he told her about the changes. She was heard in his dressing room, screaming and shouting at him.

Later she admitted: "He is very angry with me. And he has a total right to be. I should never have done that."

Then she attacked Kershner for not telling her of the changes before Ford had. "I got mad at him and it screws us up," she moaned.

Fisher's occasional tantrums were by now familiar. "She could be very funny when she was on top form, but she could also be a real down-and-out grouch," said Peter Mayhew.

Empire's best-kept secret remained under lock and key, on a soundstage away from the main activity at Elstree.

For more than a year, Lucas, Kurtz, and Kershner had been working with Stuart Freeborn on the model for Yoda, the Jedi master. Lucas loved the idea of making him a tiny, 800-year-old wizard rather than a superhero. Drawing his inspiration from a picture of an elderly Albert Einstein and his own reflection in the mirror, the balding Freeborn produced what would become the most acclaimed creature of his career. His model was a munchkin Methuselah, twenty-six inches tall, with vast baggy eyes and horizontal rabbit's ears. Kershner, Kurtz, and Lucas knew they had the star of the film the minute they cast eyes on him. To bring the wire-operated puppet to life, Kurtz hired Frank Oz, creator of the most familiar of the Muppet voices. With a few of Ben Burtt's twists and tweaks, Oz's soft croak sounded perfect. Yet filming Yoda proved the most difficult element of the entire film. Inevitably it added further to an already strained budget.

The swamp planet set was the most unpleasant anyone had ever worked on. An entire sound stage had been filled with ankle-deep water, then sprayed with mineral oils. The miasma produced noxious gases and both Oz and Kershner had to wear masks to stop themselves vomiting as they walked through. Oz's ordeal didn't end there. The puppet-master had to squeeze his 6-foot 2-inch frame into a tiny bunker within the fairytale cottage Norman Reynolds had created for Yoda's home. To simulate the model eating, blinking, and frowning, Oz and a team of assistants had to manipulate invisible wires, connected to Yoda's eyeballs, eyelids, cheeks, tongue, lips, and pixie ears. At the same time Kershner, himself well over six feet, had to squeeze himself into the doll's house–like set to supervise the shooting. Kershner described the process as being "like having a chain around your neck, hands, and feet and being dropped into a tank of water and told to direct from four fathoms." The process was so complex, it took an average of four hours to film every two lines of dialogue featuring the puppet.

At least Oz was equipped with a sense of humor. During a scene in which Luke tells Yoda he has adhered to his teachings and "followed his feelings," the set was suddenly filled with the unmistakable voice of Miss Piggy. "Feelings? Ya wanna know about feelings?" the most obnoxious of all Oz's Muppet characters announced, suddenly appearing on his arm in a lavender gown and gloves. "Get behind this couch and I'll show ya feelings, ya little runt."

Miss Piggy went on to demand someone call her agent and rant and rave about the working conditions. "I've been booked in dumps before, but nothin' like this."

CHAPTER 10

"You're Ruining My Movie"

On the morning of Wednesday, June 6, a troubled production became a tragic one.

While talking to Robert Watts in his office at Elstree, John Barry complained of a headache. Moments later he collapsed and was taken to hospital. By the next morning, news filtered back to the set that he had died at 2 A.M. that day. The events unfolded with a "suddenness that, had it been written into a film plot, would have been called implausible dramatic license," *Variety* reported days later.

The loss was another shattering blow. As production had fallen further behind schedule, Barry had been called in to direct a second film unit. The director, soft-spoken and likeable, had been unavailable when Lucas and Kurtz first approached him. After years of waiting, he had finally been given the chance to make his directorial debut on another science-fiction piece, *Saturn 3*. His joy had been short-lived, however. After a series of internal rows with producer Stanley Donen he was sacked. Barry had been welcomed back to the *Star Wars* family like a long lost son.

Kurtz was impressed with the calmness that greeted the revelation that Barry had died of infectious meningitis. "In any other country people would have been demanding inoculations and God knows what. But the British crew—although they were shattered—kept their traditional cool."

Five days later the production was closed down for the day out of respect. Kurtz led the mourners at the funeral service in Chiswick. Back at Elstree the following day he had to take over as second unit director until replacement, Harly Cokliss, arrived in London.

The shutting down of the set for an afternoon cost Lucasfilm around $50,000. The loss was tiny in comparison to the holes that had been blown in the budget by the fire and ice setbacks at Studio 3 and in Finse. By June, Kurtz estimated that the original $20 million would now end up nearer $22 million. Kurtz had by now moved to a splendid country home, Wallingford House in the village of Little Padnor, near Chesham in Buckinghamshire. Since *Star Wars* Kurtz had become an unashamed Anglophile. He and his wife, Meredith, had spent £200,000 of the *Star Wars* windfall to buy the house and another £250,000 refurbishing it. At the end of most days, Kurtz would spend evenings in his luxurious home deep in conversation with Lucas, invariably about the budget. It was not his money on the line. Yet Kurtz could not see that *Empire* was quite the risk Lucas did. "Even if he did spend $30 million, it wasn't that big a risk. It would have had to have been a pretty rough movie not to make its money back," he said. As if to prove his point, by early May 1979, *The Empire Strikes Back* was already picking up where its epoch-making predecessor had left off. On May 10, *Variety*'s front page headline proclaimed the latest landmark in the *Star Wars* saga: "EMPIRE" GUARANTEES $26 MIL-PLUS.

America's cinema owners had been asked to bid for the follow-up to the biggest film in history an unprecedented twelve months before they would be able to screen it. Even without cinemas in states where "blind bidding" was out-lawed, their tenders totaled an all-time record $26 million. "It doesn't take much to calculate that the picture will be in profit when it opens," Fox's Peter Myers crowed.

Yet to his frustration, the producer had to watch the cost of his film balloon in ways even the most creative members of his team could never have imagined. At one point the budget was inflated by the cost of a group of bodyguards hired to protect Carrie Fisher. Her mother had telephoned her from Las Vegas where she was performing, warning her of a plot to kidnap Carrie. With only days left before the end of her scenes, no one was willing to ignore the threat. The guards stayed with her at her St. John's Wood home until she left, even adopting the disguise of waiters at an extravagant party she threw at the end of her stay in London a week later.

Then a week's filming was lost when Mark Hamill sprained his thumb. The accident had happened on the day Hamill had become a father for the first time. (News of Marilou's delivery of a son, Nathan, was put on the news wires with a quote from Hamill: "So now I have a little English son. God Save The Queen.") Hamill injured the thumb filming a risky scene in which he fell from the Cloud City into the *Millennium Falcon*. As his thumb swelled, an emotional and exhausted Hamill had lashed out at Kurtz for not using a stunt man for the scene, banished a small celebration party from his dressing room and stormed off the set. He was not seen until the following Monday.

At least in that particular instance, Kurtz and Lucas were covered by insurance. When a entire day's worth of filming was lost because of an accident in the film-processing labora-tory there was no safety net.

As the costs steadily spiraled, images of Francis Coppola once more haunted George Lucas. Coppola had been all but broken financially and psychologically by the making of *Apocalypse Now* in the Philippines. A budget that had begun at $12 million had ballooned to an unheard-of $33 million. Coppola faced losing everything if the film failed.

Marcia understood the fear he felt perhaps better than anyone. "George is methodical and ritualistic. He loves to feel safe and secure," she recalled. "Any kind of threat would make him so uneasy and uncomfortable he couldn't work."

"It was very frustrating for George not being there and it not going exactly as he had envisioned it," said Bunny Alsup.

By the end of June, the inevitable had happened. Lucas had snapped. With work at ILM now taking shape and the budgetary pressures piling up on the other side of the Atlantic, he could no longer keep his distance. Lucas's reappearance on the set did little to calm fraying nerves. "It didn't help to have him around. George was always concerned about the money. He would always be saying, 'Gotta get done, gotta get done,'" said Kurtz.

Kurtz resented being told he was allowing Kershner too much time on certain scenes. No one had done more to speed the occasionally ponderous director along. "We always had pressure on Kersh. Several times I ordered him to finish scenes or abandon scenes and directed the scene myself. I knew it was important to get the momentum going and to get to the important bits," said Kurtz. It was the producer who completed the direction of scenes in which Luke escaped from the Wampa cave and Solo slices open a Tauntaun for shelter.

It was the sight of a rough cut of the still unfinished film that sent Lucas over the edge, however. Paul Hirsch had been editing throughout the filming process. More than sixty hours of film had been reduced to a two hour rough cut. When Lucas saw the assemblage he exploded. Trembling with anger he accused Kurtz, Kershner and Hirsch of sabotage. "He said: 'You're ruining my movie,'" said Gary Kurtz.

Kershner's idea of a legato second movement was utterly

alien to Lucas. "Paul had put together a rough assembly and it was pretty slow. George didn't like it at all," said Kurtz. Lucas didn't appreciate the effect the more intimate moments between Han and Leia, in particular, had on the movie's pace. "George didn't like mushy stuff. He thought it slowed the action down," said Kurtz.

Lucas took control of the editing suite and locked himself away for two days. The clear implication was that "Supereditor" was going to save the day. When he emerged, the producer, director and editor were horrified at what he had done to the film.

"It was awful," laughed Kurtz. "It was chopped into tiny pieces and everything was fast."

When the trio objected violently Lucas merely became more agitated. "I'm on the hook for the money," he told them.

"He tried to pull a power number basically," said Kurtz.

Eventually it was Hirsch who talked Lucas round. When his nerves had calmed, he admitted his anger had been directed at himself as much as his team whose dedication he could not doubt. "In the end he finally realized the whole thing needed to be finessed," said Kurtz. "I think he was overwhelmed by events at the time."

Far from being a disaster, *Empire* was clearly shaping itself into something rather special. Days after his outburst, Lucas had admitted to the director and producer that the film was "coming together beautifully." Kershner's eye for detail and attention to the actors combined with Schuzitsky's camerawork, particularly in the ethereal blue of the Dagobah sequences, had lent the film its own distinct and likeable personality. "Kersh was maddening at times. He was a bit slow, but I think in the end it paid off. I have great admiration for him," said Kurtz.

The film's problems were far from over, however. Quite the opposite, it was now on a crash course with disaster—at least as far as Lucas was concerned. By the middle of July, the film's threadbare finances finally reached breaking point. One Monday morning, in California, Lucasfilm's chief executive Charles Weber, who had put together the film's complex loan structure, was told by the Bank of America that it would not advance the production any more money. It also wanted the $22 million it had so far extended the company repaid. Weber was faced with the prospect of not being able to pay $1 million in wages at the end of the week.

Acting on estimates that *Empire* needed another $3 million to be completed, another loan, from the First National Bank of Boston, was hastily arranged. They agreed to extend a full $25 million, at a punitive rate of interest. No sooner had the deal been done, however, than it had become obvious that yet another $3 million would be needed.

This time the Boston bank also said no. It would only extend the loan if it were underwritten by a big company—someone like Twentieth Century–Fox. Lucas began to face the awful reality. He would have to crawl back to Fox, hat in hand. As it happened, his timing could not have been worse.

At the end of June, Alan Ladd Jr. stunned Hollywood by announcing his resignation as president of Twentieth Century–Fox's film division. Since taking over the reins, Ladd had become the most successful and highly paid studio head in Hollywood history. In 1973, when he had begun sowing the seeds of his "filmmaker's studio," Fox's annual revenue from its film division was around $150 million. By 1978 that figure had increased to just under $350 million.

To the commercial kudos he won with *Star Wars* and that year's big hit, Ridley Scott's *Alien*, he could add the artistic pleasure of Fred Zinneman's *Julia* with Vanessa Redgrave and Jane Fonda, Herbert Ross's *The Turning Point* with Anne Bancroft and Shirley Maclaine, and Bob Fosse's *All That Jazz* with Roy Scheider and Jessica Lange. His salary alone proved his worth to the studio whose fortunes he had transformed in the space of six years. With bonuses, his earnings for 1978 were a record $1,944,000. Yet, on the afternoon of June 27, rumors began swirling around Wall Street that he had quit. Shares dropped almost $4 in the two days when the news was confirmed.

At first Ladd had told the press he was "tired of the paperwork" and hoped to produce movies on his own. The truth, however, lay elsewhere. And if *Star Wars* had been a major contributor to his rise it also played its part in his fall.

In the wake of the *Star Wars* success, Ladd's always difficult relations with Dennis Stanfill had reached an all-time low. The gulf between the moneyman and the show-man had become an unbreachable chasm.

Ladd had resented Stanfill's introduction of new manage-ment methods. In turn, there were those who believed Stanfill resented Ladd's salary and his exalted position in Hollywood. Matters came to a head, however, when Stanfill vetoed Ladd's plans to share the *Star Wars* bonanza with his staff. Ladd, along with Gareth Wigan and Jay Kanter had benefited from the *Star Wars* windfall. The trio had pro-posed to the board that the whole of the film division should be awarded bonuses for the work they had done on *Star Wars*.

"We three—Laddie, Gareth and myself—were the recip-ients of an awful lot of money and we felt that the people in the division should have gotten more," Kanter said later. "The company was very quick to give the stockholders a special dividend and the stockholders also profited because the value of their shares increased—tremendously."

Stanfill, however, was opposed. Ladd felt aggrieved that while he could spend millions on a movie or an advertising campaign, he was prevented from rewarding his hard-working staff with a minor token of his appreciation.

"It seemed silly to us that Laddie could spend all the

production and marketing money—which in itself was in excess of $150 million a year—and nobody would question his decisions. There was no logic to the fact that he could buy $4 million of network time and nobody would question whether it was a good buy, but he couldn't give somebody a $100, $200, or a $500-a-week raise," said Kanter.

Even when Ladd, Kanter, and Wigan passed on part of their $1 million total bonus to their staff, the board refused to buckle.

Ladd also resented the lack of credit he had been given for the role he had played in turning the company around so spectacularly.

"Nobody on the corporate side ever came to us and said, 'You did a good job,' or 'The film division is 85 percent of the company and we appreciate what you're doing,'" said Ladd. "The year Fox broke all industry records, none of the corporate people ever said, 'Hey, you did a nice job.'"

Ignorance ensured the divide between corporate and creative life would never be breached. "Their attitude was almost resentful. A lot of the people on the corporate side thought, 'Well, aren't those people lucky? They just look at movies all the time, go to dinner with movie stars, take flashy trips,'" said Ladd. "What they don't see is the Mel Brooks who walks into my office, loses his temper over a problem, picks up a chair, and throws it across the room."

Stanfill ordered Ladd, Wigan, and Kanter to vacate their offices immediately. They were given a suite at the Beverly Hilton Hotel while the whole unpleasant mess was sorted out. At one point Stanfill announced that Ladd would be given other duties within Fox. "He is going to wash dishes at the Aspen ski resort," one Hollywood wag joked.

In the meantime, Ladd could not talk to Lucas about his problems on *Empire*. "If I even talk to him, I'll have a lawsuit," he had told friends.

Instead, Lucas was forced to negotiate with a new regime

led briefly by Sherry Lansing. Fox demanded a punishing 15 percent of the profits from *Empire*. After much toing and froing, Tom Pollock got them to agree to a bigger share of the distribution rights instead. The $3 million loan cost Lucas much more than his pride. Years later he claimed he was still "suffering" from the slice of his film's earnings Fox had negotiated. The Empire had bitten back—and it hurt.

As he looked around for someone to blame, Lucas found Gary Kurtz standing directly in the firing line.

At least Kurtz had been able to share some good news with Lucas. Weeks earlier they had taken Alec Guinness to his favorite West End restaurant, Neal's in Covent Garden. Guinness was reluctant to reprise the role of Obi-Wan. The character had, after all, perished in the first film. What was the purpose of bringing him back? "I didn't want to at all," Guinness said.

To Lucas, however, the senior citizen of the film was also its talisman; his imperious presence had made much of the mysticism of *Star Wars* credible. Guinness had been suffering with a severe eye problem and was not convinced. By the end of the meal he gave way, mainly out of reverence for Lucas.

Guinness's affection for Lucas extended beyond the money he had made on the back of his enterprise. Over another dinner with his fellow knight, Sir David Lean, Sir Alec paid Lucas as high a compliment as he could pay any director.

"David Lean asked me about him and I told him, 'He has the same sort of eye as you,'" he recalled. In their manner, the magisterial Lean and the apologetic Lucas were apples and oranges. "He is not the same sort of director," said Guinness. "There was none of that 'The director is on the set.' Yet he has the same sort of precision in what he saw, a great appreciation of visual detail."

Guinness agreed to make a small contribution. "I said

only if it is a smidgen of a part." To the hard-pressed Lucas's delight, he also agreed to do it for nothing. "I did it out of courtesy. I don't think I took any money for it because I thought George had been very generous and I had done very well out of it. I thought it was a day or two's work at most, so I thought I'd just throw it in," he added.

On one of the final days of shooting, Guinness arrived on the set at 8:30 A.M. By 3 P.M. he had filmed his brief scenes with Luke and Yoda on Dagobah and Luke on Hoth. Despite wincing at the harsh light after his operation and looking occasionally ill at ease acting with the wizened Yoda puppet, Guinness once more lent the film some much-appreciated *gravitas*.

Lucas was on set to greet the great man. At dinner Lucas had seemed, as he had when he first shared a meal with him in Los Angeles, "very simple, very shy, very direct." At Elstree, however, Guinness detected familiar—and un-welcome—changes in the gifted filmmaker. "He had a great entourage around him and that always rather depresses me," he said.

On Friday August 31, with filming all but over, cast and crew relaxed at the official "wrap party." Meredith Kurtz had overseen the transformation of the swamp planet Dagobah into the most surreal picnic area anyone had ever seen. The stink of the unpleasantly authentic bog gases had been replaced by the fragrant aroma of candles and tiger lilies. A false "lawn" had been spread out on the edge of the tangled forest. As each guest arrived they were given a picnic basket full of snacks. Taking full advantage of the plentiful bar, they sat at the foot of Yoda's cottage, sharing gossip and glasses of French wine. Despite the budget problems Kurtz's wife had spared nothing in giving every-one a good sendoff. "There was no hint of parsimony," the publicist Alan Arnold wrote in his journal.

Behind the smiles, however, Gary Kurtz knew his days with the Lucas empire were drawing to a close. In the black-and-white world of Lucas, there was no doubt who was to blame for the inflation the budget had suffered. "There were a lot of problems. I think he blamed me for a lot of what happened," said Kurtz. "He thought the things he felt were wrong with *Empire*, with the money and a director who was difficult, were all my fault," said Kurtz. "It really galled him that he had to go back to Fox." It had been seven years since Lucas had approached him to produce *American Graffiti*. To those who had worked with them throughout that time they had seemed two halves of a whole.

"They were an incredible team," said Bunny Alsup who had remained with the company through thick and thin. She saw Kurtz as the rock of Lucas's professional life. "Everything was hard for him. It was hard for him to direct, hard for him to write. Gary was always there helping him to get the scripts done and so on. They are both very individual and creative and they know all aspects of film together. They both know how to edit, how to direct, how to be photographers, they both know everything. That comes along so rarely," she said.

Yet the two men had drifted apart. Their divergent views of the direction in which *Star Wars* should now be heading only accelerated the process. Despite Lucas's fears, plans for a third movie, tentatively called *Revenge of the Jedi*, were already under way. More cracks appeared as the duo discussed the conclusion of what Lucas by now acknowledged as the final part in the first trilogy of a nine-part series of films. Kurtz liked the idea of concluding the trilogy in the way Lucas had ended the original treatment, with Leia crowned queen of her people and the central trio of characters heading their separate ways. "It was a bittersweet thing, that chapter in their life was over," he said.

Lucas, however, had jettisoned all the original story

threads in favor of a story featuring the Emperor as a major character. He saw Luke and the galaxy's ultimate power locked in a battle for the soul of Darth Vader.

"I thought bringing the Emperor in destroyed Darth Vader as the principal villain," said Kurtz.

It was soon apparent that Lucas did not see Kurtz being involved in the third film. Kurtz, who had been discussing another fantasy project, *The Dark Crystal* with Frank Oz, sensed it was time to move on too. According to Kurtz, he and Lucas never formally sat down and acknowledged the end of their era together. "It was messy and we were estranged for a while afterwards," admitted Kurtz.

Like so many other of Lucas's associates, it seemed, he had to pay the price for failing to fall into line with his views. Kurtz was deeply hurt when Lucas later accused him of being "over his head" on *Empire*.

"I don't think George wanted robots to direct by remote control—but he had this idea that he would create the world, pass it on to someone else who would then more or less expand it based on the way he would want to do it," sighed Kurtz.

Bunny Alsup decided to move on with Kurtz to his new company, Kinetographics, which he set up in a schoolhouse in San Anselmo. Alsup admits she was in tears the day they left. In the years that followed she was angered at the manner in which Kurtz's contribution to the *Star Wars* story had been overlooked both inside and outside Hollywood.

"He seems to be written out of history when in fact he is the key to history," she said. "I don't think George will ever make another *Star Wars* until he gets another Gary."

Ironically, Lucas's worries about losing his money on *The Empire Strikes Back* were virtually over before Kurtz had moved out of Parkhouse. Lucas needed *The Empire Strikes Back* to earn around one third of *Star Wars'* box office to be able to repay the banks. With the $26 million advance he was already within sight of that target. By the beginning of 1980, merchandising had brought in almost twice as much in advance guarantees.

Every merchandise manufacturer in the world was by now desperate to jump aboard the *Star Wars* gravy train. As outright owner of the musical rights, Lucas signed a deal with Robert Stigwood to release an *Empire* sound track album on the day of the film's release. The ink was dry on the $1 million–plus deal in June 1979, a full year ahead of schedule.

By now Kenner's toy designers were made to feel like members of the family at the ILM workshop. As *Empire* was being filmed, toys based on the new vehicles and creatures were already on the production line. Lucas even consented to the development of models not featured in the film itself. Kenner rolled out a range of personal vehicles for storm-troopers and rebels. "He allowed us to come up with products that were 'inspired by the *Star Wars* universe.' That was in a way very risky on his part, but also very wise," said senior designer Dave Okada.

Very wise indeed. Lucasfilm's cut of the $1 billion a year Kenner was making from *Star Wars* was yielding around $10 million annually on its own.

Business was equally buoyant on the book front. Ballantine/Del Rey had commissioned publicist Alan Arnold to write a journal of the making of the film and Lucas had already approved a novelization of Brackett and Kasdan's *Empire* story. Both books had been sold to Sphere in the UK for $420,000, then the highest amount a publisher had ever paid for British rights only.

The most noticeable absentee amidst all this activity was Charlie Lippincott. The man who had essentially established Lucasfilm's merchandising had left the company in 1978—another victim of the growing bureaucracy within Lucas's empire.

Lippincott's contribution to the success of *Star Wars* was beyond calculation. His duties had ranged from designing the record sleeve to the *Star Wars* sound track album to acting as a babysitter for Mark Hamill during a world tour with the film in 1978. (Lippincott had been with Hamill when he was arrested by customs officials in Australia for possession of suspicious looking plants. After an uncomfortable hour or so they finally accepted they were nothing more sinister than tulip bulbs. "I said: 'Where did you get tulip bulbs?' And he said: 'The Dutch Queen Mother.'") Yet as the empire grew, Lippincott became increasingly marginalized. As the company's best-known publicist, he had been embarrassed when he had denied rumors that Irvin Kershner had been hired as *Empire*'s director. Lippincott had also clashed with Lucasfilm's new chief executive, Charles Weber, almost immediately. Lucas had brought the tall, bespectacled former investment banker in to oversee the new business.

"He had some executive ability and that's why he was hired. But he had never been in the movie business before," said Lippincott. "He was somebody I did not like."

When Weber hired a new merchandising executive, Lippincott knew it was time for him to leave. "I chose to get out of there. Period," he said, but he was at least given a payoff by Lucas.

Even during the making of *Empire* Gary Kurtz had been alarmed at the size of the mushrooming Lucasfilm machine. The cost of Weber's trips were added to the *Empire* budget, inflating it even further.

"Everything just seemed to grow. When we were making *Star Wars* there were only six of us: myself, George, Charlie Lippincott, Bunny Alsup, George's secretary, Lucy Wilson, and Ben Burtt who was on the staff there. It was natural for it to grow a bit, but it got out of all proportion. It grew without any kind of corporate plan," said Kurtz.

From being an office of a small, happy family, Lucasfilm

had evolved into another faceless Hollywood corporation. Lucasfilm had moved in 1979 to a former egg farm on Lankershim Boulevard, near Universal Studios. George and Marcia Lucas had overseen the striking architectural work inside the modern, open-plan complex. The lavish offices were equipped with everything from its own gas station and gym to a kitchen and video-game arcade. The building had an undoubtedly creative atmosphere. Steven Spielberg would while away his lunch breaks making cookies or playing the Asteroids machine and casting sessions would be held in the vast, plant-filled atrium.

Yet there was a sense of bureaucracy gone mad. Hordes of staff would debate the finest details of each and every *Star Wars* product. Valerie Hoffman was involved in one meeting in which the concept of Wookiee bedroom slippers was analyzed. "There was this whole issue of whether the Wookiee's hair covers their toes, or do they have toes? So they go, 'Valerie, do some research and find out about a Wookiee's lifestyle,'" she said, laughing.

When more Wookiee information was demanded for a book, Hoffman went directly to Lucas with an exhaustive questionnaire. He looked on in disbelief when she asked him how Chewbacca and his family reproduced. "This is very personal," he said blushing.

"He got *really* embarrassed," said Hoffman.

Hoffman had been hired as a secretary in the aftermath of *Star Wars,* and began her working days in a trailer. "The minute we moved into the new building there was a dress code. The whole thing got to be really absurd," she recalled.

By the time she had left the organization, Lucasfilm's longest-serving employee was quietly glad to see the back of the place. "I was actually quite happy when Gary decided to leave," said Bunny Alsup. Alsup had not liked the way the Lucasfilm empire had grown—at the egg company in particular. "It became so big and corporate, like working at

Universal Studios," she said. "The feeling of the company changed. It lost that intimate family feeling for me."

As Kurtz began setting up his own company, Alsup's only advice to him was to avoid making the same mistakes. "George had no choice because *Star Wars* was so successful. He had to grow and then he had to hire these people that weren't filmmakers, which changed the tone," she said. "I kept saying to Gary, 'Please don't grow like Lucasfilm.'"

CHAPTER 11

Farewell, Sin City

In late May 1980, the State of Illinois's toll-free 800 phone system collapsed under the strain of having to deal with one newly set-up number. Ads listing the number— 1-800-520-1980—had been run in newspapers across America. Callers were promised a two-minute trailer for *The Empire Strikes Back*. The number coincided with the day— May 20, 1980—the long-awaited sequel to *Star Wars* finally opened in more than 130 cinemas. Illinois was the state unfortunate enough to have the digits 520 as its area code.

"We had ten lines processing it, they couldn't give out busy signals fast enough and the entire system for the state closed down," explained Craig Miller, then in charge of promotions at the Egg Company.

Miller and his colleagues were happy to comply with the phone company's demand that they stop all advertising and add more lines to handle the unstoppable tide of calls. The publicity the event generated was worth every dollar they sent to Illinois.

Miller, for one, had been in no doubt that *Star Wars* mania was about to be reborn since driving past the famous Egyptian Theater on Hollywood Boulevard, on Monday, May 18. Three days before the film opened he saw a small group of people camped on the sidewalk in readiness. Soon television crews were there interviewing the curious band. One of them, Terri Hardin, revealed she had seen *Star Wars* 178 times before it had been finally withdrawn in 1979. As she stood at the head of the line for its sequel, she summed up the feelings of hundreds huddled in their sleeping bags around the country. "We're waiting for our high," she smiled at each camera pointed in her direction.

If *Star Wars* had sneaked onto the screens of America with minimal fuss, the launch of *Empire* was the movie event of its year. Darth Vader stared out from the cover of *Time* magazine, Yoda's wizened features dominated the front of *People* magazine, fans were able to stand in line wearing specially designed, new Luke Skywalker outfits. The sound track album had been played on radio stations for a whole month in advance.

Fox had chosen the same novel date, the Wednesday before Memorial Day, to open the film at 127 cinemas. Within two days 125 of those cinemas were announcing new house records.

Lucasfilm and Fox did not have to rely on statistics alone for its early publicity this time. Premieres had been organized for London and Washington. At the Odeon Leicester Square, the paparazzi ate up Fisher, Ford, and Hamill curtsying before Princess Margaret.

For all the troubles it had endured, *Empire* disappointed few *Star Wars* fans. Epic in scale, more human in its sensibilities, it was preferred over the original by many. Kershner collected many of the plaudits. "Kershner, after a long, honorable, unjustly neglected career, fully comes into his own at last. He's produced a contemporary marvel," said Michael Sragow of the *Los Angeles Herald Examiner*.

"More than Kubrick's too-cool space odyssey, *The Empire Strikes Back* is a sci-fi epic that would do Homer proud."

Even the doyenne of American critics, Pauline Kael, was converted. Kael had been understated in her praise for *Star Wars*. This time, however, she left the cinema feeling euphoric. "There is no sense that this ebullient, youthful saga is running thin in imagination or that it has begun to depend excessively on its marvelous special effects—that it is in any danger, in short, of stiffening into mannerism or mere billion-dollar style," she said. "I'm not sure I'm up to seven more *Star Wars* adventures (I'm pretty sure my son is) but I can hardly wait for the next one."

"The special effects are little short of astounding," wrote Kenneth Turan in *New West*. "No one understands better than Lucas Orson Welles's famous dictum about moviemaking being the biggest toy train set a boy ever had."

Movie Scorecard for the *Empire Strikes Back*.

o/o	Of the 536 Persons Surveyed	Rated It
68	Were male	A +
32	Were female	A
63	Were under 25	A +
37	Were 25 or older	A
37	Were drawn by the subject matter/type of movie	A +
11	Came to see cast	A +
68	Couldn't wait to see the film	A +
9	Just came along with others	A
41	Said this was their favorite kind of movie	A +
10	Said they attended movies often	A

If there had been a worry within Fox, it was that the bubble may have burst for the science-fiction boom. Neither Paramount's *Star Trek: The Movie*, nor Disney's *The Black Hole* had come close to the phenomenal box office returns of *Star Wars* the previous year. Within less than a week, however, their fears were allayed. After six days the box office had passed through the $9 million barrier. Fox was already negotiating to bring forward plans to spread the film to another 575 cinemas at the end of June. "Everybody wants to get on the bandwagon," Peter Myers boasted. The sense of déjà vu continued throughout the summer. After nineteen days the box office stood at $23 million; by the end of the first month $31.3 million. As July dawned it was clear that *Empire* had achieved what *Star Wars* had pulled off. By now its weekly box office was more than double its nearest rival, John Landis's *The Blues Brothers*. The summer's other main contenders, *Fame*, *Brubaker*, *Rough Cut*, and *Can't Stop the Music* had been steamrollered in its wake. As *Empire* passed the $50 million mark in early July, rival studios began to ask industry analysts to begin compiling alternative statistics— one set with *Empire* and one without. "It should be in a category by itself," one complained to *Variety*.

If Fox had learned a lesson from *Star Wars* internationally, it had been to waste little time in moving the film into other territories. Soon Japan was once more rewriting its record books as *Empire* earned just under $4 million in its first ten days in nine cities. In September the Odeon in London's Leicester Square took in more in one week, $277,000, than any other week in its history. By August, with the film playing in ten countries, the box office had been bloated by $30 million worldwide and the *Empire* total had sailed through $100 million. Only a few territories remained immune. Once more Darth Vader left Scandinavia cold. Sweden insisted the film was too violent for children under fifteen. Soon the sequel had gone the way of its predecessor—despite the familiarity of its snow scenes.

In October 1980, flanked by lines of Caterpillar bulldozers busy reshaping the valley above Bull Pit Ranch, George Lucas posed proudly for the photographer from *Fortune* magazine. Dwarfed by the rolling Marin hills behind him, Lucas overlooked his domain with pride. He had every reason to.

As America's bible of the rich and famous pointed out, he had in the space of three spectacularly short years built a personal fortune of $100 million. He was chairman and sole shareholder in Lucasfilm Ltd.—a corporation of 200 employees with a net income of $1.5 million a week. With *Empire*'s world box office now in excess of $170 million, he had been able to reclaim his $20 million personal investment back while the company sat back to wait for $51 million in profits from the film to pour in.

Lucas admitted that having won the biggest gamble of his life, he would now put the money somewhere safe—like real estate and boring municipal bonds. "I'm a coupon-clipper by nature," he told *Forbes*.

His caution was already frustrating Charles Weber at the Egg Company. Lucas had only given the go-ahead for two films, a $3 million cartoon fantasy, *Twice Upon A Time*, to be made with Alan Ladd Jr. at his new Ladd Company, and *Raiders of the Lost Ark* with Steven Spielberg. Both, however, were being financed by the studios, Warner Bros. and Paramount, respectively.

"I keep telling Charlie that moviemaking is a risky business only a fool would invest in," he smiled.

If Lucas had ever had any doubts about the wisdom of his retreat to northern California, they had been removed in the wake of the release of *The Empire Strikes Back*. By now the ways of Hollywood frustrated him more than ever. In June, a

Federal judge finally ruled against Fox in its action over *Battlestar Galactica*. He called the two works as different as apples and oranges. And he summed up the unpalatable reality for Lucas. If copyright infringement depended on finding "five, ten, or fifteen elements infringed upon, then there could be hundreds of films guilty of infringing on *Star Wars*."

In its two years before the judge, the case had at least proved two things. The only winners were the three legal firms paid millions by Fox and Universal and Hollywood was every bit as duplicitous a place as George Lucas imagined it. During its hundreds of hours the case produced endless eye-opening moments. First it was revealed that Fox had happily rented the old ILM warehouse at Van Nuys to Universal as Dykstra, Nelson, and company filmed there. Fox had even rented its rival a sound stage to record *Galactica*'s musical score.

Then it emerged that a number of high-ranking Universal executives had been among those furiously buying Fox shares after seeing a sneak prerelease screening of *Star Wars*. Ned Tanen also suffered the humiliation of being revealed by his old adversary, Lucas, as the man who turned *Star Wars* down within Lew Wasserman's citadel.

If there was one moment that had Lucas and everyone unconnected with the business shaking their heads and muttering "only in Hollywood," however, it came only a month before the case's conclusion in July 1980.

As Glen Larson was being savaged by Fox's lawyers inside the court—at one point vilified as a man "who had made a profitable career of other people's works" and accused of turning *Butch Cassidy and the Sundance Kid* into *Alias Smith and Jones* and *Coogan's Bluff* into *McCloud*—the company's television department was signing him up to head their operation. "We feel we have acquired the premier dramatic producer in television today," Harris Katleman, Fox TV's chairman said of Larson outside court shortly before the judge ruled.

There had been some consolation for Lucas three weeks later when his dispute with Jeff Berg at ICM had gone his way. An independent arbitrator had ruled he had been within his rights to negotiate the *Empire* deal on his own. The decision was a hammer blow to the giant agency, whose parent company, Marvin Josephson Associates, had to reassure Wall Street that the fact it would receive nothing in commissions from *The Empire Strikes Back* would not harm the company. Their words were clearly unconvincing. Josephson shares fell by $3 the next day.

The victory had been hollow, however. Lucas was still fuming at the most maddening and ludicrous Hollywood brouhaha of all. Lucas had been a member of the Director's Guild of America since his *American Graffiti* days but had had little to do with its plethora of petty rules and regulations. He regarded the union as little more than a bunch of bureaucrats. "The Hollywood unions have been taken over by the same lawyers and accountants who took over the studios," he once said.

He could barely believe his eyes when, soon after *Empire* was released, the DGA announced it was fining him $250,000 for failing to show Irvin Kershner's credit at the beginning of the film. Both he and Kershner found the argument close to insane. Leaving the director's credit to the end was his house style. He had not credited himself until after the end of *Star Wars* either. Yet the DGA ruled that, by flashing the Lucasfilm credit after that of Twentieth Century–Fox before the film opened, Lucas was taking his own "personal" executive producer credit before the titles. According to the DGA rules, Kershner should therefore have been credited at the same time.

Lucas was not sure whether it was the arrogance or the idiocy of the decision that annoyed him the most. "My name is not George Lucasfilm any more than William Fox's name was Twentieth Century–Fox," he fumed. Worse was to come, however. When his application for an exemption, filed with Kershner's full backing, was turned down, the DGA insisted he remove the film from every cinema it was showing in while he changed the titles.

Rather than going to the normal arbitration, an incandescent Lucas insisted on going to court. The DGA then told Kershner he would be fined if they lost—he had worked for a company that did not have a valid Guild contract.

Lucas eventually settled out of court for £25,000. Weeks later the Writer's Guild forced him to pay $15,000 for crediting Kasdan inadequately.

Within his Old Testament morality it was the final straw. "You can pollute the Great Lakes and not get fined that much," he fumed.

It took him a few months to organize his troops, but by April the following year Lucas had his middle finger to wave a final farewell to Hollywood. *Daily Variety* broke the news: GEORGE LUCAS CUTS H'WOOD TIES.

"Often considered an enigma and never a Hollywood filmmaker, George Lucas has severed his last direct ties here with resignations from the Director's Guild of America, the Writers Guild of America, and the Academy of Motion Picture Arts and Sciences."

The story went on to explain that he had coincided his resignation from each of the pillars of the Hollywood establishment with the closure of his last office in Los Angeles. The latter move had become inevitable. Even from northern California, Lucas had been able to see how obscene the indulgences at the Egg Company had become. The ranks of BMWs and Mercedes now filling the company parking lot was a symbol of the profligacy. "We were one step away from giving the delivery boy a Porsche," Lucas laughed later.

Clashes with Charles Weber over the direction the company should take had proved the final straw. Weber had suggested pumping $50 million into investments, including the doomed DeLorean car company. When he suggested the emerging Skywalker Ranch was a "drain," Lucas summoned the courage to fire him. The vast majority of the staff were laid off and the building on Lankershim Boulevard was sold and later demolished.

Sitting in the his new offices, adjacent to ILM on his site in San Rafael a few weeks later, Lucas sounded more like his father than ever. He did not quite call Los Angeles "sin city"—but he may as well have. "Down there, for every honest true filmmaker trying to get his film off the ground, there are a hundred sleazy used-car dealers trying to con you out of your money," he told the *New York Times*. "I've never made a picture in Hollywood—now I'll never have to," he smiled, with a hint of triumphalism.

Lucas left the film capital in the midst of another of its perennial crises. As one empire finally took shape, so another seemed to be once more foundering. *The Empire Strikes Back* had been the runaway success of a lackluster year. For the second year running, the movie industry as a whole was experiencing an overall drop in its audience. Even Twentieth Century–Fox had to report a drop in its earnings. Apart from *Empire* it had little to boost its balance sheet. As the film was withdrawn in the autumn its net income dropped by sixty percent. As surely as they had contributed to the industry's salvation in the 1970s, Lucas and the leaders of the "New Hollywood" were seen in some quarters as the culprits. Coppola's profligacy on *Apocalypse Now* had been topped by the wastefulness of Michael Cimino's $36.5 million disaster *Heaven's Gate* and John Landis's overblown $30 million comedy, *The Blues Brothers*. (As if slighted, the Godfather of the new era was spending $23 million on new computerized storyboards and other innovations on Zoetrope's *One From The Heart*. It would turn out to be the film that damaged him more than any other.) The whizz kids had become wastrels.

Even worse in the eyes of Hollywood, they had deserted the sinking ship. Lucas and his ranch was the most visible example of the movement away from Los Angeles itself. Elsewhere Robert Redford was preparing to move to the Sundance Institute of Film and Video in Provo Canyon, Utah. A school of new directors, led by Robert Benton, Martin Scorsese and Woody Allen, had restored New York to a preeminence it had not enjoyed since California usurped its power with the establishment of the first flimsy moving picture factories in the orange groves of Hollywood sixty-five years earlier. The last six Best Picture Oscars had gone to filmmakers based in or originally from the Big Apple.

There were those who wondered whether Hollywood might even have reached the end of its road. "I just don't know how Hollywood will bounce back," Benton told *Time* magazine. "The person who comes up with the answer has my nomination for the Nobel Prize."

As a new empire took shape, there was no question who its leader was. And there was equally no doubt about the means with which he would remain there. As Steven Spielberg succinctly put it: "Lucas has a bank called *Star Wars*."

Lucas's decision to cut himself off from the professional bodies induced a mild state of panic in the normally unflappable Howard Kazanjian.

"That's just what you want as you are planning the biggest movie of the year," said his old USC pal.

Gary Kurtz's replacement, popular with Lucas for his tight control of *More American Graffiti* and *Raiders of the Lost Ark*, had already begun work on *Revenge of the Jedi*. His major headache now was that Lucasfilm's lack of affiliation with

America's guilds meant his director would need to be a non-DGA member. The problem ruled out the one director Lucas wanted more than any other. Steven Spielberg and he had talked about the possibility of him directing *Jedi* while they had been filming *Raiders of the Lost Ark* in north Africa and Elstree in 1980. Spielberg, steeped in the same *Boy's Own* culture and blessed with an ability to film at a breakneck speed even Lucas found dizzying, had proved an ideal foil. It was, perhaps, no coincidence that Gary Kurtz's demise coincided with the beginning of what proved a long and phenomenally successful partnership between the two young geniuses of the New Hollywood. "George wanted Steven to direct the third one and Steven toyed with the idea," said Gary Kurtz. Spielberg was too much a Hollywood insider to want to risk riling the DGA, however.

In the absence of Spielberg, Lucas was determined to find a director whom he would be able to control more easily. He did not want another Irvin Kershner intellectually pondering over every line and camera angle. In effect he was looking for a surrogate.

"In his mind he wanted to hire a director who would be creative, but did everything exactly the way he wanted it," said Gary Kurtz. "It doesn't work."

Of all the directors he met, Richard Marquand, a Cambridge-educated Welshman, fitted the mold best. Marquand had cut his theatrical teeth working with the likes of Derek Jacobi, Trevor Nunn, and David Frost. He had graduated via the BBC to documentaries and then Hollywood. *The Legacy* with Katherine Ross for Universal and *Eye of the Needle*, a World War II spy thriller with Donald Sutherland for United Artists were the brief highlights of his movie resumé to date.

When Marquand volunteered to uproot his family to Marin for the six-month planning process Lucas envisaged, the job was his. From July to December 1981, he, Kazanjian, and Lawrence Kasdan spent each day constructing the storyboard. Once more the film would revolve around three major, set piece acts: an opening act in the court of the villainous Jabba the Hutt and aboard his sailbarge in the deserts of Tatooine, the second and third divided between the planet Endor and the new Death Star. While Elstree's nine soundstages would once more house the *Millennium Falcon* and all the major interiors, Kazanjian and Lucas agreed to look closer home for the two key outdoor locations.

Buttercup Valley, near Yuma, Arizona was chosen for its barren, otherworld sand dunes. A giant redwood forest in Crescent City, on the California/Oregon border, was earmarked for the lush landscape of Endor.

As the spring of 1981 arrived in the sleepy community of Crescent City, California, the 2,500 or so locals paid little attention to the small army of trucks and bulldozers that came with it. The trucks rolled through the town then disappeared up an unmarked dirt road high into the vast redwood forests overlooking the town and the clear, cobalt waters of the Pacific.

Along with fishing, the region's economy relied on the timber companies who owned swathes of the land along the stunning stretch of coastline. The sight of such equipment was far from unusual. In its long history, however, Crescent City had not witnessed a spectacle quite like the one that began unfolding high in the hills above the sea. In its way, no spectacle summed up the sheer, inflated scale of the *Star Wars* phenomenon so well.

Filming on the third installment in the saga, *Revenge of the Jedi* was not due to begin for another year. The first draft of a script had not yet been delivered. The film itself would not be seen for more than two years. Yet in the woods, producer Howard Kazanjian had begun relandscaping the ancient scenery in readiness for two weeks of filming the following spring. A network of smooth paths and tracks were installed between the three-hundred-year-old trees. The paths were then surrounded by some 17,000 baby ferns. "What was the madness behind that? We knew we were going to film scenes with the Ewoks there. They had to run and jump and we didn't want their little feet tripping over roots and stuff like that," he smiled. "We waited the full year for the ferns to grow back and look undisturbed."

Similar scenes were under way a thousand miles or so away in the barren wastes of Buttercup Valley outside Yuma, Arizona. Like some modern day Pharaoh, Kazanjian and his unit production chief, Louis Friedman, were there reclaiming part of the Arizona desert. The raw statistics might have made even Ramses blush.

Lucasfilm had negotiated rights to the Buttercup Valley for six months from the state's Bureau of Land Management. To prepare the site, a tanker spent each day of the first three months doing nothing but pumping water from a nearby canal to dampen the dunes into a packed-earth road. Two million gallons were poured into the sand. In the meantime work began on a giant sand barge. The craft was six stories tall, 120 feet wide, and 150 feet long. At one stage more than 400 people were at work on the site.

Kazanjian, from a family of Armenian jewelers, had a reputation in Hollywood as one of the most iron-willed disciplinarians in the business. Lucas admitted once that he had hired him on *Raiders* because he needed someone who "would not be a nice guy." He had never seen an operation quite like this, however.

Kazanjian realized the measure of the operation when the first bills began arriving back in the U.S. production office. "The first bill was for $99,000 worth of lumber. The next was for 11,000 pounds of nails," he recalled. Kazanjian would later learn that at the time it was the largest film site built on location in cinema history. No one was quite sure if they had taken the record from *Cleopatra*!

Kazanjian had exercised such tight control over *Raiders of the Lost Ark*, the film had—to the astonishment of Paramount—come in ahead of time and under budget. After the financial horrors of *Star Wars* and *Empire*, Lucas entrusted his old USC supporter with the role of making it third time lucky. He knew that this time, more than ever, ILM would hold the key.

Lucas had allocated at least a third of his projected $30 million budget for the development of the monsters. *Star Wars'* cantina creatures had suffered through lack of funding. He still found it hard to watch the ragtag collection of oddities he and Gary Kurtz had crammed into the scene. On *Empire* he had—inspiringly—channeled all his resources into producing a credible Yoda. This time he was determined to deluge the screen with fantastical characters. Crucial to the opening act would be Jabba the Hutt, the intergalactic Godfather he had discarded in *Star Wars*. His court would be populated by a menagerie of monsters, from an insect-like sycophant Lucas had himself christened Salacious Crumb, to a gruesome, gargoyle giant, to which Luke would be thrown like a piece of meat, the Rancor.

At the heart of the film, however, would be a new race of creatures, the Ewoks. Lucas refused to discard anything he regarded as a good idea. With money now no object, he resurrected the idea of the Wookiee race he had envisaged conducting the final shoot out in *Star Wars*. He came up with the idea of sawed-off Chewbaccas, furry, tree-dwelling teddy-bear-like creatures who would join in the climactic end of the trilogy.

Kazanjian had been considering using Rick Baker or Hollywood's highest-profile "monster maker" Stan Winston when ILM's Phil Tippett asked to be considered. Tippett had worked primarily on the stop-motion photography elements of the first two films. His enthusiasm and ideas impressed Lucas and he was given a shot at pleasing his persnickety paymaster, an experience he later described as "terror all the way."

A full year before filming was due to begin, a warehouse adjacent to the ILM building was converted from scratch into a fully-fledged creature shop to rival Jim Henson's world-leading facility in London.

In *Star Wars*, Jabba the Hutt had sported "a handlebar moustache and a Scots' brogue" according to Tippett. With ILM designer Nilo Rodis-Jamero, Joe Johnston, and Lucas, Tippett spent more than a year in pre-production on a more credible villain. The Sidney Greenstreet similarities many would detect later were real. The quartet imagined Jabba as an inflated version of the corpulent villain of the Humphrey Bogart movies, "more ridiculous than horrible, more *Alice in Wonderland* than an *Alien* slime monster." The vast, sluglike creature they came up with was originally cast in clay. At two tons, it was so large no clay oven could accommodate it. An entire room at ILM was converted into an oven instead.

Lucas was as relentless in his perfectionism as ever. Only sixty or so of the hundreds of creatures made at the so-called Monster Factory made it into the final movie—regardless of the fact that some were the product of hundreds of hours of work.

During the planning stages, Lucas had envisaged the Ewoks and a race of "tall, skinny-legged" animals, the Yuzzums, as the film's main, new creatures. The Monster Factory devoted long hours to the task of designing prototype, ostrich-like models. Dozens of the elaborate, twenty-foot tall creations, to be mounted on stilts, were readied. Kazanjian had even spent weeks tracking down expert stilt walkers to operate the creatures. An entire troupe of professionals had been located in Venezuela. "We were starting to work out the details, availability, visas, and all of that when George came back and said: 'Scratch the idea of Yuzzums.'"

Photographically, Lucas had decided, the spindly Yuzzums would not fit in the same frame as the squat Ewoks.

No one could bear to see the hard work go entirely to waste. "We did in the film have a Yuzzum," said Kazanjian. "He's there in Jabba's palace. Out of the eighty creatures we did clay figures of there was one, a tribute to the Yuzzum," smiled the producer.

Everywhere Lucas's old mantra from *Star Wars*, "faster—more intense," seemed to apply. A high-speed chase through the forestry of Endor featuring sleek Imperial "speeder bikes" had been an element in the very earliest drafts of the script. ILM veterans Dennis Muren and Joe Johnston considered a number of ideas—from erecting a vast, overhead cable system to carry the bikes, to fitting a cameraman with a James Bond–style jet-pack to create a sense of speed.

In the end the scenes were filmed relatively simply, using a cameraman fitted with a finely balanced "steadicam" camera to film footage as he walked through the forestry, filming the bike and its riders against a blue screen and combining the elements in the effects laboratory afterwards. The film in the camera was run at one-thirtieth of its normal speed. Run through a projector at normal speed, it seemed as if the camera was strapped to a Grand Prix car.

George Lucas had finally acquired the biggest electric train set a boy could wish to have. The ILM operation now boasted the most sophisticated computers anywhere within the industry. More than $3 million a year was being spent on research into expanding the boundaries of filmmaking.

Lucas was able to go for broke in the space battle finale attempting many of the effects that had been an impossible dream on *Star Wars*.

"When you look at the space battle in the first one, the ships were moving very slowly, there's not more than two or three ships in a shot and there's no continuity between shots—the ships don't fly out of one shot and into another," he enthused. In *Star Wars* the most complex shots were made up of at most a dozen different elements. In *Jedi*, the blizzard of X-Wings and Y-Wings, Imperial Destroyers and TIE fighters at the film's end was made up of sixty-seven layers of film. "The public demands a special-effects extravaganza," said Joe Johnston. "Something that will blow them away for their five dollars. We were never sure whether the film was a vehicle for the effects or for the story."

CHAPTER **12**

The Lost Emperor

On January 13, 1982, George Lucas telephoned his wife in California with a request. "Marcia, could you send me a trunk of warm clothes, I think I'm going to be here a while."

He may have told himself he was capable of keeping his distance. The reality was that *Star Wars* had become the consuming obsession of his life. As filming on *Jedi* got underway his priorities were now simple. "I'm only doing this because I started it, and now I have to finish it," he was soon telling visitors to the Elstree set. "I've got to get my life back."

Lucas had visited London before Christmas, returning to Marin for the festivities while the set was closed down. Howard Kazanjian had produced two movies with his old USC friend and thought he knew his habits. "Usually if he's not directing he comes in for the first two weeks, watches it, maybe comes back mid-way and maybe the last week. On *Jedi* he was there every day," said Kazanjian. "He never went home. He was there riding in the car with me at 5 A.M. and going home at night with me at 7 P.M."

Lucas and Kazanjian knew they could not extend their director the artistic autonomy Irvin Kershner had enjoyed. In Marquand, they found a more malleable talent. The director agreed to allow Lucas an active role during filming and consented to hand most of the postproduction and editing over to him.

He rationalized the situation elegantly enough. "The way I reconciled it was this: I think of *Star Wars* as a symphony. The music for the next part was there, but they needed a conductor who could come in, rehearse today, and tape tomorrow. I'm that conductor, [and] the composer happens to be alive."

Marquand was not entirely averse to expressing an opinion. It had been his idea that Yoda be reintroduced in the film. In the original draft, Luke had simply referred to a conversation he had had with his master before he had died. "I insisted we put him back. I felt we needed to see the conversation," Marquand said at the time.

If the production had its own Yoda, however, there was no question who it was as far as cast and crew were concerned. No matter how hard he tried, Lucas could not avoid being asked "a million questions a day." Nor could he resist offering advice. When he found Marquand rehearsing Hamill for a lightsaber sequence he chided him for allowing the actor to wield it one-handed. (Kershner had, to Lucas's annoyance, allowed Dave Prowse to do so in *Empire*.) "You hold it like a samurai sword," he told him. On another occasion he found Carrie Fisher standing in a curiously upright position on the set of Jabba the Hutt's court. Fisher, disguised as a male in the scene, had been told by Marquand to "stand like an English sentry." Lucas frowned and suggested: "Carrie, you're standing like an English sentry. You want to be more swashbuckling."

Lucas later claimed he hated being constantly asked, "Can these creatures do this?" "What is the history of this character?" "No matter how much I think everybody knows about *Star Wars* now, they don't," he moaned at one point. "I've given Richard the answers to a million questions over the last year, filled everybody in on everything I can think of, and yet when we get here the crew comes up with a thousand questions a day—I'm not exaggerating—that only I can answer."

Of course, he had the option of walking away. Deep in his heart, however, he knew he could not do so. "It's like marriage. You know what they say, 'You can't live with them, and you can't live without them,'" he said with a thin smile at one point.

Gary Kurtz had been filming *The Dark Crystal* on an adjoining sound stage at Elstree. He spent time with the old friends he had made on the *Star Wars* crew and observed Lucas and Marquand at work. Lucas had taken the path that had driven a wedge between him and his old producer. The story revolved around the redemption of Luke's relationship with Darth Vader and the Emperor's efforts to finally draw him to "the dark side." Marquand had recruited the distinguished stage actor Ian McDiarmid to play the Emperor.

Kurtz was not surprised at what he saw—or the results a year later. "George harassed Richard Marquand into more or less doing what he wanted and I think the film suffered because of that," he said.

Carrie Fisher had been the most vociferous voice among the cast in the negotiating stages. She was insistent that Leia was made a stronger woman this time around. Lucas relented, stripping her of her suffocating sackcloth and replacing her in a skimpy outfit forced on her by the slobberingly sexist Jabba the Hutt.

Fisher's metallic bikini made her the focus of the red-blooded male crew's attentions. Her breast plates would often slip. "After shots the prop man would have to check me," she said. "The hooters in place? Tits all right?" Fisher learned to laugh at the situation. "I was embarrassed at first with one hundred guys going crazy over my revealed self. Dignity was out of the question."

Under the watchful eyes of Kazanjian and Lucas, the Elstree section of filming was finished close to time and budget. The arrival of the *Star Wars* set on American soil brought its own set of headaches, however. Harrison Ford may have nicknamed it Boring Wood but the beauty of Elstree was that it was secure. During the final weeks of their *Star Wars* careers, Harrison Ford, Carrie Fisher, Mark Hamill, and the rest were officially employed on a horror movie called *Blue Harvest*. Curious onlookers were greeted by burly men in T-shirts reading "Blue Harvest: Horror beyond imagination." On the morning "call sheets," where Hamill was listed as "Martin," for the first time in years, strangers referred to Han Solo as "Harry." Lucasfilm even went so far as to announce filming on *Jedi* had actually switched to Germany. But the ruse lasted less than two weeks. After the *Los Angeles Times* reported the lengths Lucas was going to to film secretly in his home state, crowds began to gather every day. Harrison Ford fans were the most persistent, screaming his name incessantly whenever he loped into the viewfinders of their long-lensed cameras.

The secrecy surrounding the script was, if anything, even more intense. By now Fisher, Ford, and Hamill found the whole folderal incredibly silly. The big surprise this time would be the revelation that Leia was in fact Luke's sister. When the scene in which Luke breaks the news to Leia was filmed, she recalled, "They asked the crew—even the sound man—not to listen."

She confessed to being relieved at being let in on the secret in advance. "I'd have laughed on camera if Mark had told me for the first time then," she said. "It would've been like, 'Carrie, your dad isn't Eddie Fisher. Hitler is.'"

Even Lucas's security system could not account for the

accidental eavesdropper, however. Anthony Daniels had found himself a quiet spot in a glade and was settling down for a snooze when he heard Ford and Fisher rehearsing their most significant exchange.

Lucas had remained loyal to the British band of brothers he had assembled back in 1976. After being hidden from the world inside R2-D2, Kenny Baker had even been given his moment of glory, playing Wicket the Ewok who befriends Leia. On the morning of his first scene, however, Baker was laid low by stomach cramps. Explanations varied. Howard Kazanjian believed the diminutive actor had been sunbathing au naturel. Another explanation was that he had eaten a substandard chili dog.

For too many of those involved, *Jedi* seemed an adventure too far. Harrison Ford in particular had simply outgrown the production. *Raiders of the Lost Ark* and *Blade Runner* with Ridley Scott had allowed him to extend his repertoire. He was already looking for a script that would take him away from the fantasy genre altogether. (It would arrive, a year later, in the shape of *Witness*, the film that would win him an Oscar nomination and his longed-for step up into more "serious" roles.)

He had fought hard to have Solo killed off so as to add more emotion to the story. "I was convinced that Han Solo should die," he said afterwards. "I told George: 'He's got no mama, no papa, and he's got no story. Let's kill him and give some weight to this thing.'"

Lucas was used to Ford's feisty contributions to story conferences. By now Ford had become the leading man of Lucas's repertory company. His dry-as-the-Dead-Sea-Scrolls humor had found a perfect vehicle in the daring Doctor Indiana Jones. He had also grown in confidence under the direction of Steven Spielberg, who had encouraged him to ad-lib to great effect on *Raiders of the Lost Ark*. "Harrison has always had opinions about things. Harrison is not someone who doesn't question what's going on. And so he's been very involved," he said.

On this occasion, however, despite the tigerishness of his argument, he had to accept his position in the *Star Wars* chain of command. "That was the one thing I was unable to convince George of," he shrugged during filming.

Instead, his contribution was reduced to a by-the-numbers numbness. Required to do little more than react to action or effects, he made little effort to hide his unease at what he regarded as his enslavement to George Lucas's dark Empire. "Massa George says ah kin go at the end of 'eighty-five—a freed man," he said, semi-jokingly on the set.

Richard Marquand found Harrison as opinionated as Kershner had. "He doesn't suffer fools gladly. If you don't know what you're going to do on the day he gets a little confused and upset," he said later.

When *Time* magazine arrived on set to conduct exclusive interviews with the cast, they found him disinterested. "There is no difference between doing this kind of film and playing *King Lear*. The actor's job is exactly the same: dress up and pretend," he yawned.

He was not the only one who found the pretending more ludicrous than ever amid the monster factory of *Jedi*, however. "Special-effects movies are hard on actors," Hamill said, summing up all their feelings. "You find yourself giving an impassioned speech to a big lobster in a flight suit."

More than any of the leading trio, Hamill had been driven down a cul-de-sac by *Star Wars*. Even a well-received portrayal of Mozart in *Amadeus* on Broadway had done little to persuade casting directors to look at him. He had pestered Alan Parker for the lead in *Midnight Express*—to no avail. "I don't even get a chance to fail," he opined.

In the years that followed his sense of bitterness would deepen. Of all *Star Wars*' senior figures he would find it the most difficult to escape the chains of his enslavement to Lucas's empire. Hamill would remain the voice of Skywalker on a *Star Wars* radio series and a succession of talking books. He would also contribute to the CD-Rom games Lucas later developed with his LucasArts company. On the rare occasions Lucas talked of the possibility of more *Star Wars* films he talked of Hamill waiting in the wings to play an older, wiser Luke. "If he is old enough?"

More than a decade later Hamill's anger would be mixed with resignation. "In the end, when all is said and done, I've got a big '© LUCASFILM' stamped on my ass!"

Aware of the significance of the moment, Kazanjian and Lucas had given the go ahead for lavish "wrap parties." At the end there was a clear divide between those who were glad the ordeal was over and those who dearly wanted life in the *Star Wars* universe to go on.

For Carrie Fisher, the saga soon seemed a picnic compared to her troubled private life. After seven stormy years with Paul Simon, she married him later that year. Within eleven months the marriage had collapsed and she had descended further into the darkness of her drug dependency. Her excesses eventually landed her in a hospital emergency room where she had her stomach pumped. "I always wanted to blunt or blur what was painful," she came to confess. "My idea was pain reduction and mind expansion, but I ended up with mind reduction and pain expansion." No one suffered more amidst the trials and tribulations of the *Star Wars* era. Her triumph in overcoming her problems, and her subsequent success as the author of the scabrous, semi-autobiographical *Postcards From the Edge* and *Surrender the Pink*, was more impressive than anything Princess Leia ever pulled off.

Some, like Peter Mayhew, walked away from the experience with nothing but fond memories. "There was a party at the end of each shoot. It was very sad, but we did at least have a feeling that we had done something that was going to be in the history of the cinema forever," he said. Mayhew, like Dave Prowse and Kenny Baker, returned to England and relative obscurity afterwards. While Prowse picked up the reins of his London gymnasium and continued to make personal appearances as Darth Vader and Baker returned to the cabaret circuit, Mayhew quit at the top. Two decades after joining the *Star Wars* circus he was working in a timber mill in the Yorkshire town of Keighley. "After a couple of years, when the work was not coming in I decided to get out," he said. He, at least, is content with the memories and the occasional appearance at a science-fiction convention where the affection for his character—and the trilogy of films—has never waned. "There has never been anything like them. I was just glad to be part of it."

For Lucas, however, it was the end of the most significant chapter in his life. He talked of spending more time with the new family he and Marcia had finally begun with the adoption earlier that year of two-year-old daughter Amanda. "When you have a daughter it changes things," he said. "You can't put a kid on hold and say, 'Wait, I've got one more picture to do, you just stay tight. You know she's only going to be two once, and she's great and I'm not going to miss it.'" If he was ever to pick up the pieces of the *Star Wars* saga it would only be by putting his family before his films. "If I can't make that work, then there won't be any movies," he said.

He talked of taking two years off and studying social psychology, returning to racing cars, and learning to play the guitar. "Or I may just end up being an ex-workaholic sailing a boat around the world." At the heart of his dreams for the future was the filmmaking Shangri-la whose name acknowledged its debt to *Star Wars*, Skywalker Ranch.

Most of all, however, he simply wanted to wake up in the mornings no longer worrying. "It's been ten years," he said.

"Every time I kick it down, it comes rearing its ugly head back up again. This time I've kicked it down for good, I think..."

In April 1983, Albert Szabo had begun the search for thirty new staff members at the Avco cinema in Westwood, Los Angeles. "There's no excuse to be undermanned," the sixty-four-year-old cinema manager had told his disbelieving bosses at the General Cinema Corporation. Two months later the sagacious smile on Szabo's face said it all. By now thirty pairs of hands did not seem enough.

Three years after *Empire*, the lines had begun forming a full eight days before *Jedi* opened. By Wednesday, May 25—the sixth anniversary of the first extraordinary scenes at the Avco and the Chinese Theaters—the house records were tumbling once more.

Two days later the figures flew straight on to the pages of the major newspapers. More than one and a half million people had lined up to see *Jedi*. The box-office total of $6.2 million was the biggest opening day in history by a margin of $800,000. "What makes the achievement so remarkable is the fact that the record was set on a Wednesday," said the *New York Times*.

The lines had begun forming at the Egyptian Theater on Hollywood Boulevard on the prior Thursday. Six days later the first ticket holders were allowed in at one minute past midnight on the opening day.

For the new, rationalized Lucasfilm empire, *Jedi* was a perfect showcase for its new technology. The Avco in Westwood and three other cinemas around America had forked out $15,000 to be fitted out with a new sound system by Lucasfilm engineers. With a nod to his roots, Lucas had christened the high-clarity, low-distortion system THX Sound. He had set up a new company, Skywalker Sound, to market it.

The accompanying gravy train also proved more lucrative than ever. If *Star Wars* had been pulled along by a merchandising version of Stephenson's Rocket, it was now being hauled by the equivalent of a Japanese bullet train.

The upper reaches of the *New York Times'* bestseller list was dominated by no less than five *Jedi* books. The Kenner toy catalogue alone now ran to forty pages with as many furry versions of the Ewoks alone. Top-of-the-line, $50 models of Salacious Crumb and Jabba the Hutt came complete with a trap door and a version of the film's subterranean dungeon in which to cast hapless victims.

Star Wars had also taken its first step into the burgeoning new video arcade market. Atari, then leaders in the field, signed a deal to put $3,000 coin-operated consoles in thousands of malls, arcades and cinemas in time for the launch. The game, in which players took on the role of Luke Skywalker attacking the Death Star and were rewarded with Obi-Wan's voice promising "Remember, the Force will be with you, always," was the company's most advanced yet.

For the first time the battle had been taken from the shops into the heart of the shopping malls themselves. Hundreds of American shopping arcades had been fitted out with "*Jedi* Adventure Centers," complete with earpieces to tune in to dialogue from the film and photo booths which allowed their image to be transposed alongside Luke, Leia and the rest of the gang. It almost went without saying that the venture was "the largest simultaneous movie/shopping mall promotion ever undertaken."

In his few interviews, Lucas sounded half-hearted as he fended off suggestions the films had shown their true commercial colors. "A lot of people say the films are just an excuse for merchandising. 'Lucas just decided to cash in on the teddy bear?'" he bridled. "Well it's not a great thing to cash in on. If I were designing something original as a market item, I could probably do a lot better." He conceded that without the stream of funds provided by toys he would not have been able to develop much of the computer technology ILM had harnessed for the effects in *Jedi*. "People tend to look at merchandising as an evil thing. But ultimately, a lot of fun things come out of it, and at the same time, it pays for the overhead of the company and everybody's salary."

By the first Friday of the Memorial Day weekend it was clear that history was once more repeating itself. The record of Wednesday had lasted two days. On the Friday *Jedi* collected $6.437 million at the box office. On Sunday it raked in $8.44 million. By the following Wednesday it had more than doubled even *E.T.*'s remarkable opening week. Even the most hardened Hollywood head shook at the $45.3 million it had taken.

More than any other film, it had been *Star Wars* that had transformed the release of a major movie into an exercise in statistics rather than salesmanship. By now the number-crunchers controlled as much space as the critics. There may have been some among that fraternity who were protesting at their newfound impotence in the face of modern cinema's self-fulfilling prophecies. Most reviewers disliked *Jedi* for more straightforward reasons, however.

The film appeared to have been somehow lost in hyper-space. Selfreverential and humorless, overreliant on the dazzle of the ILM effects and at times incomprehensible in its story structure, *Jedi* was—to most minds—by far the poorest of the three films. Its overpopulation with creatures so clearly designed with at least half an eye on the merchandising shelves also left a nasty taste in the mouth. "This time the toys have taken over the toy store," wrote Peter Rainer of the *Los Angeles Herald Examiner*.

"The innocence that made *Star Wars* the movie phenomenon of the 1970s, has long since vanished. It has become its own relentless Empire, grinding out Fun with soulless efficiency," *Newsweek*'s David Ansen added.

In the run up to the film's release Richard Marquand had anticipated hostility. "You know the old saying, the third soldier through the gap is the one who gets it," he joked. The snipers were waiting. Pauline Kael's conversion to the cause proved short-lived. She accused Marquand of taking "the fantasy out of fantasy."

Most—correctly—laid the blame at George Lucas's door. One went so far as to call it his "Waterloo."

Yet their remarks made absolutely no difference whatsoever. By the end of the summer of 1983 *Jedi* had become the third *Star Wars* film to overwhelm its competition. By the time the final ticket had been sold, Americans had paid $232 million to see the end of the trilogy. The worldwide market earned half as much again. *Jedi* slipped in behind *Star Wars* and *E.T.* in the top three most successful films of all time.

It was Pauline Kael who best encapsulated the divide that now separated the "serious" cinema from the world of Lucas and his friend Spielberg. "It is one of the least amusing ironies of movie history that in the 1970s, when the 'personal' film-makers seemed to be gaining acceptance, the thoughtful, quiet George Lucas made the quirkily mechanical *Star Wars*—a film so successful that it turned the whole industry around and put it on a retrograde course, where it's now joining forces with video-games manufacturers," she despaired.

To Albert Szabo and the men on the front line, however, Lucas was simply the savior of his industry. "He is in the mold of Louis B. Mayer, Jack Warner, Adolph Zukor, and Darryl F. Zanuck," said the most knowledgeable cinema boss in Los Angeles. "No one tells George Lucas what to do or how to do it. He is the epitome of America—and were getting better entertainment for it."

A week or so after *Jedi*'s release, staff at the Lucasfilm office in San Rafael were called together for a staff meeting. The trades scattered over the desks were proclaiming the latest record-breaking box-office figures. A sense of genuine euphoria still permeated the office.

As an ashen George Lucas began addressing the audience, however, the mood changed immediately.

In a faltering voice, Lucas told his loyal staff that, after fourteen years of marriage, he and Marcia were seeking a divorce. Throughout the brief speech, he and Marcia held each other's hands. The tears that rolled down their cheeks were visible on the faces of many others.

Friends were stunned by the news. There seemed to have been no indication of any problems within what had seemed a genuinely perfect marriage. Indeed, throughout his interviews before the release of *Jedi*, Lucas had talked of little else but how he now wanted to devote time to Marcia and Amanda.

At first it made little sense. Yet when friends like Howard Kazanjian, who with his wife had double-dated with Lucas and the then Marcia Griffin way back in the 1960s, took time to think, they cursed themselves for not having spotted it sooner.

At the end of *Jedi*, Kazanjian had assumed that Marcia would be an automatic choice to help cut the film. With no sign of her, he had asked Lucas whether she would be helping out? "George said 'You're gonna have to ask her,'" he recalled. (Marcia worked on the film. Yet, perhaps significantly, the emotional credibility she had always given her husband's films—"the dying and crying" as he called it—was absent.)

On previous films, Kazanjian, Marcia, and Lucas would go out to dinner three nights a week on average. During a year of making *Jedi* he struggled to recall one evening meal with Marcia. "I think once we went out to dinner," he recalled. "George would go home and Marcia would stay in the editing room." Kazanjian was in Japan, overseeing the film's release there when he heard the news. "My heart went to my foot. I sat down and nearly cried. And then I said 'Boy, Howard are you blind?'"

"Everybody said, 'Didn't you know, Howard?' There were so many arrows and so many things telling me. But I didn't know. You could say, 'you idiot,' but it didn't click because they were the perfect couple."

Others, however, had detected the signs of strain within their marriage years earlier. George's inability to let go of his work had been a persistent source of irritation to Marcia.

"George would take problems to bed with him and she said this had caused a lot of problems," said Charlie Lippincott, who interviewed Marcia in depth for a proposed book on the making of *Star Wars* back in 1976. "At the time of *Star Wars* she swore she would never edit another film with George," he added. "If she ever had to work with him again, she felt it would be the end of their marriage."

Lucas had acknowledged the problem in the run up to the opening of *Jedi*. "It's been very hard on Marcia, living with somebody who is constantly in agony, uptight, and worried, off in never-never land," he had confessed. The tragedy was that his words had come too late.

While the complex divorce got under way, news leaked out to the wider world. Eventually it emerged that Marcia had been seeing another man, Tom Rodriguez, a worker on Skywalker Ranch, whom she later married.

For Lucas the loss was almost too much to bear. Having poured every ounce of his being into making *Star Wars* successful and establishing Skywalker Ranch, he had lost the only person he had been interested in sharing it with. At first he reacted by transforming himself. Suddenly the checkered shirts, jeans, and tennis shoes were replaced by slacks and smarter designer shirts.

Friends had often heard Marcia laugh at the fact George wore the same, thick-rimmed glasses, shirt, jeans and tennis shoes every day of his life. And his idea of the perfect evening was watching the television news in bed. (When he asked Mark Hamill out for dinner on one occasion, the two dined at Lucas's local Taco Bell. "I should have known George wouldn't go to a place where there were tablecloths and waiters," Hamill said.)

"George never wanted to do anything," said one friend. "She loved talking to people, going places, having parties, going to the opera, skiing, Hawaii. They were so opposite that's what made them work."

"After he lost her, he wore contacts, started taking guitar lessons, he would go racing and go to the opera," said another friend. If it was a message to Marcia, it fell on deaf ears.

Soon he was embarking on a short-lived romance with the singer Linda Ronstadt, an affair that had the word "rebound" written all over it. Ronstadt's reputation as something of a man eater had been earned in short-lived, high-profile relationships with California Governor Jerry Brown, *Rolling Stone* journalist Pete Hamill, and songwriter J.D. Souther and an up-and-coming young comic, Jim Carrey. For Lucas it seemed the unlikeliest of matches.

His divorce cost him most of his $50 million-dollar fortune. He paid Marcia rather than lose Skywalker Ranch, now the one thing he cared about that he had left. It took Lucas four years to publicly acknowledge the devastation caused by the split. By then he had adopted another daughter, the second of three who would come to fill the void left by Marcia.

He had no hesitation in blaming the success of *Star Wars* for his troubles. "That kind of success is very difficult to deal with, very disruptive to one's personal life," he told the respected *New York Times* writer, Aljean Harmetz. "It took eight years and a lot of creative energy and emotional torment to complete the movies. Then the divorce. Divorce is a very difficult thing financially and emotionally."

Lucas told Harmetz he was only now pulling out of "a several-year tailspin."

If there was a common force at work within the lives of the two men who had brought *Star Wars* to life, it seemed a dark and destructive one in the years that followed the end of the on-screen saga. While Lucas picked up the pieces of his life, Gary Kurtz endured an even more painful sequence of events. In 1983 he and his wife Meredith went through their own divorce. It had little of the civility of the Lucas's action.

Kurtz had wound up Kinetographics soon after filming *The Dark Crystal* in 1982. While well-received by the critics, *The Dark Crystal* failed to set the box office ablaze. By the time Kurtz had invested in Walter Murch's debut as a director, a woeful "sequel" to the *Wizard of Oz*, *Return to Oz*, in 1985, he had hit serious financial problems.

In July 1986, Kurtz, a proud and private man who had often said in interviews that he disliked talking about money, was forced to lay his soul bare in a London bankruptcy court. As the producer of *Star Wars* and *The Empire Strikes Back*, he told the court he had earned $10 million. As of that morning, however, he had $150 to his name.

The chain of events almost beggared belief. After instigating the divorce, Kurtz had been obliged to pay off a $5 million debt run up by a publishing company his wife had set up in California. In addition, his films had left him with a $3 million debt to Chemical Bank of New York. Kurtz had hoped to sell his various properties, in Sausalito near San Francisco, Los Angeles, Sacramento, British Columbia, and Buckinghamshire to pay both the bank and his wife. As delays mounted on the sales of each, however, the massive interest had begun to cripple him.

Kurtz told the court that every dollar of the $1.7 million he was still due from his *Star Wars* profits would go directly to Chemical Bank. "My ex-wife controls all my personal effects in America," he said with resignation.

The ordeal left Kurtz, then forty-five, understandably disillusioned. Afterwards the producer left the film industry altogether, remarrying and spending time in a new home in the rolling hills of the Wye Valley near the Welsh border. "I got fed up for a while and withdrew. I didn't have anything to do with the business at all," he said.

He is now happy to measure his life by something other than the box office. There are echoes of George Lucas in his voice. "For me it was about how much time is there in the day to do the things I want to do. And I didn't see it happening," he said. "It is very difficult to have any sort of ordinary life."

Today he is working on an animation series for the BBC, content to watch the world of mainstream moviemaking from a distance. After years of estrangement, he and Lucas have resumed their friendship.

In molding the century's most powerful piece of mass mythology Kurtz had, with Lucas, tapped into the tradition of the ancient storytellers. "There's no reason why the *Star Wars* story could not have been told as a Greek myth, or as an American western or a World War I love story. It would have fitted perfectly into all those genres," he said. "And I think that is one of the reasons it had a strong impact on people's lives."

If his own life turned into a variation on a Greek tragedy, at least Gary Kurtz can now treat it with a philosophical smile. "If all you want to do is make a lot of money there are a lot of easier ways of doing it than making movies," he said.

EPILOGUE

Set alongside the still waters of a reed-filled creek, the center-piece of Skywalker Ranch is the manse-like building known as Main House. With its vast winding staircase, Victorian library, fine antiques, and Tiffany chandeliers, it is a home to match the most extravagant antebellum mansion. It is where Charles Foster Kane would have lived if he had married Scarlett O'Hara. When the actor Robin Williams first set foot there, he cried: "Tara, I'm home!"

By the summer of 1995, however, the sight of the man whose millions built and furnished the magnificent house was as rare as the collection of Norman Rockwell originals on its walls. Generally he visited the building just once a week, on Fridays.

He reserved the last day of the work week for the minutiae of this business life. The day was organized around answering his mail and attending board meetings, talking to lawyers and catching up on news within his diverse empire.

He reserved the rest of his week for spending time with his three adopted daughters. George Lucas had finally regained control of the life he had lost. Or at least, so it seemed.

In the years that followed the end of the *Star Wars* saga, Lucas had become one of the more intriguing mysteries in the entertainment world. If he was not quite the Howard Hughes of modern Hollywood, he was certainly not the Donald Trump either. His public appearances were few, his public utterances even fewer. He had remained as dismissive and disinterested in Hollywood as he had ever been—as Old Testament in his lack of forgiveness too. Even his elevation to the company of Hitchcock, Zanuck, DeMille, and his hero Disney, with the presentation of the honorary Irving Thalberg Award at the 1991 Oscars did little to heal the wounds of the past. He did not rejoin the Academy, the Director's Guild, or any of the industry's other establishment enclaves afterwards.

The benefits of his new, relaxed regime were obvious. Bar the occasional fleck of distinguished gray in his beard and hair, he looked, at the age of fifty-one, lean and well-preserved. His face still carried a glint of youthfulness, as did his clothes. The student-issue jeans and checkered shirt seemed as well-worn as his Nike sneakers. Yet, a dozen years after he drew down the curtain on the *Star Wars* saga, all was far from well in the empire Lucas had spent more than a decade building. As an executive producer, his name had been associated with a quartet of box office disappointments. If 1988's *Tucker*—the true story of the car designer Preston Tucker—had at least redeemed his relationship with Francis Coppola, there was nothing positive that could be said of the $35 million disaster *Howard the Duck*, released to mockery in 1986. *Willow*, a fantasy directed by Ron Howard in 1988 and *Radioland Murders*, directed by Mel Smith six years later, had been merely lackluster. Only the Indiana Jones movies had brought success on the grand scale. Unlike *Star Wars*, the second great trilogy of Lucas's cinematic career improved with age. In 1989 *Indiana Jones and the Last Crusade* had witnessed Spielberg, Harrison Ford—and Sean Connery as the dashing archaeologist's father—at the peak of their powers.

Epilogue

On the debit side, however, Lucas had not fared well with a television spinoff. By 1993 *The Young Indiana Jones Chronicles*, based on the teenage character played by River Phoenix in the *Last Crusade*, had been canceled by ABC television after twenty-eight hours of its projected thirty-two-hour run.

More worrying still were the clouds now gathering above the northern California skies of his business interests. His plans for Skywalker Ranch had aroused anger and resentment within his corner of Marin County. By 1985 he owned 4,750 acres in the Lucas Valley area. His plans to move ILM and its staff of 200 to a 300,000-square-foot new building on the ranch became the subject of the most protracted public debate the area had ever seen. Cartoons in his local newspaper lampooned him as "Lord Lucas," a Darth Vader–villain hovering over the unspoiled countryside in a sinister spaceship. The locals' fury was only fueled by disclosures that he had been buying yet more land in the name of his accountant. "Lucas sneaked in behind our backs," the local homeowners's association protested. "Do you think the county would let Standard Oil do this?" His inept handling of the situation left his main businesses, ILM and Skywalker Sound, marooned in San Rafael.

For more of the decade that followed *Jedi*, both companies remained the industry's technological torch-bearers. Oscar statuettes adorned every corner of ILM's futuristic complex, testimonials to state-of-the-art effects on films from Spielberg's *E.T.* and *Jurassic Park* to Jim Carrey's *The Mask* and Tom Hanks's *Forrest Gump*. ILM was routinely referred to as "Hollywood's secret weapon." It formed the heart of the kind of integrated multimedia company the old giants of Hollywood all yearned to become. Nonetheless the head start it had built from the *Star Wars* bonanzas of the 1980s had been eaten away by the new conglomerates of the 1990s. Once ILM's collection of Silicon Graphics supercomputers had been the envy of even the Pentagon. As computer companies like Bill Gates's Microsoft forged new alliances within Hollywood, the competition began closing in—and fast.

In 1994 Lucas was forced to close Skywalker Sound's Los Angeles offices and wind down his expensive experiments with a company exploring the "new media." At the same time he lost a number of his most talented staff, some to rivals, others amid rumors of drift and dissent within his empire.

Outwardly, the setbacks hardly amounted to a crisis. Lucas was routinely listed among the industry's most powerful players and America's richest men. Yet like the Wizard of Oz, he knew that behind the magical façade all was not what it appeared.

So it was that on the last Friday of May that year, Lucas climbed the spiral staircase to his office on the first floor of the Main House ready to meet a rare visitor from Hollywood, Rex Weiner, a reporter on one of the two daily bibles of showbusiness, *Variety*. Weiner had needed no second invitation to fly up from Los Angeles that morning. His interviewee may have been out of sight for a decade, but he had never once slipped out of mind.

As Lucas eased himself into a chair and began his first major interview in years, he wasted little time in getting to the point of his audience with Weiner. Afterward the reporter also wasted little time in dispatching the story back to his office. On Monday morning *Variety's* front page headline ran: "LUCAS THE LONER RETURNS TO WARS."

Rumors of three more *Star Wars* films had surfaced and sunk again with monotonous regularity. This time, however, it was straight from the horse's mouth. Lucas revealed that he had already begun work writing three more adventures, as he had always hinted, concentrating on the period that preceded the *Star Wars* trilogy and the relationship between the young Obi-Wan Kenobi and Anakin Skywalker before his transformation into Darth Vader. To the genuine amazement of many, however, he also revealed that he had decided to return to directing. His would be the name after the credits of the first of the new trilogy films.

In the early years that followed the release of *Jedi*, Lucas had been as good as his word and kept *Star Wars* under lock and key. The remainder of his epic story had sat untouched in the five three-ring binders he kept in the "treehouse" writing room he had built with Marcia in an outbuilding at Parkhouse. Yet, as he explained to the man from *Variety* he had always intended returning to the saga when he felt the technology was available.

It had been ILM's achievements with *Jurassic Park*, Spielberg's dazzling adaptation of Michael Crichton's novel about genetically engineered dinosaurs, that had finally convinced him, he said. The company's breathtaking computer-generated T-Rex had been to the first half of the 1990s what its lumbering space cruisers had been to the latter half of the 1970s. At the box office, *Jurassic Park* had gone on to rewrite many of the records *Star Wars* had set seventeen years earlier.

"The fact that you can make a realistic thing, as real as anything on the set and have it walk around and talk was the big breakthrough," Lucas told *Variety*. With that technology now available he was free to make "more interesting" *Star Wars* stories. Crucially, however, he would be able to do so at what he described as "a reasonable cost." Lucas estimated each of his new movies would cost between $60 and $70 million—at 1995 prices, a far from outlandish outlay.

The news sent Hollywood into a spin. For some the burning question was, why? Did Lucas need the money to regenerate his companies? Had the middle years of his life left him frustrated? Was he merely fulfilling his destiny in completing the nine *Star Wars* stories he had promised?

Epilogue

For the major players of Hollywood, however, such puzzles soon paled in the face of the one certainty of the situation. It soon emerged that Lucas intended to sell the right to distribute the films. To its new owner's fury, Fox had lost the rights to *Star Wars* in the mid-1980s when Rupert Murdoch acquired the studio from the Texan oil billionaire Marvin Davis. Lucas had implemented a "key man" clause relieving him of his old ties to the studio if a new overlord arrived.

The contrast with the situation he had faced more than twenty years earlier could not have been more overwhelming. From Disney to Universal, Fox to SKG DreamWorks (Steven Spielberg's newly formed venture with David Geffen and Jeffrey Katzenberg), Hollywood became a sea of blank checkbooks. Like its owner, *Star Wars* may have been out of sight, but its power had never strayed out of mind.

In his rare moments of public reflection in the wake of *Jedi*, Lucas had rejected any idea that his films had left more than a minor mark on their era. "It's given people a certain amount of joy in a certain time of history," he said. "In a thousand years, ten thousand years, it will be nothing more than a pretty minor footnote in the pop culture of the 1970s and 1980s."

Yet it took only the most cursory glance at the business of modern movie-making to recognize the remark as a serious attack of over-modesty. Far from being a footnote, *Star Wars* had, in many ways, been the central story of its era. Its legacy permeated the entertainment industry of the 1990s.

In 1977, movie merchandising tie-ins were halfhearted marriages. Now mainstream Hollywood was able to generate three times a film's box-office revenue by selling the baseball cap and the computer game, licensing the theme park ride and the hamburger Happy Meal. In 1977 special-effects movies were virtually nonexistent. Two decades later it was a rare box-office chart that did not have at least one work of computer-generated genius at its apex, most of them produced by the wizardry of ILM. In 1977 the summer was a time for cinematic sleepers, two months to keep the seats warm for winter. By 1995 every studio trained its biggest guns on the last week in May and Memorial Day. "George Lucas effectively moved the summer forward two weeks, from the middle of June to the end of May," said Tom Sherak, Twentieth Century–Fox's senior film executive. "The Wednesday before Memorial Day is called 'George Lucas Day.'" Perhaps most significantly of all, a new generation had been converted to the sheer joy of a night—or day—at the movies. As they hissed at Darth Vader and cheered Luke Skywalker, they may not have been attending high church. Yet at least audiences had returned to weekly worship. More than any other movie, *Star Wars* had been the film that paved the way for the multiplex generation.

The stampeded to the gates of Skywalker Ranch began almost as soon as the interview was published. Fox wasted no time in pitching its tent for what were soon being referred to as the "prequels." Once Lucas had sworn he would never allow *Star Wars* to be released on video. Adding fuel to he fear his empire may need the money, he had soon accepted Fox's offer to finance a lavish repackaging of a boxed set of the trilogy. Those who had cast doubts on *Star Wars'* shelf-life thought again when they sold 22 million copies in America alone in just six months in 1995.

Soon Fox had persuaded Lucas to rerelease the trilogy theatrically to mark the twentieth anniversary of its unheralded premiere back in 1977. By the time teaser trailers were shown in American cinemas at the end of 1996, ILM had been able to add three to five minutes of new, digitally generated footage to the original movie.

Fox's hopes for the special editions had not been harmed by the success of *Independence Day*, the $400 million alien invasion heavyweight of the summer. "There's no better time than now," Tom Sherak said as a new wave of science fiction was prepared in its wake. "*Star Wars* was the mother of all sci-fi movies."

Yet by the summer of 1996, no one was any closer to winning the rights to the new movies—or indeed even seeing Lucas to discuss them. Sherak was only half-joking when he said in August: "When Lucas comes here, we won't let him out of the room."

If the deals being done elsewhere only added to Hollywood's anxiety, they added to the rest of the world's anticipation. Few were surprised when Lucasfilm announced a link-up with a food manufacturer. After all, if *Star Wars* was the mother of sci-fi movies it was the father of the modern, merchandising mega-deal. Yet no one could quite believe the scale of the partnership when it was forged in May that year.

McDonalds, Coca-Cola, and Pepsi had been at the head of the line of multinationals vying for the rights to associate themselves with the new films. Pepsi, with its restaurant chains Taco Bell, Pizza Hut and Kentucky Fried Chicken, emerged triumphant, paying a mind-bending $2 billion to carry *Star Wars* characters on its products for the next five years. *Variety* called the tie-in "the largest in size and scope the entertainment industry has ever seen." Twenty years after it began rewriting the records books, it seemed as if *Star Wars* had never been away. If there was a sense of the world having turned full circle, the early months of pre-production on the new films only added to it.

In the autumn it was revealed that preproduction on the prequels had begun, once more on the outskirts of London rather than Hollywood. The new Millennium Studios, at a former Rolls-Royce factory site at Leavesden in Hertfordshire, had beaten out Elstree, Shepperton and Pinewood to land a deal estimated to be worth $1 billion. Naturally it was comfortably the biggest in British film history.

Epilogue

At the same time, Tunisia was once more being prepared for an invasion. With much of the story clearly destined to be set back on Tatooine, the country's unique supply of architectural oddities were once more being sized up. A network of honeycomb-like ksars—or fortified granaries—built by the Berbers on Jerba and a crumbling, clifftop fortress near the border with Libya were among the potential locations being lined up by Lucas's new producer Rick McCallum.

McCallum had caught Lucas's eye working on the *Young Indy* series for television. As he put together a new-look team, with production designer Gavin Bocquet and supervisor David Brown picking up where John Barry and Robert Watts had started, McCallum found himself hindered by a lack of continuity. Many of the sites seen in the first film in particular had been lined up to reappear in the prequels. With no surviving log of the 1976 expedition, McCallum had to rely on a particularly fanatical *Star Wars* fan to find the original sites of the Mos Eisley cantina and Obi-Wan's home on Jerba.

Star Wars' unique brand of onset secrecy returned too. Systems were tightened at both ILM and Leavesden, where the set was protected by a militaristic checkpoint and barbed-wire fencing. Leavesden had been converted into a studio for the return of James Bond in the successful *GoldenEye*, in 1995. Even 007 might have been hard-pressed to crack the security surrounding casting and storylines.

Of the original cast, only Kenny Baker and Anthony Daniels were likely to return for the first three prequels at least. Lucas had always seen the ageless R2-D2 and C-3PO as the constants within the turmoil of the hundred-year-long saga. Daniels's links with Lucas had remained strong. Once the most recalcitrant of the cast, he was now Lucas's "golden boy," contributing to robot's voice on a radio series based on the saga and writing a column for his in-house magazine.

Elsewhere, however, Lucas was once more involved in a search for new stars to populate his universe. Casting director Robin Gurland had been focusing on young actors for the parts of the young Anakin Skywalker, Obi-Wan Kenobi, and a young queen, presumably Leia and Luke's mother.

Ironically it was the role of Obi-Wan Kenobi that became the only one connected with an established name. A persistent, not to say intriguing, rumor that Kenneth Branagh had signed up for the role failed to disappear even after an official denial from Lucasfilm. The choice made sense from Lucas's perspective, at least. Who better than the most gifted Shakespearian stage actor of his generation to bestow some Guinnesslike gravitas to the next trilogy?

As production drew closer, easily the most encouraging echo of the past was the mood of George Lucas himself. Coaxed away from his writing to celebrate the twentieth anniversary of ILM towards the end of 1996, he seemed born again in the face of the challenge. Bunny Alsup, Gary Kurtz, and the founding fathers of the Lucas empire would have recognized the boyish excitement in his voice. Lucas had waited patiently for ILM to perfect the technology to bring his dreams to life. The wait had seemed worthwhile from the moment he began tinkering with his first three movies. Thanks to the new CHI, computer-generated imagery perfected on *Jurassic Park*, even the most cumbersome creatures could now be brought to life. Lucas had restored Jabba the Hutt to the Mos Eisley sequence in *Star Wars*. Even Yoda was able to walk. "Suddenly all the constraints are lifted. It's like you've been plowing fields in one hundred-degree sun, with a seventy-pound backpack and lead balls chained to your ankles, and someone comes along and puts you in an air-conditioned tractor," he told the special-effect trade's magazine *Cinefax*.

For Lucas, the greatest contrast between 1996 and 1976

boiled down to perhaps the most precious commodity of all—control. "Part of *Star Wars* was a bold gesture by a headstrong kid saying 'I want to tell a big story' without actually saying 'Okay, how am I going to pull it off?'" he admitted. This time he knew he would be the master of the technology available to him. "With digital technology I can get the cost down and thus make the films more epic, grander in scale and tell much more sweeping stories," he said. "That's where the real thrill of it all comes. That's what's bringing me back to doing it, in a way—just the fun of it."

And so the world must wait. It will not be until the end of the present millennium that we will be allowed our first glimpse of the vision once more forming in Lucas's extraordinary mind. After the first prequel's release in 1999, Lucas hopes to release the next two films in 2001 and 2003. It is his ambition that within ten years of that the cycle of nine films would then finally be completed. It would be perhaps George Lucas's greatest achievement of all if he still considered the process "fun" at the end of that remarkable journey.

The path ahead is a daunting one. No films will ever have been so eagerly anticipated. Yet no filmmaker in history will have been burdened by the same weight of expectation. Lucas will need more than time and technology. To succeed he will require a flash of magic beyond even his marketing and merchandising millions. His will be a formidable force. More than ever, however, he must hope that force is with him...

SELECT BIBLIOGRAPHY

Arnold, Alan, *Once Upon a Galaxy: A Journal of the Making of The Empire Strikes Back*, Ballantine, 1980.

Baxter, John, *Steven Spielberg: The Unauthorized Biography*, Harper-Collins, 1996.

Brode, Douglas, *The Films of Steven Spielberg*, Citadel Press, New York, 1995.

Champlin, Charles, *The Creative Impulse: The Films of George Lucas*, Harry N. Abrams, New York, 1992.

Evans, Bob, *The Kid Stays in the Picture*, Aurum, 1994.

Farber, Stephen, and Green, Marc, *Hollywood Dynasties*, Deliah, 1984.

Gelmis, Joseph, *The Film Director as Superstar*, Doubleday, 1970.

Goodwin, Michael, and Wise, Naomi, *On the Edge: The Life and Times of Francis Coppola*, Morrow, New York, 1989.

Halberstam, David, *The Fifties*, Ballantine, 1993.

Harmetz, Aljean, *Rolling Breaks and Other Movie Business*, Knopf, 1983.

Jacobs, Diane, *Hollywood Renaissance*, Delta, 1980.

Lentz, Harris M. III, *Science Fiction, Horror and Fantasy Film and Television Credits*, McFarland, 1983.

Litwak, Mark, *Reel Power: The Struggle for Influence and Success in the New Hollywood*, Morrow, 1986.

McClintick, David, *Indecent Exposure*, Morrow, 1982.

Madsen, Axel, *The New Hollywood*, Cromwell, 1975.

Parish, James Robert, and Terrace, Vincent, *The Complete Actors' Television Credits, 1948-1988*, Scarecrow Press, 1989.

Phillips, Julia, *You'll Never Eat Lunch in This Town Again*, Mandarin, 1991.

Pollock, Dale, *Skywalking: The Life and Films of George Lucas*, Harmony Books, New York, 1983.

Pye, Michael, and Myles, Linda, *The Movie Brats: How the Film Generation Took Over Hollywood*, Faber & Faber, 1979.

Rosenfield, Paul, *The Club Rules: Power, Sex, Money and Fear: How It Works in Hollywood*, Warner, 1992.

Silverman, Stephen, *The Fox That Got Away: The Last Days of the Zanuck Dynasty at 20th Century–Fox*, Lyle Stuart, 1988.

Worrell, Denise, *Icons—Intimate Portraits*, Atlantic Monthly Press, New York, 1989.

ACKNOWLEDGMENTS

Research for this book was conducted in London and Los Angeles where I was assisted by the *Hollywood Reporter* and *Los Angeles Times* writer Todd Coleman. My first debt of thanks is to Todd whose industry and enthusiasm, not to mention his impressive contacts book, were invaluable. Indeed without him this book would have been almost impossible to write. I look forward to combining forces with him again.

Between us, Todd and I were able to speak to a disparate band of people, each bound by the experience of having been part of the extraordinary events of two decades ago. On this side of the Atlantic, I would like to pay particular thanks to Gary Kurtz, whose generosity extended beyond the many hours he spent talking to me. I am also deeply grateful to Sir Alec Guinness for the time and trouble he took as he recovered from illness. I must also single out Dave Prowse for his assistance not only in recalling his days as Darth Vader, but in pointing me in the direction of other members of the cast.

In Los Angeles I am particularly grateful to Charles Lippincott, John Dykstra, Jim Nelson, Dorothy Alsup, Johnny Friedkin, Gareth Wigan and Howard Kazanjian, each of whom cleared time in busy schedules to spend long hours reminiscing about the events of two decades ago.

Other interviewees to whom I am particularly indebted include Peter Mayhew, Kenny Baker, Anthony Waye, Dave Okada, Fred Roos, Tim Deegan, Ray Gosnell, Craig Miller, Valerie Hoffman, Louis Friedman, Jonathan Dana. As ever, there were those who preferred I did not mention their names.

Research was conducted at both the Academy of Motion Pictures, Arts and Sciences Margaret Herrick Library in Los Angeles and the British Film Institute library in London. I would like to extend my personal thanks to the staff at the latter where, once more, I found their collective resourcefulness and enthusiasm peerless. Elsewhere I am grateful to Paul Y., Geoff S. and Brian O. for their contributions of material.

More than ever I must thank Cilene for putting up with a particularly painful deadline and my frequent disappearance into an alternative personality as I fought to meet it.

Finally thanks must go to the team at Simon & Schuster, Ingrid Connell for her eminently sensible and helpful editorship, Matthew Parker for his support at the project's birth and, once more, Helen Gummer, without whose assured advocacy this book would never have left the ground. I hope this has justified her faith.

INDEX

ESB = *The Empire Strikes Back*
F = film; GL = George Lucas;
RJ = *Return of the Jedi;*
SW = *Star Wars*

Academy Awards (Oscars), 183–84, 259, 260
Adventure Theater (TV), 1–2, 54, 166
Aldrich, Robert, 195, 203
Alexander, Dick, 84
Alias Smith and Jones (TV), 229
Alice Doesn't Live Here Any More (F), 81
Alien (F), 213
All That Jazz (F), 213
Allen, Irwin, 42, 141, 145, 167
Allen, Woody, 183, 233
Alsup, Dorothy "Bunny," 31, 46, 51, 56, 98, 111, 218, 219, 222–23, 267
Altman, Robert, 27, 45
Amadeus (play), 246
American Graffiti (F): filming of, 28–35, 52, 66, 110; finance, 30, 32, 36, 40–41, 50–51; success of, 47–49, 53–54, 59, 72
American Zoetrope, 18, 19, 26, 57, 232
Andromeda Straing, The (F), 63
Annie Hall (F), 183
"Anakin Skywalker," 39, 61, 267
Ansen, David, 251
Apocalypse Now (F), 26–28, 57, 79, 82, 178, 210, 232
Arnold, Alan, 198, 202, 217, 220
"Artoo." *See* R2-D2.
Ashley, Ted, 18, 19, 26–27
Avco Cinema (Los Angeles), xii, 146, 162, 249
Aykroyd, Dan, 177

Baker, Kenny: as R2-D2, 89, 96, 98, 107–8, 109, 127; later career, 248, 266
Baker, Rick, 134, 237
Ballard, Carroll, 57, 135
Bancroft, Anne, 213
Barry, John, 95, 100, 117, 183, 208–9, 266
Barwood, Hal, 12, 18, 57, 60, 148, 179, 194
Batchelor, Ruth, 161

Battlestar Galactica (TV), 185–87, 188–89, 229
Bel Aire Associates, 164–65
Belfrage, Julian, 110
Belushi, John, 177
Benchley, Peter, 55, 145
Benton, Robert, 233
Berg, Jeff, 38, 40, 41, 46, 68, 72, 74, 192, 230
Berg, Jon, 134
Beswick, Doug, 134
Betsy, The (F), 83
"Biggs Darklighter," 148
Big Red One, The (F), 194
Big Sleep, The (F), 193
Black Hole, The (F), 185, 227
Blade Runner (F), 245
Blalack, Robert, 183
Blazing Saddles (F), 45
Blues Brothers, The (F), 227, 232
Bocquet, Gavin, 266
Boone, Ashley, 116, 133, 142, 146
Brackett, Leigh, 193–94
Branagh, Kenneth, 267
Brando, Marlon, 185
Broccoli, "Cubby," 38
Brooks, Mel, 45, 68, 215
Brown, David, 266
Brown, Jerry, 255
Brown, Phil, 86
Brubaker (F), 227
"Buck Rogers," 186
Burtt, Ben, 60–61, 131, 184, 188, 206
Butch Cassidy and the Sundance Kid (F), 229
Butler, Wilmer, 17
Buttercup Valley (Ariz.), 235, 236

"C3PO," 37, 39, 60, 89–90, 95, 96–97, 107, 132, 133, 170, 175, 266
Campbell, Joseph: *Hero With a Thousand Faces, The*, 37, 55
Canby, Vincent, 156, 158
Can't Stop the Music (F), 227
Cantwell, Colin, 61, 76, 122
Captain Blood (F), 141
Carol, Sue, 44
Carpenter, John, 82
Carr, Pat, 108

271

Index

Index

Index

Index

Liska, Laine, 134
Lisztomania (F), 202
Livingston, Alan, 169
London, 181–82, 225, 227
London Symphony Orchestra, 140
Loomis, Bernie, 174
Love Story (F), 55
Loze, Donald, 164–65
Lucas Arts company, 247
Lucas family, 3–5
Lucas, George, Sr., 1–6 passim, 55
Lucas, George Walton: APPEARANCE: 11, 22, 87, 254–55; CHARACTER: determination and hard work, 13; idealism, 17; interests, 5–8; Luke Skywalker as alter ego, 53, 99; pessimism, 4; perfectionism, 124, 238; religion, 9, 36–37; shyness, 16, 20, 84; FILMMAKING: and animation, 13–14; awards, 183, 259, 260; creative genius, 130; directorial style, 20, 30, 90, 106, 117, 118, 216–17; editing, 13–14, 23, 120–21, 147–48; films, *see American Graffiti; Empire Strikes Back; Return of the Jedi; Star Wars; THX 1138;* other films, 12, 17, 259; proposed *Star War* series, 261–68; relations with cast and crew, 51, 101–4, 110–12, 113, 124–25, 134–35, 176, 188; relations with Hollywood, 35, 48, 68, 183, 228–33; script-writing, 16–17, 29–30, 35–37, 38, 51–59, 194; *see* Lucasfilm; GEORGE LUCAS DAY," 264; HEALTH: x, 14, 104–5, 124; LIFE: childhood, 1–8; car accident, 8–10; student days, 10–14; marriage, 18–19; divorce, 253–55; daughters, 248, 253, 255, 258; later life, 258–59
Lucas, Marcia (neé Griffin): career, 27, 81, 120, 125, 148, 183–84; marries GL, 18–19; married life, 50, 53, 57, 104–5, 148–49, 211, 248; divorce, 253–55; and SW success, x–xii, 120, 180
Lucasfilm Ltd.: beginnings, 31, 51, 65; development, 144, 163, 170, 172–73, 191, 200, 209; expansion and break with Hollywood, 221–23, 228, 230–32, 249, 265. *See also* ILM.
"Luke Skywalker," 37

M*A*S*H (F), 27
M*A*S*H (TV), 135
McCallum, Rick, 266
McCloud (TV), 229
McCune, Grant, 183
McDiarmid, Ian, 243
McGovern, Terry, 53
McGrath, Earl, 176–77
McGraw, Ali, 155
McKenna's Gold (F), 16
Maclaine, Shirley, 213
McOmie, Maggie, 20
McQuarrie, Ralph, 60–61, 67, 70–71, 88, 90, 122, 154, 201
McQueen, Steve, 141, 145
McQueeney, Patricia, 160, 203
Majors, Farrah Fawcett, 137
Majors, Lee, 137
Mann, Ted, 146, 175
Marquand, Richard, 234, 242–43, 246, 252
Marvel Comics, 77, 172
Marvin, Lee, 194
Marvin Josephson Associates, 230
Mask, The (F), 260
Mather, George, 129
Mattel company, 137–38, 173–74
Matter of Time, A (F), 103
Mayhew, Peter, 88, 100–101, 102, 115, 206, 247
Mazursky, Paul, 45
Medium Cool (F), 19
Méliès, George, 71
merchandising, 73–74, 75–78, 136–39, 170–74, 182, 219–21, 263–64
Metropolis (F), 60
Mexico, 181
MGM, 26, 42, 64, 65
Michaeljohn, 261
Michener, James, 80
Microsoft, 261
Midnight Express (F), 246
Mifune, Toshiro, 28, 83
Miles, Sarah, 80
Milius, John, 12, 13, 18, 27, 48, 53, 148
Mill Valley, GL's house in, 19, 22, 23, 26, 31, 34, 35
Miller, Craig, 224–25
Minnelli, Vincente, 103
"Miss Piggy," 207
Modesto (Cal.), 1, 3, 5, 7–8, 9
Modesto Junior High School, 8

Index

Index

Index